CHRISTIANITY AND
PAGANISM, 350–750

North Sea

Baltic Sea

Iona

Lindisfarne
Jarrow
Wearmouth

Armagh
Birr
Kildare
Bangor

York

THURINGIA

HESSE

BAVARIA

Canterbury

Antwerp
Ghent
St. Amand

Rouen
Paris
Reims

ATLANTIC

OCEAN

Orléans
Tours
Loches
Bourges

Auxerre
Luxeuil

Milan
Turin
Bobbio

Verona

Vienne

Bordeaux

F
R
A
N
K
S

L
O
M
B
A
R
D
S

Adriatic Sea

Ravenna

Arles

Lérins

Rome

Nola

PYRENEES

Braga

Toledo

V
I
S
I
G
O
T
H
S

Mediterranean Sea

Carthage

Hippo

Ruspe

0   100   200   300   400   500 miles

CHRISTIANITY AND PAGANISM, 350–750

THE CONVERSION OF WESTERN EUROPE

Edited by J. N. Hillgarth

UNIVERSITY OF PENNSYLVANIA PRESS

Philadelphia

1986

The Middle Ages

a series edited by
Edward Peters
Henry Charles Lea Professor
of Medieval History
University of Pennsylvania

First published in 1969 by Prentice-Hall Inc.
under the title
The Conversion of Western Europe, 350–750

Revised edition first published in 1986 by the
University of Pennsylvania Press

Library of Congress Cataloging in Publication Data

Main entry under title:

Christianity and paganism, 350–750.

    (The Middle Ages)
    Rev. ed. of: The conversion of Western Europe, 350–750. 1969.
    Bibliography: p.
    Includes index.
    1. Church history—Middle Ages, 600–1500—Sources.
2. Europe–Church history—Middle Ages, 600–1500—Sources.
I. Hillgarth, J. N. II. Title: Conversion of Western Europe, 350–750. III. Series.
BR200.C47   1985   274'.02   85-1154
ISBN 0-8122-7993-X
ISBN 0-8122-1213-4 (pbk.)

Printed in the United States of America

CONTENTS

PART ONE   CHRISTIANITY IN THE TRANSITION FROM THE ROMAN TO THE BARBARIAN WORLD

Contents

ACKNOWLEDGMENTS

I HAVE TO THANK THE FOLLOWING FOR PERMISSION TO USE COPYRIGHTED material which was already granted in 1969: Brepols, Turnhout, for Corpus Christianorum, Series latina, XXIII, pp. 420–21; CXVII, pp. 408–10, 419, 421–23; CXLVIIIA, pp. 1–12, 265–70, 275–80; Hermann Böhlaus Nachfolger, Weimar, for K. A. Eckhardt, ed., *Lex Salica, 100 Titel-Text*, Germanenrechte N.F. (Weimar, 1953), pp. 82–84, 86–90; The Clarendon Press for Gregory of Tours, *History of the Franks*, trans. by O. M. Dalton, II (Oxford, 1927), pp. 67–70; *The Conflict Between Paganism and Christianity in the Fourth Century*, ed. A. Momigliano (Oxford, 1963), pp. 6, 9, 10; F. J. E. Raby, *A History of Christian Latin Poetry*, 2d ed. (Oxford, 1953), pp. 115, 123; Charles Plummer, ed., *Venerabilis Baedae Opera Historica*, I (Oxford, 1896), pp. 364–76, 405, 408–23; Deutschrechtliches Institut für Geschichtsforschung, for F. Beyerle, ed., *Leges Langobardorum 643–866*, Germanenrechte N.F. (Witzenhausen, 1962), pp. 118, 139–40, 155–56, 185–86; Firmin-Didot, Paris, for *Le Liber Ordinum*, ed. M. Férotin, Monumenta Ecclesiae Liturgica, V (Paris, 1904), cols. 149–53; The Abbaye de Maredsous, for G. Morin, ed., *S. Caesarii Arelatensis Opera Omnia*, III

(Maredsous, 1942), pp. 297–323; *Revue bénédictine*, XLVIII (1936), pp. 232, 233; The Rev. Fr. Jacobus Mulders, S.J., for his *Saint Victrice de Rouen, Son "De Laude Sanctorum,"* *Texte et commentaire* (Rome, 1953); Paulist/Newman Press, for *The Letters of St. Paulinus of Nola*, Ancient Christian Writers, 35–36, trans. by P. G. Walsh (Westminster, Md., 1966–67), I, p. 7; II, p. 273; Princeton University Press, for *The Theodosian Code and Novels and the Sirmondian Constitutions*, trans. by Clyde Pharr (Princeton, 1952), pp. 70, 440–42, 447, 449, 473–74, 476, 483–84; and Sheed and Ward, Ltd., London, for *The Anglo-Saxon Missionaries in Germany*, trans. and edited by C. H. Talbot (London/New York, 1954), pp. 71–72, 75–78, 84–86, 91–92, 93–95, copyright 1954 Sheed and Ward, Inc., reprinted with permission of Andrews, McMeel and Parker, all rights reserved; S. P. C. K., London, for P. R. Coleman-Norton, *Roman State and Christian Church*, II (London, 1966), pp. 524–25; Weidmannsche Verlagsbuchhandlung, for E. Diehl, *Inscriptiones Latinae Christianae Veteres*, I–III (Berlin, 1961), I, No. 1513 (p. 289), Nos. 1549, 1616, 2349, 2483; II, Nos. 3485, 3863; Yale University Press, for C. W. Barlow, *Martini episcopi Bracarensis Opera Omnia*, Papers and Monographs of the American Academy in Rome, 12 (New Haven, 1950), pp. 183–203.

To this list should be added the following acknowledgments which concern this edition (those to Hölder-Pichler-Tempsky and those to the Monumenta Germaniae Historica were omitted by error, for which I apologize, in 1969): Brepols, Turnhout, for Corpus Christianorum, Series latina, CLIX, pp. 460–62; The Clarendon Press, Oxford, for *Cáin Adamnáin, an Old-Irish treatise on the Law of Adamnan*, ed. and trans. by Kuno Meyer (Oxford, 1905), pp. 3f., 15f., 21–33; The Dublin Institute for Advanced Studies, for *The Irish Penitentials*, trans. L. Bieler, Scriptores latini Hiberniae, V (Dublin, 1963), pp. 97–107; Walter de Gruyter and Co., Berlin, for Roger E. Reynolds, *The Ordinals of Christ from Their Origin to the Twelfth Century* (Beiträge zur Geschichte und Quellenkunde des Mittelalters, 7) (Berlin, 1978), p. 58; The Henry Bradshaw Society, for E. C. Ratcliff, *Expositio antiquae liturgiae gallicanae* (London, 1971), pp. 3–16; Hölder-Pichler-Tempsky, Vienna, for Corpus scriptorum ecclesiasticorum latinorum, 7 (1881), pp. 35–36; 16 (1888), pp. 165, 234–35, 237, 239–40, 503–5, 507; 30 (1894), pp. 255, 261; 56 (1918), pp. 154–55; The Pontifical Institute of Mediaeval Studies, Toronto, for *Mediaeval Studies* 41 (1979), pp. 260–62; Spicilegium Sacrum Lovaniense, Leuven, for M. Andrieu, *Les "Ordines Romani" du haut moyen age*, II (1948), pp. 69–74; Monumenta Germaniae Historica, Munich, for Monumenta Germaniae Historica, Auctores Antiquissimi, VI, 2, pp. 75–76; X, p. 340; Leges, I, 1 (1902), pp. 77–78, 165, 259, 379–80, 424; II, 1

(1883), pp. 1–3, 11–12, 15, 19–23; Scriptores rerum Merovingicarum, III, pp. 158–59; V, pp. 373–94, 428–49, 483–84.
 I would like to stress the fact that, with the exception of the relatively few older translations acknowledged as being used here, the responsibility for all the translations in this book is my own.

PREFACE

THE FIRST VERSION OF THIS BOOK—COMPRISING ABOUT TWO-thirds of the present volume—was published by Prentice-Hall in 1969 as *The Conversion of Western Europe, 350–750*. The reason why the former title has become a subtitle is my wish to emphasize the *incomplete* nature of the process documented here. Western Europe, Britain, and Ireland were very imperfectly Christian in 750. Only the preconditions for the penetration of Christianity had been established. If pagan idols had been overthrown, pagan customs and beliefs were only beginning to change. What was emerging in many places was less the clear victory of the Christian Creed than a mixture or fusion of the old and the new.

The main changes from the book as it appeared in 1969 concern Part Two and especially Part Two, Chapter 3, "Christianity in the North," and Chapter 4, "Liturgy." I have regretted the lack of attention paid to Ireland in the 1969 version. I attempt to remedy this here as far as is possible in a small space. I have also inserted a section on the Frankish Church in the seventh century. The new section on the Liturgy gives some examples of the "liturgical community" as it was developing in the sixth and later centuries.

In my selection of texts I have not included some very well known and important documents such as the *Rule of St. Benedict* or the works of St. Patrick. (The *Rule* is available in *Monks, Bishops and Pagans*, edited by Edward Peters for the University of Pennsylvania Press, 1975.) I have often referred to other documents available in translation so that those interested can carry research further. I have concentrated on topics underemphasized in the past, such as the cult of Relics in popular Christianity, the emergence of consciously Christian monarchies in Europe, and the gradual penetration of the Church's influence in a world which remained pagan long after Constantine. My only reservation as regards my earlier selection of topics concerns the cult of Relics. In recent works, notably Professor Peter Brown's *Cult of the Saints* (1981) and his *Society and the Holy* (1982), the cult of a dead saint has been singled out as characteristic of the Latin West as distinct from the Christian East, where the live holy man is rightly seen as playing a central role. This distinction appears to be principally based on the works of Gregory of Tours (for whom see Peters's book, already cited). I have argued elsewhere that even in Gregory one finds considerable emphasis on living as well as dead saints, while, if one looks at other evidence, especially the lives of saints coming from Merovingian France, the picture is very different. While in the cities of France, including Gregory's own Tours, one finds living saints co-existing with the shrines of those long dead, in the countryside, where the vast majority of the population lived, the presence of living missionaries is overwhelming. (One example of such a missionary is Amand, whose *Life* is translated here for the first time.)

No one who has studied the religion of the fifth and later centuries would be inclined to underestimate the importance of Relics and shrines. I suggest that they should be seen in proportion and that without the presence of the living saint the greater part of Western Europe would have remained permanently alien to the new religion. In this the Christian West does not appear to me to differ significantly from Syria or Asia Minor.

I began the first version of this book largely at the stimulus of Professor Robert Lee Wolff of Harvard University, the general editor of the series "Sources of Civilization in the West" in which the book appeared. Professor Wolff's tragically premature death prevents me doing more than express here my indebtedness to him. I would wish to thank Professor Edward Peters of the University of Pennsylvania for his kindness in encouraging me to revise and expand the work for the present edition.

Professor Herbert Bloch of Harvard University much improved the translation of several passages in the first version of this work. In preparing the sections on Ireland and the Liturgy, which appear here for the first time, I

Preface

am much indebted to the advice of my colleagues at Toronto, Professors Ann Dooley and Roger Reynolds.

In 1968 I referred in the Preface to my mother, "to whom," as I wrote, "I owe my first interest in history and much encouragement over many years." My mother's liking for the book and her urging me to undertake a new, enlarged edition have been in my mind as I prepared the present volume. It is dedicated to her memory.

ABBREVIATIONS

Beyerle, *Leges*	F. Beyerle (ed.), *Leges Langobardorum 643–866*, Germanenrechte N. F. (Witzenhausen, 1962).
Boretius	A. Boretius, *Capitularia regni Francorum*, MGH, *Leges*, II, 1 (Hanover, 1883).
CCSL	*Corpus christianorum, Series latina* (Turnhout, Brepols).
CSEL	*Corpus scriptorum ecclesiasticorum latinorum.*
MGH, AA	*Monumenta Germaniae Historica, Auctores antiquissimi.*
MGH, SRM	*Ibid., Scriptores rerum Merovingicarum.*
Pharr, *Theodosian Code*	Clyde Pharr (trans.), *The Theodosian Code and Novels and the Sirmondian Constitutions* (Princeton, 1952).
PL	*Patrologia latina*, ed. J. P. Migne.
Scott, *Visigothic Code*	S. P. Scott (trans.), *The Visigothic Code* (*Forum Judicum*) (Boston, 1910).

INTRODUCTION

THE PROBLEM OF THE "DECLINE AND FALL" OF ROME, WHICH FASCI-
nated men's minds even before it became an inescapable fact in the
fifth century, tends to be seen today rather in the light of a "*transformation* of the Roman world."[1] It is necessary to understand the long-term
progression which took place. The centralized, despotic Empire of 300,
stretching from Britain and Spain to Armenia and Egypt, from the Danube
to the Sahara, had evolved into the fragmented world of 700, where the
transformed Roman (now Byzantine) Empire, with its capital at Constantinople, only survived effectively in Asia Minor and the Balkans. Meanwhile
Western Europe was divided among a number of barbarian "successor-states"
and Islam had engulfed the Middle East and North Africa. To understand this
progression involves studying the fourth to the eighth centuries as a unit,
rather than dividing this period artificially into "ancient" and "medieval"
history. It also means discarding a number of prejudices inherited from the

1. See Lynn White, ed., *The Transformation of the Roman World, Gibbon's Problem After Two
Centuries* (Berkeley and Los Angeles, 1966), also S. Mazzarino, *The End of the Ancient World*
(New York, 1966).

humanists of the Renaissance and still alive. An age of radical transformation is not necessarily one of unmitigated catastrophe. Much was lost with the collapse of Roman power in Western Europe but much was also achieved from the fifth to the eighth century. Two of the most crucial changes in European history were well under way by the eighth century: the process by which the Mediterranean-centered Greco-Roman civilization spread into Northern Europe, and the conversion of Western Europe to Christianity. These changes were intimately connected. It was a Christianized Greece and Rome which, evangelizing the Teutonic and Slav peoples, incorporated the Northern European plains into civilization and so laid the basis for the Europe of later ages. This book is intended to provide some of the materials for the history of the conversion of Western Europe, for the "realistic evaluation of the impact of Christianity on the structure of pagan society,"[2] which Professor Momigliano has pointed out we still lack. I hope that it will also illustrate some of the difficulties and limitations of "conversion."

When Constantine entered Rome in 312 as the victorious ruler of the Roman Empire in the West, he immediately began to favor the Christian Church, which had only just emerged from very severe persecution. It is generally agreed that he was taking a considerable risk. In contrast with the East, where whole provinces were already largely Christian—but which Constantine was not to conquer until 324—Christianity in the Latin West, except in North Africa, was the religion of a small minority. During the fourth century the conversion of the Roman aristocracy and of the middle classes of the towns advanced greatly but it was by no means complete by 400. The first effective and general prohibition of all pagan worship by the Roman State only came in 391–92 (p. 47); it inspired the last serious attempt by the Roman aristocracy to support a pro-pagan pretender to the Empire. It required repeated and increasingly severe legislation to drive paganism in the towns underground. It took centuries more before Christianity really began to penetrate the vast mass of the population of Western Europe, the peasants, slaves or semifree "coloni," who provided food for their masters, Roman or barbarian, and for the shrunken and decaying cities. It is apparent from the documents in this book that, for the majority of the rural population, down to the eighth century (and often much later still), some form of ancestral paganism was at least as attractive as Christianity.

The Church's difficulties were greatly increased by the Barbarian Invasions of the fifth century. The invaders were almost all pagans. When they became Christians they did not adopt Catholicism but the Arian heresy.

2. Arnoldo Momigliano, "Introduction," *The Conflict Between Paganism and Christianity in the Fourth Century* (Oxford, 1963), p. 6.

Arianism had constituted the main challenge to the Catholic Church in the fourth century. The issue it raised was of vital concern to every Christian. Was Christ identical with the Supreme God? If he was not, how could his Incarnation have saved mankind? How could he be, as Christians believed, the central pivot in the universe and the turning point of history? But if Christ *was* the Supreme God how could one avoid polytheism, by worshiping not only God the Father but the Son (and also the Holy Spirit)? Arius argued that Christ and the Holy Spirit were secondary gods, mediating between God the Father and the world. In reply, the Catholic doctrine of the Trinity in Unity was worked out. The distinction between the Three Persons of the Trinity was necessary philosophically but it was less important, to most Christians, than the affirmation that Christ was equal to God the Father, that the Supreme God had truly "become flesh" and that men were saved by his Passion. Catholics detested Arianism because they saw it as the betrayal of the central truth of Christianity, the truth by which they lived.

In 381 the Catholic doctrine of the Trinity was officially accepted within the Roman Empire. But, before or shortly after this time, the Visigoths were converted to Arian Christianity: they had been approached by missionaries of their own race, armed with a Bible in their own tongue. Visigothic missionaries and influence gradually converted the other barbarian tribes invading the Empire to Arianism also. Hence the religious opposition, which often took a violent form, between the Catholic leaders of the native population of Western Europe and North Africa and the invading Arian barbarians. (See Part One, 4, A.) The turning point only came about 500 with the conversion of the Franks from paganism to Catholicism. After the overthrow of the Arian Ostrogoths and Vandals by the Catholic Byzantine (East Roman) Emperor Justinian (527–65) the Arian Visigoths also became Catholics (587–89). (See Part One, 4, B.)

By 600 the Catholic Church had emerged from the barbarian crisis and had attained an extraordinarily powerful position in Western Europe, one which it was to retain in many countries until the French Revolution. It was a great landowner, it included among its members the ruling classes, and it had converted and was actively supported by all the barbarian successors of Rome, except for the Arian Lombards and pagan Anglo-Saxons who were definitely converted by 680. The barbarian kings sought to help Church Councils to stamp out any form of deviation or dissent, receiving, in return, the Church's consecration of their troubled rule. For almost two centuries the Church in the West had not been faced with any intellectual opposition, and it had never been disturbed by inner divisions, heretical or schismatic movements comparable to those that plagued the Byzantine East and North Africa.

The triumph of Catholic Christianity over Roman paganism, whether intellectual or popular, and over heretical Arian or pagan barbarism was certainly due in large part to the support it received, first from the declining Roman State (Part One, 2) and later from the barbarian monarchies (Part Two, 2). It was also due to other considerations, some of which will be discussed more fully under the heading "The Christian Appeal" (Part One, 1).

From the fourth century onward "the Church attracted the most creative minds, . . . almost all born rulers, . . . men who in the past would have become excellent generals, governors of provinces, advisers to the emperors. Moreover, the Church made ordinary people proud, not of their old political institutions, but of their new churches, monasteries, ecclesiastical charities. Money which would have gone to the building of a theater or of an aqueduct now went to the building of churches and monasteries. The social equilibrium changed—to the advantage of the spiritual and physical conditions of monks and priests, but to the disadvantage of the ancient institutions of the empire."

The Church "provided space for those whom the State was unable to absorb."[3] The Greco-Roman world had seen the poor as negligible and slaves merely as "talking-stock," who lived in barracks on large estates close to the animals ("semivocal stock") and were hardly, if at all, better treated.[4] One has only to consult the sixth-century *Life of St. Caesarius of Arles* (Chap. 61 on p. 42 of this book), with its insistence on Christians paying the same attention to their sick slaves' salvation as to that of their relations, to see a change has taken place. One of the new features of Western Europe by 600 is the cult of the poor. It stands out in all the leading writers of the time, Pope Gregory the Great, Gregory of Tours, Caesarius of Arles. The reversal of standards announced in the Magnificat (Luke 1:51–53) had, to an extent, been achieved. Preachers dwelt on the Parable of the Banquet (Luke 14:16–24), with its stress on "the poor, the maimed, the blind and the lame" inheriting the Kingdom of God, and on the story of the damnation of the rich man and the salvation of Lazarus (Luke 16:19–31). Gregory the Great emphasized that "God has chosen those the world despised."[5] The Church's "identification" with the poor was not confined to sermons. In the *Life of Caesarius* one can see how a bishop was the main support of his city's population, founding hospitals, liberating prisoners of war, never shutting

3. Momigliano, *loc. cit.*, pp. 9, 10.

4. See Max Weber, *Gesammelte Aufsätze zur Sozial-und Wirtschaftsgeschichte* (Tübingen, 1924), pp. 289–311, cited by Mazzarino, *op. cit.*, pp. 137–48. Also F. W. Walbank, *The Decline of the Roman Empire in the West* (London, 1946).

5. *In Evangelia*, II, 36, 7, *Patrologia latina*, 76, col. 1269C. For his use of the story of Lazarus, see *ibid.*, 40, cols. 1301–12.

himself away from the poor, guarding his people in the sixth century against the feuds of barbarian kings as, a hundred years earlier, he had protected them against the rapacious officials of the dying Roman State.

Two of the dominant notes of the Christian world emerging in Western Europe seem particularly strange to us: its completely unscientific approach to reality—its acceptance of miracles, demons, and witchcraft as normal—and its worship of asceticism, of every form of bodily mortification. To nineteenth-century students of the age these things seemed the clearest proof of a tragic decline from the standards of classical antiquity. Today we know that neither an unscientific view of the world nor the exaltation of asceticism were the creatures of Christianity but were leading features of the world Christianity entered. The irrational side of much of Greek life and thought has been brought out in many recent studies.[6] It is clear that the vast majority of the population of the Roman Empire at *any* time felt the need for religion and that even among the educated the number of pure sceptics was probably always very limited. Greek science virtually ceased to advance after 200 B.C. and what science there was might more properly be called occultism, connected with magic and sorcery, appealing to revelations and dealings with the supernatural. The pagan intellectuals, from the Emperor Julian down, who opposed Christianity in the fourth century were no more critical or "scientific" than any Christian, and were quite as dogmatic in their adherence to Homer and other authorities as Christians were in their appeal to the Bible.

A type of physical "dualism," which involves a depreciation, if not hatred of the body, was also common to both pagans and Christians. As Gilbert Murray said, the Emperor Julian was probably as proud of the lice in his beard as any monk in Egypt.[7]

The advantages that the Catholic Church possessed over its pagan rivals, notably the Eastern "Mystery Religions," such as Mithraism, and over paganism generally, may be briefly stated, following, if slightly modifying, Gibbon, as: a clearer and much more *precise* mythology; a more *organized* asceticism, linked closely to moral teaching; an organized hierarchy; an exclusive and intolerant Creed; and a complete frame for life, beginning with Baptism and ending in the tremendous vision of the Last Judgment.[8]

6. See E. R. Dodds, *The Greeks and the Irrational* (Berkeley and Los Angeles, 1951) and *Pagan and Christian in an Age of Anxiety* (Cambridge, 1965); B. Farrington, *Science and Politics in the Ancient World* (London, 1939); A.-J. Festugière, *Personal Religion Among the Greeks* (Berkeley and Los Angeles, 1954).

7. *Five Stages of Greek Religion* (London, 1935), p. 197.

8. Gibbon, Chap. 15. See G. B. Ladner, "The Impact of Christianity," in *The Transformation* (n. 1), pp. 59–91.

Unhistorical minds—and pagan minds were quite unhistorical—were naturally fascinated by the historical precision of the Bible, with its dates, its lists of kings, and the connections between the Old and New Testaments. These were already stressed, for instance, by St. Matthew's Gospel, which always points out how Christ, by entering *history* in Incarnation, *fulfills* prophecy, and by St. Paul (see, for example, 1 Corinthians 10, where the Israelites' passage of the Red Sea is seen as a prototype and anticipation of Christian Baptism and manna in the desert of the Eucharist). One finds the same appeal to Biblical *history*, in simplified form, in Martin of Braga's sermon for rustics (Part One, 3), while Benedict Biscop used pictures to relate the Old and New Testaments in his attempt to reach the illiterate in Northumbria (Part Two, 3).

Many pagans were as convinced as most Christians that the way to grace or wisdom was through punishing—or at least thoroughly disciplining—the body, but there did not exist in paganism the organized communities of monks and nuns which arose among Christians in Egypt and spread with great rapidity to Western Europe. Nor were pagan rites linked to clear moral teaching such as existed in the Christian Church. Paganism also lacked the Church's unity, with its hierarchy of bishops, meeting, when necessary, in provincial or General Councils to enforce dogmatic agreement or discipline on the recalcitrant.

From the first, Christianity was "a missionary and exclusive religion."[9] It had all the strength of Judaism's refusal to compromise, to join (and be dissolved) in the syncretic welter of beliefs and cults that characterized the Later Roman Empire. No Christian would have agreed with the tolerant statements of such representatives of paganism on the defensive as Symmachus—when defending the retention of the Altar of Victory in the Senate in 384—that all paths led to the same goal. On the contrary, Christians were sure that only baptized and orthodox believers would attain God: others would go to Hell. The insistence on the necessity of Baptism for salvation and on the Last Judgment, with its clear and intelligible system of rewards and punishments, is central to all Christian popular propaganda.

The advantages possessed by Catholic Christianity, together with the support of the Roman State (definitely secured from the accession of Theodosius in 379), the backing of the poor, and the corresponding disunity of paganism, are sufficient to explain the Church's virtually complete triumph by 400 in the sphere of government and law, among the literate ruling classes and in the towns, where it took over responsibility for the impoverished middle

9. E. Emerton, *The Letters of St. Boniface* (New York, 1940), p. 3.

class and proletariat. From about 400 the Church began to concern itself actively with the rural masses (Part One, 3). As I have indicated, this mission *within* the Roman world was to continue for centuries. In the fifth and sixth centuries the Church was also confronted with the barbarian tribes which gradually occupied all Western Europe. Its reactions to the barbarians will be examined in Part One, 4 and in Part Two. The *external* mission to pagans outside the old boundaries of the Roman Empire only developed from the seventh century onward (Part Two, 3).

The poverty of our sources for these centuries has rightly been called "more qualitative than quantitative." We are relatively well informed as to the actions of some princes and bishops, as well as to theological controversies, but incomparably worse off concerning the majority of the population. However, we are somewhat less badly situated for religious than for economic or social history, or rather it is *through* religious sources that we have perhaps our best chance of gaining information on social and economic conditions.

Late Roman culture was predominantly literary and was displayed mainly by the apt quotation, the polished compliment, or epigram. Yet those who could follow the elaborate satire of St. Jerome's letters or indeed the dialectic of St. Augustine's *City of God* were few in number. It is no accident that a large part of this book consists of sermons and lives of saints. From the fifth century onward there was an attempt to write more simply, to reach the people at a time when the lettered class was shrinking with the closing of most public schools owing to the barbarian invasions. This attempt took two main forms—sermons and lives of saints. Although lives of saints would only be read in full by clerics, monks, and a few laymen, they could be and often were read aloud in church or used as the basis for sermons. Similarly, although only a few bishops were great preachers, their sermons circulated and were repeated verbatim (as they were intended to be) by inferior clergy and also by their less brilliant colleagues (see Martin of Braga's sermon, written for the use of another bishop).

I have given preference to works (letters, sermons, lives of saints, laws) which were aimed at a concrete and identifiable audience—whether a recently converted king or barely converted peasants—and which directly reflect the aspirations of the clergy and monks who were forming the new ideals of Christian Europe. Much of the literature of this age is rhetorical and most of the writers of the time would have subscribed to Ennodius of Pavia's claim that "Rhetoric rules the world."[10] Eloquence was indeed not to

10. Quoted by F. J. E. Raby, *A History of Christian Latin Poetry*, 2nd ed. (Oxford, 1953), p. 115.

be despised by a Roman world deprived of arms and faced with barbarian conquerors. At times it is difficult to penetrate beyond this rhetoric, but in its better examples, for instance in Victricius' sermon on the martyrs' arrival at Rouen (Part One, 1, B) or in Avitus' letter to Clovis (Part One, 4), the style tells us much of the audience as well as of the writer. Both Victricius and Avitus were masters of an elaborate style but they were also bishops, charged with souls, and, as such, concerned to speak as directly as possible to their flock or to the barbarian king who had suddenly become a Catholic.

This book virtually ignores the higher level of Christian philosophical thought as it developed in the West from before Augustine to the Carolingian age. The speculation of Augustine or Boethius was inaccessible and would have been unintelligible even to most educated men of the time. The influence of these works was felt far more clearly from the ninth century. If Augustine is represented here, it is for his complete faith in the power of the relics of a martyr to heal, one of the most powerful and widespread beliefs of the age.

PART ONE

Christianity in the Transition from the Roman to the Barbarian World

1

THE CHRISTIAN APPEAL

A. A New Frame for Life

A CEREMONY THAT PROMISES FORGIVENESS OF SINS, AS THE GATE TO A NEW life, possesses an obvious attraction. A number of parallels to Christian Baptism existed in the world in which Christianity emerged, both among the Jews and in the pagan "Mystery Religions," notably Mithraism.

Baptism was principally administered at Easter. Until the fifth century most of those baptized were adults and their Baptism during the solemn Vigil service on the night of Holy Saturday was the culmination of a long period of instruction, very necessary for converts from paganism. This included inquiry and examination into the convert, special rites, especially exorcisms, and sermons stretching throughout Lent which were intended to give the new Christian a solid doctrinal formation.

The ceremony took place in a special building, the baptistery, attached to the cathedral—in principle Baptism was only administered by the bishop in his cathedral. The converts (naked, men and women separately) entered a large font, where water was poured on them and the words of Baptism were pronounced, "I baptize you in the Name of the Father, and of the Son, and of the Holy Spirit" (see Martin of Braga's sermon, p. 61). The baptismal water was seen as the mother womb of the Church, which the Holy Spirit had made fruitful. Confirmation—laying on of hands and the administration of holy oil by the bishop—and the convert's first Communion followed at once. In the Vigil Liturgy the newly baptized stood out as a group by the snow-white linen robes they had been given when they emerged from the font (see Avitus' letter to Clovis, p. 77).

I include here two very short addresses given by Bishop Zeno of Verona (d. c. 372) to the candidates for Baptism, immediately before its administration, and an inscription written by one of the greatest theologians of the fifth century, Pope Leo the Great (440–61), shortly before he became Pope. Set up in the baptistery attached to the Cathedral of Rome, the Lateran Basilica, it is still to be seen there, as it was seen by the pagans and unbaptized Christians who still formed a large part of the population of Rome. The inscription was mainly addressed to these groups.

The new Christian suffered from two main threats to his existence. He was liable at any time to become a victim of the military despotism under which he lived. He was also open to attack by invisible foes. The extent to which men's minds were dominated by demons is difficult for us to realize. In these centuries everyone, pagan and Christian alike, believed in the existence of demons. Demons were in the air you breathed, the water you drank, and the meat you ate. The Christian John Cassian in the early fifth century tells us that "the air between heaven and earth is so crammed with spirits, never quiet or finding rest, that it is fortunate for men that they are not permitted to see them." To understand the mentality of these centuries, one might consider equatorial Africa today. Christ's power over demons, over *visible* appearances of evil, especially in the form of demon possession, is perfectly intelligible, believable, and is of the utmost importance to modern African converts to Christianity.

The Church was the one refuge against both earthly and spiritual enemies. A conscientious bishop like Augustine (or Caesarius of Arles, later) tried hard to protect his people against exploitation by the State and extralegal intimidation by the rich.[1] The Church also offered men protection against evil demons. Candidates for Baptism were repeatedly exorcised as part of the normal rite. Those considered to be "possessed" by demons, that is most ill people—most obviously epileptics and the insane, but also the deaf, paralytics, etc.—were "treated" by being taken to the nearest priest, bishop, or monk who was thought to possess the power to heal. Christ had exercised this power in his ministry and was believed to have transmitted it to his disciples. Casting out devils was a standard test of sanctity for a Christian ascetic. For him it was part of his incessant battle with demons, whom he identified with

1. See, for instance, Augustine's four letters, 113–16, written on behalf of one tenant farmer, in *Fathers of the Church*, 18, trans. Sr. W. Parsons (New York, 1953), pp. 256–60.

the old pagan gods (see Martin of Braga's sermon, chap. 7, etc.). When a saint's personal presence could not be secured the next best thing was a document signed by him. Large numbers of papyri containing magical invocations still survive; the fragment translated here shows they were current in Gaul, as well as Egypt, in the sixth century.

The inscriptions I have selected illustrate Christians' expectation of a future life, and the ways they thought it could be secured. Orientius' long poem, the *Commonitorium*, probably written about 430, is mainly interesting for the reaction it displays to the Barbarian Invasions of Gaul (see pp. 70–71). It ends with an impressive vision of the Last Judgment.

Baptism: The Way to a New Life

1. Zeno of Verona, *Tractatus*, II, 30, 33, *PL*, 11, col. 476, 479, with some readings from J. B. Giuliari (Verona, 1883).

Brothers in Christ, rejoice, fly to receive the heavenly gifts. Now the saving warmth of the eternal fount of salvation invites you, now our Mother adopts you that she may bring you forth, but not by the law by which *your* mothers bore you, when they gave you, as prisoners, to this world, groaning with the pain of giving birth, while you were weeping, filthy, wrapped in filthy rags. Now your Mother is joyful and you rejoicing, she and you are heavenly; she is free, you are freed of all sins; she brings you up not from stinking cradles but from sanctuaries fragrant with the sweet odor of the sacred altar. Through Our Lord Jesus Christ.

You who differ in birth, age, sex, condition will soon be but one. Fly to the ever flowing womb of the Ever Virgin Mother. There your faith will ennoble you and you will enjoy as much happiness as your faith deserves. Admirable and truly divine, most holy birth, in which she who gives birth does not groan and he who is born again knows no tears. This is rebirth, this is resurrection, this is eternal life. This is the Mother of all, who has made one body of us who are gathered out of all races and nations.

2. Pope Leo the Great, Inscription in the Baptistery attached to the Lateran Basilica, Rome (432–40), in *Inscriptiones latinae christianae veteres*, ed. E. Diehl, I (Berlin, 1961), no. 1513, p. 289.

A Race destined for Heaven is born here of holy seed
Which the Spirit begets from life-bearing waters.
Plunge, sinner, in the holy flood which will make you clean,

For the wave which receives the old man will bring him forth as new.
There is no difference between those reborn,
Whom one font, one Spirit, one Faith have made one.
The children Mother Church has conceived in her virginal womb
By God's Breath, she bears in this stream.
If you wish to be guiltless you must wash in this bath,
Whether Adam's sin or your own presses you down.
This is the fount of life, which has cleansed the whole world,
Flowing from its source, Christ's Wound.
Only those reborn here may hope for the Kingdom of Heaven:
The blessed life is not for those born once.
Let no one fear the number or the nature of his sins:
The man born in this stream will be holy.

THE CHURCH FREES MEN FROM DEVILS

Vitae patrum Iurensium . . . Eugendi 11 (Gaul, 6th century), ed. B. Krusch, MGH, SRM, III (Hanover, 1896), pp. 158–59.

In the parish of Segny a certain girl, of high rank in the world, was seized upon by a cruel demon; she was not only shut up in a convent but even bound with iron chains. When many people, in the usual attempts to cure her, twined formulas of exorcism round her neck (the authors [of these formulas] being personally unknown to her), she, through the unclean spirit, jeered (sad to say) at their names and claimed that those who had written these texts had exhibited more vices in the past and had been guilty of that and that specific sin, which had been hidden from men's knowledge. Then one of the bystanders said to the possessed woman: "What are these others' sins to us? You terrify us by your own vices, Unclean One! Truly, in Christ's Name, I shall fasten not only the writings of those men whom you slander, but, if I can, of all the Saints, round your neck, so that you may be overcome by the crowd of those who command you, if you dare to despise these few." "You can," said the devil, "load me with cargoes of Alexandrian papyri, if you like, but you will never be able to expel me from the vessel I have got possession of, until you bring me the order of the monk of the Jura, Eugendus." Immediately, seizing on this last speech, they hasten with full faith to the most blessed man, and, fallen at his feet, relate what had happened, declaring that they would not return home, unless he would convey the Mercy of Christ to the oppressed girl.

The Father, conquered either by argument or by their prayers, after long prayer, sent a short letter to the most unclean one, as Gregory the Great formerly did to Apollo, writing and declaring as follows: "Eugendus, servant of Jesus Christ, in the Name of Our Lord Jesus Christ, of the Father and the Holy Spirit, Our God, I order you by this writing: Spirit of Gluttony and Rage and Fornication and Love and of the Moon and Diana, and of Midday and the Day and the Night and Every Unclean Spirit, go out from the human being who has this writing with her. I adjure you by the True Son of the Living God: Go out quickly and beware, lest you enter her again. Amen. Alleluia." Praying and folding up the text, he gave it to the suppliants to take with them. What more is there to say? They had not yet gone half way back when, behold, that villain, gnashing and howling, went out from the possessed before those returning had crossed the threshold of the house.

EXPECTATION OF A FUTURE LIFE: INSCRIPTIONS

1. Sicily, 4th century. From E. Diehl, ed., *Inscriptiones latinae christianae veteres,* I, no. 1549.

To Julia Florentina, sweetest and most innocent child, made one of the faithful, [her] parents placed [this stone]. She was born a pagan on [March 6], before it was light, under Zoilus, Governor of the Province. Eighteen months and twenty-two days later, while dying, she was [baptized], at the eighth hour of the night. She lived another four hours, so that she received communion again, and died at Hyble [near Catania, in Sicily] at the first hour of [September 25]. When both her parents were weeping for her without ceasing, at night the voice of Divine Majesty was heard, forbidding lamentation for the dead. Her body was buried in its coffin by the presbyter near the Martyrs' tombs on [October 9].

2. Die (in Gaul), *c.* 500. Diehl, II (1961), no. 3485.

Here Dalmata, redeemed by the death of Christ, rests in peace and joyfully, with the Saints interceding, awaits the Day of Future Judgment.

3. Briord (in Gaul), 501. Diehl, I, no. 1616.

Here reposes in peace Arenberga, of good memory, who lived twenty-eight years. She died in peace on [April 24], the Most Distinguished Avienus being consul. She freed [by her will] a [slave] boy, by name Manno, for the redemption of her soul.

4. Como (Italy), late 6th century, Diehl, II, no. 3863.

Here there rests in peace the servant of Christ, the Honorable Lady Gun-
telda, who lived in this world some fifty years. She was buried on [August
30]. There also repose here Basil, her son, together with his son, Guntio,
who lived in this world about fifty years. I adjure you all, Christians, and
you, the custodian of St. Julian's [church], by the Lord and by the tremendous Day of Judgment, that this tomb may never at any time be violated,
but be preserved to the end of the world, that I may without hindrance return
to life, when He shall come, who is to judge the living and the dead . . .

5. Bologna, probably 7th century. Diehl, I, no. 2349.

The body of Martin, cleric and doorkeeper of this church, is buried here
in peace. May Peter the Key-bearer absolve him from the bond of sin! He
died November 6 in the Fourth Indiction. I beg you, priests, that you will
pray for me a sinner!

6. Crypt of Abbot Mellebaudis, near Poitiers, late 7th century. From E. Le
Blant, ed., *Nouveau recueil des inscriptions chrétiennes de la Gaule*, Collection de
documents inédits sur l'histoire de France (Paris, 1892), nos. 247–48, pp.
259–60.

In the Name of God. Here I Mellebaudis, a debtor and servant of Jesus
Christ, constructed this cave for myself, where I lie, unworthy . . . [This is]
my tomb, which I made in the Name of the Lord Jesus Christ, Whom I
loved, in Whom I believed. It is truly right to confess Him as the living
God. His glory is great; in Him are peace, faith, love. He is God and man
and God is in Him. If there [is] someone who does not love to worship the
Lord Jesus Christ here and destroys this work, may he be Anathema Mara-
natha forever [Accursed in the Coming of the Lord].
  [Another inscription.] Alpha and Omega. The Beginning and the End.
For all things become every day worse and worse, for the end is drawing near.

THE VISION OF FUTURE JUDGMENT

Orientius, *Commonitorium* (early 5th century), II, vv. 309–46, ed. R. Ellis,
CSEL, 16 (Vienna, 1888), pp. 239–40.

Why should I inspect further the different crimes which will torment men [in the future life]? . . . Whoever has denied the Lord of Creation, bowing down his head to stocks and stones, he will be pitiable indeed but will be pitied by no one. He will suffer alone every torment. Innumerable worms will live in his always dying body and there will be no end to the fire.

On the other side will stand the crowd of pious friends of God. Those who, though injured, have not returned evil for evil, have given help to the wretched and food to the beggar, affection to their friends and obedience to their fathers, these will shine as the lights of the flaming sun, their shining limbs clothed in togas white as snow. Above all those whom both night and day find ready to fulfil the Law of Christ, who vowed never to pollute the snow-white baptismal robes by contact with women, who are chaste not only in body but in heart . . . they are already happy—this is the beginning of Glory—who have conquered the charms of the world and of the treacherous body, who, seeking the true life for the Name of Christ, have not feared to lay down their dedicated lives. And this holy army will include priests and monks withdrawn from the tumults of men, who, spurning the allurements of earthly fame, hope for the prizes of the Judgment Day. Free from care, leading a life of quiet leisure, they live well now, as they deserve, and will live better. For, when the Lord shall come as Judge of the world, they will crowd round their King in dense array, and, wherever the Lamb goes, they will go, transfused with the true Light, the Light of God. And their quickened faces will receive so much beauty that the eyes of men will not be able to gaze on them.

B. New Heroes and Ideals

One of the traits of their religion which Christians emphasized from the first was that it was a revolt "against the old ways." Against the extreme conservatism of pagan intellectuals of the fourth century, who held, in Macrobius' words, that "antiquity is always to be adored," against Symmachus' plea to respect the religion under which Rome had grown to greatness, Christians exulted in the inevitable overthrow of the old and corrupt by the new, in the radical changes Christianity was bringing about.

To pagans the most startling way in which the novelty of Christianity appeared was in its substitution of new ideals for old, in the invasion of a

From the Roman to the Barbarian World

bureaucratic world by charismatic heroes. Instead of the service of the Roman State and a gradual ascent through public office, many a young Christian, from the highest aristocracy down, chose, in the fourth and fifth centuries, a different way. He gave up his possessions, did not marry, or—if he was already married—ceased sexual relations with his wife, and dedicated himself to attaining union with Christ, by means of an ascetic existence and the service of Christ's poor, in the expectation of His Second Coming. To put such views into practice on a large scale, particularly during the Empire's political decline, was inevitably to provoke strong opposition.

In the first three centuries A.D. many Christians had lived celibate and ascetic lives, but separation from the world's normal standards was made more dramatic with the appearance of monasticism. The first monks appeared as hermits in Egypt and Palestine at the end of the third century. By 360 Egypt and Syria had large organized monastic communities and the movement was spreading to Asia Minor and, more slowly, to the West. There it met with considerable hostility. In the 380's a crowd rioted against monks in Rome. At least one Pope was very sceptical of the movement. Monks were jeered at in Carthage, persecuted in Spain. The first great monastic hero of the West, Martin, Bishop of Tours 371–97, came from what is today Hungary. Despite his miracles and ascetic life he was a highly controversial figure, with many enemies among the more conventional bishops of Gaul. It was after his death that his name became widely known through the *Life* and other writings dedicated to him by Sulpicius Severus.[2] A large part of these writings cannot be described as anything except a defense of a difficult cause.[3] Sulpicius (c. 363–c. 420) and his friend Paulinus of Nola (c. 353–c. 431) were young Roman aristocrats who had left the world and entered the monastic movement, still relatively new in the West. Paulinus, although settled at Nola in Southern Italy, kept in close touch with his native Gaul, not only with Sulpicius but with a number of ascetic-minded bishops, notably Victricius of Rouen in Normandy.

The monastic movement, with its hero in Martin of Tours, was especially devoted to the cult of the martyrs—the first heroes of Christianity—who had died during the persecutions of the Church by the Roman State. A considerable literature arose in the fourth century in the martyrs' honor.[4] Paulinus built two large churches at Nola in honor of the local saint Felix; his descriptions of the buildings and of the celebration of the anniversary of Felix's holy death by the surrounding peasantry are valuable.[5] At the same time Paulinus, together

2. Translated in *The Western Fathers*, ed. F. R. Hoare (London – New York, 1954).

3. See now J. Fontaine, *Vie de St. Martin*, 3 vols. (Paris, 1967–69), a new edition with translation and full commentary.

4. See, for instance, the Spaniard Prudentius' poems, *Peristephanon*, trans. H. J. Thomson (London and Cambridge, Mass., 1953).

5. See R. C. Goldschmidt, *Paulinus's Churches at Nola* (Amsterdam, 1940).

with the great St. Ambrose of Milan (d. 397), promoted the spread of the cult of the martyrs through the distribution of their relics. These were, at this time, not the martyr's whole body but a fragment of him or even a cloth which had touched his body or his tomb.

The rising tide of martyr and relic worship, closely linked to the monastic movement, was strongly disliked, not only by pagans, to whom the martyrs were simply "criminals" properly executed by the State for breaking the law, but by the party in the Church which opposed extreme asceticism. But neither rational criticism nor an imperial law of 386, forbidding traffic in relics, could stem the popularity of relic worship. Victricius of Rouen's *In Praise of the Saints* (*c.* 396) shows the heights that worship could reach. This work combines the original sermon delivered on the arrival at Rouen of the relics of different martyrs (the *second* consignment Victricius had received, both evidently from St. Ambrose) and a (presumably later) theological treatise explaining the cult. My translation is concerned with the sermon.

Letter 18 of Paulinus of Nola describes Victricius as a former soldier and as a monk and itinerant apostle before becoming a bishop.[6] Monks and nuns from the monasteries he founded play a prominent role in the procession which he describes as greeting the relics on their arrival. Victricius attempted to convert his rural diocese by establishing groups of monks in the countryside. He was probably, as his translator Mr. Walsh says, "one of the most influential missionary figures of his age." Some of his rhetoric may seem to us absurd but it was not so to his hearers and his thesis is clear. He presents the Christian ideal, expressed in the martyrs and in the male and female ascetics who fill his procession and *are* the new martyrs, since their life is a daily martyrdom. He presents his ideal as *new*, in deliberate opposition to the glories of the Roman Empire, symbolized in the emperor's entry into a city, which Victricius contrasts with the entry of the relics of martyrs into Rouen, followed by a very different escort, the heroes of the new age. Camille Jullian observed, "This entry of Relics surpassed, in emotional force, all spectacles and ceremonies which Gaul had yet seen." All those who took part believed that they now held at Rouen, in tangible, visible form, the *power* of the martyrs, of Christ's saints, to heal men and to forgive sins. Harnessing the monastic movement to this powerful belief certainly assisted it to triumph in the West. Relic worship also probably enabled Christianity to penetrate strata of the popular mentality which might otherwise have remained closed to it.

In 415 the body of the first martyr of Christ, St. Stephen, was discovered at Jerusalem. Its discovery generated almost as much enthusiasm as the finding of the True Cross almost a century before. It helped on the popularity of relics of martyrs. Shrines to Stephen sprang up all round the Mediterranean, including St. Augustine's North African See of Hippo.

6. In "Ancient Christian Writers," 35, trans. P. G. Walsh (Westminster, Md., 1966), pp. 167–77.

From the Roman to the Barbarian World

In dealing with the cult of martyrs, Augustine had always tried to maintain the proper theological balance. As he said in Sermon 318, "The Martyr Stephen is *honored* here but the Rewarder of Stephen is *adored.*" But Augustine's four sermons (given here as taken down in shorthand) on the miraculous cure of a brother and sister at St. Stephen's shrine at Hippo about 425 completely acquiesce in accounts (often read in church at Hippo) of miracles and visions due to relics. Augustine appears to sanction an element of competition among rival shrines to St. Stephen which foreshadows later competition among pilgrim centers. Paul's (the brother's) account of his misfortunes was clearly drawn up by Augustine. Coming from a Greek-speaking area, Paul could not have commanded Augustine's Latin or his theological references. These miracles of 425 were used by Augustine in *The City of God*, XXII, 8, where he states that in 424–26 almost seventy miracles had occurred at the shrine at Hippo.

For Augustine, relics were not strictly magical devices, since their efficacy depended on the intercession of the saint (ultimately on Christ), not on the relic itself. But in the sixth century Bishop Gregory of Tours explicitly rated dust from a martyr's tomb as more effective, *per se*, than a pagan wizard.

From the fifth century onward the cult of the ascetic confessor, monk, or bishop begins to rival the popularity of that of the martyr. Like the martyrs, ascetics were seen as "defenders" of their local city, replacing its ancient gods, as their shrines replaced pagan worship throughout the West, protecting their people against barbarians, plague, fire, and drought. They were the "omnipresent 'gendarmes' of the bishops, completing his action," invoked by him to punish malefactors, the incredulous, and the disobedient.

St. Martin of Tours was generally acclaimed the greatest ascetic of the West. In 473 a great new pilgrim church was built in his honor at Tours. The inscription over the entrance tells the pilgrims what to expect. It refers to some representations of Martin's miracles during his life but, more important to the pilgrims, it speaks of the continual chain of miracles wrought by him *now*, after his death. For another reference to the miracles at Tours, see the Letter from Nicetius of Trier (p. 79); by 565 Martin's shrine is associated with those of the other bishop-saints of Gaul but it is still pre-eminent.

Lives of saints, although providing much of our information on these centuries, differ, of course, in value: many were written long after their subject lived or are too stereotyped to be valuable. The *Life of Caesarius of Arles* has been called, by H. G. J. Beck, "by far the most complete and authoritative of Merovingian lives of the Saints." It was written within seven years of Caesarius' death by men who knew him well. It is most exceptional in preserving what appear to be genuine quotations from Caesarius' conversation. I have translated the greater part of Book I, which is concerned with Caesarius' public life.

Caesarius was bishop of Arles and Metropolitan (presiding bishop) of his ecclesiastical province for forty years (503–43), at a time when Arles and Provence were disputed among Visigoths, Franks, Burgundians, and Ostrogoths. His biographers are probably correct in ascribing credit to him for the relatively peaceful transition, first from Visigoths to Ostrogoths (508), and then (536) from Ostrogoths to Franks. He possessed the gift of fearlessness before kings—and both the kings he dealt with were Arians, not Catholics. He represents the role the native Gallo-Roman bishops played in the confused century between the collapse of Rome and the assured hegemony of the Franks.

Caesarius also represents the definite triumph of monasticism in the Gallic church. A monastic bishop, in the tradition which went back to Martin of Tours, he was faithful to both vocations. He made his clergy live or at least eat together—a painful experience for some of them—in order to enforce greater clerical discipline. He founded one of the first convents for women in Gaul and also wrote *Rules* for monks and nuns which were widely adopted and adapted. He made every effort to get the laity to participate in church services, to listen to sermons, and to memorize them. (In his sermons he also urges them to memorize biblical stories.) He allowed his presbyters and deacons to preach in his place and wrote sermons on every possible subject for their use. He made efforts to improve the recruitment of the rural clergy. A Church Council, over which he presided in 529, established a type of rural seminary for aspirants to the clergy.

Apart from the *Life of Caesarius* we also have his sermons.[7] Among these sermons, 1 (an address to the bishops and clergy), 6, and 13 (admonitions to the people) are perhaps particularly notable. I shall return to these sermons when speaking of Martin of Braga.

The literature of classical antiquity was written by and for the educated upper and middle classes, whose disinterest in manual work and inventions which might ease its burden for the majority of the population was complete. With Christianity the voice of new classes was heard. Fascination with demons, common to the peasantry of the Mediterranean world, entered *literature* for the first time with the New Testament. The Evangelists and St. Paul also made manual work respectable.

In these ways, as in others, monasticism was the prolongation of the New Testament. Physical labor soon became a laudable and integral part of communal monasticism, which most Christians agreed was the highest life open to man. In monastic *Rules* in the West and in the lives of monks such as Ursus, manual work appears, together with prayer and reading, as a basic part of life. From the fifth century onwards many of the vast forests, marshes, and wastelands of Western Europe were invaded by monks who brought them into cultivation. Monks, since they could not depend on abundant slave-labor, were also interested in labor-saving devices such as water-mills, known to, but little used by, the Romans. In men like Ursus and his monks, Christianity

7. Almost all the sermons appear in "The Fathers of the Church" series, 31 and 47, trans. Sr. M. M. Mueller (New York, 1956–64).

contributed to what Lynn White has called "The Agricultural Revolution of the Early Middle Ages" (*Medieval Technology and Social Change*, Oxford, 1962). By this revolution the life of the rural masses was significantly improved, perhaps for the first time in history.

Together with abundant literature on martyrs, monks and bishops, we have some fifth- and sixth-century accounts of nuns (notably of Ste. Geneviève of Paris) but hardly any of laymen, other than princes. Our information on the ideals they adhered to comes mainly from inscriptions, which naturally record the deaths of only the relatively rich. The main virtue the laity were required to display was that of almsgiving. One of the more interesting inscriptions is that of the merchant Agapius, found at Lyon, who died in 601. It says: "[Below] the epitaph you see, reader, rests the body of Agapius, the merchant of good memory. He was a place of refreshment for the miserable, and a door for the needy. Good to all, he was a constant visitor to the Saints' shrines and practiced almsgiving and prayer. He lived in peace 85 years. . . ."[8]

The Christians of the West were divided by language, and often also by ecclesiastical schism, from the Greek-, Syriac-, and Coptic-speaking East, but very much of their inspiration, in ascetic practices, in monasticism, in liturgy and art, as well as many of the relics they prized, came from the East. Pilgrimage to Palestine was undertaken by many Western Christians, laity as well as clergy. Our first detailed record of a pilgrimage to the East (from Bordeaux) dates from 333. Numerous other itineraries (translated for the Palestine Pilgrims' Text Society) and scattered references to pilgrims survive to show that the practice continued with scarcely a break, despite political and ecclesiastical difficulties.

Paulinus of Nola wrote about 410, "No other sentiment draws men to Jerusalem but the desire to see and touch the places where Christ was physically present, and to be able to say from their very own experience: 'We have gone into His tabernacle, and have adored in the place where His feet stood' (Psalm 132:7)."[9]

No doubt many pilgrims' motives were mixed, combining, at times, curiosity and tourism with asceticism (given the length and difficulty of the journey). But one may compare the desire to "see and touch the places" where their religion began with devotion to relics, which conveyed to men the physical presence of saints. In Palestine, Western Christians could see everything they knew from the Old and New Testaments, from the place where Abraham spoke with angels, and Lot's wife still frozen in stone, to the couch on which Christ reclined at the wedding at Cana in Galilee, "upon which," a sixth-century pilgrim remarks, "we reclined and upon which, I, unworthy that I am,

8. E. Diehl, ed., *Inscriptiones christianae latinae veteres*, I, no. 2483.

9. Letter 49 in "Ancient Christian Writers," 36, trans. P. G. Walsh (Westminster, Md., 1967), p. 273.

wrote the names of my parents." The *historicity* of the Incarnation and of the whole Bible was *verifiable*, as it were, by a pilgrimage to Palestine. This, too, was part of the Christian appeal.

The Martyr and His Relics

Rouen celebrates the arrival of relics (*c.* 396).
Victricius of Rouen, *De laude sanctorum*, ed. Jacobus Mulders, S.J., Thesis (unpublished), *St. Victrice de Rouen. Son "De Laude Sanctorum"* (Rome, 1953). This text will appear in *Corpus Christianorum, Series latina,* LXIV (1985).

1. We are taught, beloved brethren, by the present increase of spiritual benefits, that we belong to the Mercy of God and the Omnipotence of the Savior. We have seen no executioners, we have not known swords drawn against us and yet we set up altars of Divinity. No bloody enemy assails us today yet we are enriched by the Passion of the Saints. No torturer has stretched us on the rack yet we bear the Martyrs' trophies. No blood is shed now, no persecutor pursues us yet we are filled with the joy of those that triumph. Let us plunge ourselves in tears of joy for great joy is resolved in rich mourning. See how great a part of the heavenly army deigns to visit our city; our habitation is now among a legion of Saints and the renowned powers of the heavens. It is no slight mitigation of sins to have with you those you may charge with your cause, those you may assuage. . . . I regret, and in some sort, in human terms, I am sad that the dwellers in our hearts should have come so late: they would have found fewer sins had they come before. So, beloved, let this be our first petition to the Saints, that they may excuse our sins as merciful advocates and not search them out as judges. . . .

2. [To the bearers of the Relics.] Give them up, then, give! Why do you delay? Give me these temples of Saints. We must act rather than speak. If a light touch of the hem of the Savior's garment could cure, there is no doubt that these dwelling places of Martyrdom [the Relics], carried in our arms, will cure us. For this reason this labor brings on no fatigue. We bore our Apostles and martyrs already by Faith. The Saints come for the second time to the city of Rouen. They had already entered our hearts, now they honor the church of the city. [To the Saints.] Every age is at your service, each, in its devotion, tries to excel the other. Here are presbyters and deacons and every member of the clergy, known to you by his daily service. . . .

3. Known and long continued service feels greater awe of God. . . . And such a soldier [that is, Victricius himself] appears to serve you, who has been

tried by time . . . He is accustomed to consider himself infinitely enriched every time his hands are honored [by touching] the Relics of the Saints.

Here there presses the crowd of monks, with their faces emaciated by fasting, there the sonorous joy of innocent boys bursts out. Here the choir of devout and untouched virgins carries the ensign of the Cross. There the multitude of continent [men] and widows, wholly worthy of entering in this procession, for their life is all the more splendid that their lot has proved the harder. For the conflict is hard, when one has to resist known pleasures. If you do not know them the very nature of your ignorance defends you. If you do, your very knowledge is your enemy. The coldness of the death of her husband has extinguished the ardor of this woman and all her desire is enclosed in a sad monument. The surviving husband of another has kept her love but he has been seduced by the promise of eternity. Their lots have been different but their reward is the same. This other woman refused, in honor and shame, sexual relations while her husband lived; she lives today for the memory of the dead. Such great zeal for religion is its own justification, for where there is no thought of pleasures, there chastity dwells. A good conscience does free homage to the Saints. It presents nothing which scandal might harm or the slightest suspicion vex. The display of modesty and abstinence is praiseworthy zeal. [In this procession] no dress of Tyrian purple dazzles you, no carefully studied walk sets off floating and rustling silks. Here are no pearls and no gold necklaces. Human things inspire disgust to those concerned with the divine. As the Apostle teaches: "I have esteemed all these as dung that I might win Christ" (Philippians 3:8). These women advance in brilliant array, glowing with the intoxication of chastity. They advance, their only adornment the gifts of God. Their hearts are filled with the riches of the Psalms. There is no vigil night in which such jewels do not shine forth. There is no religious festival which such finery does not adorn. The crowd of the chaste is the joy of the Saints, the multitude of widows and continent attracts the heavenly powers. Hence old men's joy is mixed with tears, hence mothers' vows. These joys even take hold on the souls of children so that the whole people has only one feeling towards Your Majesty [the Saints].

4. Have mercy on us, have mercy! You can forgive. . . .

5. Now let us, beloved brethren, offer to the Holy Relics the words of the Psalms steeped in milk and honey. Let our sobriety, drunk with vigils and fasts, demand the forgiveness of our sins. Let us draw down on us the favor of the Saints, while their coming is still fresh. Their dwelling is on high but let us invoke them as our guests. . . . You, holy, inviolate virgins, chant, chant, and let your chants ascend the ladders that lead to Heaven, I mean

these Saints, who truly enjoy forever the clear light of Paradise, troubled with no clouds. Yes, strike these ladders with your feet, tire them with your assaults. . . .

6. Stretched out on the ground, and watering the earth with our tears, let us call out with one voice, so that you [the Saints], who inhabit forever the Holy Relics, may purge our bodies. Nor, Venerable Saints, will our offering [the new church] seem mean in your sight. This house is worthy to be inhabited by so many victors. Here you will find John the Baptist, he, I say, who stood, covered with blood in the common contest, but ascended crowned to Heaven, whom the Lord Himself accounts the greatest among the children of women. Here are Andrew, Thomas, Gervasius, Protasius, Agricola, Euphemia, that virgin with a man's soul, who did not pale under the butcher's knife. In fact there is here such a multitude of the citizens of Heaven that we would have had to find another place for the coming of Your Majesty today if you were not all united by your secret and by the unity of your power. . . .

You come from yourselves to yourselves. You will find Saints here, serving the altars of the Lord Jesus Christ. John the Baptist awaits you with open arms; Thomas, Andrew, Luke, the whole heavenly multitude calls you to itself. It is not a new host who greets you. It is those with whom you share the heavenly battle. But it will be a particular cause for joy to unite in their Relics those who are [already] united in spiritual light. . . .

9. Let no one, deceived by vulgar error, think that the truth of the whole of their bodily Passion is not contained in these fragments of the Just and in this apostolic consecration. We proclaim, with all our faith and authority, that there is nothing in these Relics that is not complete. For where healing power is present the members are complete. We say that the flesh is contained in coagulation of blood and we affirm that the spirit, bathed with the shedding of blood, has received the [Divine] Word's enflamed ardor. Since this is so, it is completely certain that our Apostles and Martyrs have come to us with all their powers. . . . A flame sheds forth its light but does not suffer loss by its radiation. So the Saints are munificent without suffering loss, they are whole without need of addition, and came to us without the fatigue of a journey. . . . The sun and the stars, the earth and the other names of these vain things are corruptible, because their origin is not spiritual.

10. But the Passion of the Saints is the imitation of Christ, and Christ is God. Therefore, no division is to be inserted in fullness, but in that division which is visible to the eye the truth of the whole is to be adored. . . . We see little Relics, a little blood. But truth perceives that these fragments are brighter than the sun, for the Lord has said in the Gospel: "My Saints shall

shine as the sun in the Kingdom of My Father" (Matthew 13:43), and then the sun will shine more brilliantly than today.

11. Add to this that no less curative power resides in the parts than in the whole. Do [the Saints' Relics] heal the sick in different ways in the East, at Constantinople, at Antioch, at Thessalonica, at Naisus [Nich], at Rome, in Italy? . . . John the Evangelist, who leaned on Christ's breast until the Consecration [of the Lord's Supper], cures at Ephesus and in many other places, and his same curative power is present among us. Proculus and Agricola cure at Bologna and we also contemplate their Majesty here [at Rouen]. Anthony cures at Piacenza, Saturninus and Troianus in Macedonia, Nazarius at Milan, Mutius, Alexander, Datysus, Chindeus spread the grace of salvation to large areas. Ragota, Leonida, Anastasia, Anatoclia cure. As the Apostle Paul says: "In a perfect man, in the measure of the age of the fullness of Christ, with one and the same Spirit, who works all in all" (Ephesians 4:13; 1 Corinthians 12:6, 11). I ask you, the healing power of the Saints I have named, is it different with us and with others? If, wherever there is anything of the Saints, they defend, purify, protect in the same way those who honor them, we have only to add to their cult, not to question their Majesty. . . . I show you with my hand what you are searching for. I touch remnants but I affirm that in these Relics perfect grace and virtue are contained. . . . He who cures lives. He who lives is present in his Relics. Apostles and martyrs cure and wash away sin. In their Relics they are bound together in the bond of all eternity. . . .

12. And so, beloved, while the [coming of the] crowd of Saints is recent, let us exert ourselves, and put forth sighs from the deepest veins of our bodies. Our advocates are here; let us throw open the history of our sins in prayer. Our judges are favorable. They can mitigate the sentence, for it was to them that it was said: "You shall sit on twelve thrones, judging the twelve tribes of the Children of Israel" (Matthew 19:28). They are always judges because they are always Apostles. But my speech has been spun out, less by interest in oratory than by the service of the Faith. . . . The Apostles and Martyrs have come—the bishop should not be silent. Altars are set up; let the people's joy begin with that of their priest. . . .

If some prince of the world came to our city today every street would be crowned with garlands for a festival, matrons would cover the roofs, the gates would vomit out a flood of people. People of every age, grouped in their guilds, would chant triumphal airs and songs of war. [The prince's] brilliant military uniform and Imperial purple would dazzle everyone. These treasures of the Red Sea and "frozen tears of wild beasts" would draw all eyes. And yet—they are a pretty sight but to be despised, if you consider, for in the end they are only stones. Yet the people would gape at all this. But, my beloved brethren, now that the triumph of the Martyrs and the splendor of their virtues come under our roofs, why do we not dissolve in joy? Eloquence is not necessary, only the pure simplicity of joy. What is lacking to stir our admiration? Instead of the royal cloak there is the clothing of eternal light. The Saints' togas have drunk this purple. Here are diadems adorned with the various splendor of the jewels of wisdom, intelligence, science, truth, counsel, strength, tolerance, temperance, justice, prudence, patience, chastity: in each of these stones is expressed and inscribed one of these virtues. The artist who has adorned with these spiritual jewels the Crowns of the Martyrs is the Savior. It is toward these jewels that we should set the sails of our souls: there is nothing fragile in them, nothing that decreases, nothing which can feel the passage of time. They flower more and more in beauty. The blood which the fire of the Holy Spirit still seals in their bodies and in these Relics shows that they are extraordinary signs of eternity. We rejoice, beloved, as often as we see darkness dispelled by light. Why should we not burst into greater joy when we see the saving splendor of eternal light arrive here? Today seems to me to be infused with a clear and serene joy. And rightly so, for, as I said, the Martyrs are seven times more resplendent than the sun.

But now, beloved, for us it is not enough to speak, we have to pray that we may repel every attack of the Devil, who enters our heart by a secret fall. Strengthen, O Saints, your worshipers, and found our heart on the cornerstone. The enemy is strong and fearful. He explores every approach, every entrance gate. But we have nothing to fear. Here is a multitude of Saints who come to us. When so great a number of soldiers and kings comes to our aid from the castles of Heaven let us seize on the arms of justice and prudence and protect ourselves with the shield of faith, not with an earthly breastplate but with that of temperance and modesty. In our right hands let us always brandish the weapons of faith and patience. Let us strike at once if any enemy attacks. Such arms the Apostles bore once. Armed with them they broke the necks of intemperance, lasciviousness, cupidity, ambition, wrath and pride. . . . Let no one desert the standards of the Savior. He has given us His example. He sends us aid. Victory is certain when one fights with such companions in arms and with Christ as Commander. The priest's helmet will shine on my head if your love looks on me in the battle. It is a spur to glory to fight before your eyes and at your head. . . .

Let there be no day, dearest brethren, in which we do not meditate on the stories [of the Martyrs]. This Martyr did not pale before the torturer, that other was swifter than the slow executioner in hurrying [to his death], another greedily swallowed the flames around him, another was cut in pieces but remained whole, another said he was happy that it was he who was to be crucified. Another in the butchers' hands, hastening to execution, lest he suffer delay, ordered rivers to turn back toward their source. That girl, as a daughter, sorrowed for her father's tears, but, as a Martyr, she despised them. Another girl, eager for death, by inciting him, excited a lion's wrath against herself. Another, while her child was fasting, stretched out full breasts to the wild beasts. That virgin bared her neck to the sword, with no other adornment than the jewels of eternity. There are thousands, dearest brethren, of examples of miraculous power which the holy page commemorates. But since we are exhorting rather than teaching we have plucked a few from many. For to the faithful a few things suffice, to the unfaithful many are of no use.

Let us not put off further the desire of the Saints. Why delay? Let this church open to the Divine Martyrs. Let their Relics be united and their favors. Let these first fruits of the Resurrection come together. Meanwhile let our confession be made quietly. The [heavenly] powers delight in the forgiveness of sins.

It was not without reason, dearest brethren, that, wishing to build, I appropriated the land for this basilica. The coming of the Saints justifies my ambition. It was they who, by the secret logic of my desire, ordered a palace to be prepared for them. Yes indeed, it was they. We have laid the foundations, we have prolonged the walls, and today we learn for whom our zeal for the work grew. That is why all delays are blameworthy. We are still too slow and idle for my taste. I enjoy rolling great stones along and carrying them on my shoulders. Let the earth drink my sweat—alas that it cannot drink my blood, shed for the Name of the Savior! At least let it drink my sweat, this earth which will receive the altars. If our Apostles and Martyrs see us faithful in this work they will invite other [Saints] to join them here.

Miracles wrought by the relics of St. Stephen at Hippo.
Augustine, *Sermones* 320–23 (a shorthand report, *c.* 425), *PL*, 38, col. 1442–46.

320 (Easter Day). On a man healed by the prayers of St. Stephen.

We are accustomed to hear accounts read of miracles obtained by the prayers of the Most Holy Martyr Stephen, but today the presence of this young man replaces a book. You who recall what you lamented to see him suffering, now joyfully read what you see, so as to glorify Our Lord God more fully, and to engrave in your memory what is written in him. . . .

321 (Monday after Easter). We said yesterday, as Your Charity recalls, that the presence of this man here is proof of his healing. But, since he has told us some things which you should know, which will excite in you a more lively wonder and make you glorify Our Lord still more in the shrines of His Saints . . . it is right to read the account which contains all we have heard from him. Tomorrow you will hear it.

322 (Tuesday after Easter). Yesterday we promised Your Charity the reading of the account of the healing of this man, of the things you could not see. . . . Let us have the brother and sister appear before you, so that those of you who have not seen what he suffered may see it by what she still undergoes. Let them both, then, stand forth [on the sanctuary steps], the one who has been healed by God's Grace, and the other, for whom we must pray for mercy.

Copy of the account given by Paul to Bishop Augustine

I pray you, Blessed Bishop Augustine, to order the recitation of this account to the holy people, which I have presented at your command.

While we still inhabited our fatherland, Caesarea in Cappadocia, our elder brother assailed our mother with atrocious and intolerable insults and went so far as to strike her. We, the rest of her children, who were all present, took this quietly. None of us asked our brother why he treated our mother in this way. Outraged by this treatment she resolved to punish her son by cursing him. While she was hurrying at cockcrow to the Baptistry to call the wrath of God down on her son, she saw appear before her some demon, in the shape of one of our uncles, who asked her where she was going. She answered, to curse her son for the intolerable insult she had received. That enemy [of mankind], when he found easy access to the heart of this enraged woman, persuaded her to curse all her children. This advice of the serpent inflamed her rage. She prostrated herself at the sacred font and, with her hair dishevelled and her breasts bare, begged God that, exiled from our land and wandering over the earth, we might appal all men by our example.

The vengeance of Heaven followed soon after these maternal prayers, and our elder brother was seized by a horrible trembling in every limb, such as Your Holiness saw in me three days ago. Then all of us, by order of birth, were seized, within a year, by the same punishment. Our mother, seeing her curses so efficacious, could not endure any longer the knowledge of her impiety and men's contempt. She strangled herself with a rope and ended a sad life by a sadder death. Then we all left our city, being unable to bear our shame, and dispersed. Of the ten of us the second was cured, we have heard, at the shrine of the Glorious Martyr St. Laurence which has just been set up at Ravenna. As for me, who come sixth, with my sister, who comes after me, wherever I learnt that there were holy places, where God worked miracles, I traveled there for the great desire I had to regain my health. To say nothing of other famous shrines of Saints, I came to Ancona in Italy, where the Lord works many miracles by His Most Glorious Martyr Stephen. But I could not be cured except here, because this place was chosen by Divine Predestination. I did not leave out Uzali in Africa, where the Blessed Martyr Stephen is said to work many miracles. But, three months ago, on the Kalends [1st] of January, I and my sister, who is here with me, still suffering from the same torment, were taught by a vision. An old man, venerable for his brilliant aspect and white hair, told me that within three months I would receive the health I wanted. My sister, in another vision, saw Your Holiness [that is, Augustine] just as we see you today. By this we learnt that we should come here. And indeed I have often seen Your Holiness in other cities on our journey, as I see you today. Taught by clear Divine Authority we came to this city about fifteen days ago. You have seen my suffering and my miserable sister still displays before you what we all underwent. And all those who see in her what I was can know the greatness of the grace the Lord has worked in me by His Holy Spirit. I prayed every day, shedding floods of tears, in the place where the shrine of the Most Glorious Martyr Stephen is. On Easter Sunday, as those who were there saw, while I was praying and crying, holding on to the bars [of the shrine], I suddenly fell down. I lost my senses and did not know where I was. After a little I rose up and did not feel that horrible trembling in my body. Full of gratitude for such a gift of God I have offered you this account, in which I have set down what you did not know of our calamities, and what you know of the perfect cure I have received, so that you may deign to pray for my sister and thank God for me.

323. [After the reading of the above account, the brother and sister having gone down from the sanctuary steps, Augustine speaks.]. . . . For us, my brethren, let us hasten to thank God for the man who has been cured and pray for his sister who still suffers greatly. Let us bless God, who has found us worthy to see this wonder. For what am I, who appeared to this brother and sister without knowing it? They saw me without my knowing it and were told to come here. Who am I? A man like many others. And, to tell Your Charity the truth, I greatly wonder and rejoice at the grace given us. This man could not be cured at Ancona, or rather he could very easily have been cured there but he was not, because of us. Many of you know how many

miracles are done there by the Most Holy Martyr Stephen. Hear something which will amaze you. The shrine of Stephen at Ancona is ancient. Perhaps you will say: "His body was only discovered recently. How could there be a shrine to him at Ancona before that?" The reason is hid from me but I will not conceal what I have heard. When St. Stephen was stoned, innocent men and especially those who already believed in Christ were present. It is said that a stone struck Stephen on the elbow and then rebounded at the feet of one of these Christians. He took it and kept it. He was a sailor. His voyages took him to Ancona and it was revealed to him that he should leave this stone there. He obeyed; from then on there is a shrine of St. Stephen at Ancona, and, since the truth was not known, men thought that Stephen's arm was there. . . . Miracles did not begin there until after the body of St. Stephen was discovered. If this young man was not cured there, it was because God kept the sight for us. . . .

While Augustine was speaking the people began to cry out from the shrine of St. Stephen: "Thanks be to God! Praise to Christ!" While this clamor went on, the girl [just] cured [the sister of the narrator Paul] was led to the sanctuary. As soon as the people saw her, it broke into joy and tears and continued to shout for some time, with no words audible but only noise. When silence was at last restored, Bishop Augustine said: "It is written in a Psalm, 'I have said: I will confess my sin to the Lord My God, and Thou hast forgiven me the sin of my heart' (Psalm 32:5). 'I have said: I *will* confess'; I have not confessed yet. . . . I recommended this wretched girl to your prayers (or rather, she who *was* wretched). We were *about* to pray and we were heard. Let our joy be a thanksoffering. Our Mother the Church is heard sooner than [that girl's] mother was heard, for her destruction. Let us turn to the Lord. . . ."

THE ASCETIC CONFESSOR: ST. MARTIN OF TOURS

Inscription at the entry to the new church of St. Martin at Tours (completed 473), addressed to the pilgrims. Paulinus of Périgueux, *De orantibus*, ed. M. Petschenig, *Corpus scriptorum ecclesiasticorum latinorum*, 16 (Vienna, 1888), p. 165.

When you have bowed down to the earth, your face sunk in the dust, your wet eyes pressed to the beaten ground, raise your eyes, and, with a trembling glance, perceive wonders and commit your cause to the best of patrons. No book can include such great achievements though they are here recorded in

stone and inscriptions. The earth does not shut in [Martin's] labor, which the
Royal Court of Heaven has received and the stars inscribe in shining jewels.
If you seek the help of Martin, rise beyond the stars, touch heaven, inspect
the angelic host in the aerial region. There, joined to his Lord, seek for your
patron, as he steadily follows the steps of the Eternal King. If you are doubt-
ful, look at the miracles you see here, by which the True Savior honors His
servant's merit. As you gaze on what should be recounted and retell what
you have seen, you have become the last of many thousands of witnesses.
All the wonders the Holy Scriptures recount, [Martin] renews by God's aid.
The blind, the lame, the poor, the possessed, the tormented, the sick, the
feeble, the oppressed, the captive, the afflicted, the indigent, all profit by
his gift. Every cure shows forth miracles worthy of the Apostles. He who
comes in weeping, goes out rejoicing. All clouds are dispelled. [Martin] is
the remedy which calms remorse. Ask for his assistance: it is not in vain
that you knock at this door. His generous goodness extends over the whole
world.

The Pastoral Bishop: St. Caesarius of Arles (470–543)

Vita S. Caesarii Arelatensis a discipulis scripta, I, ed. G. Morin, *S. Caesarii
Arelatensis Opera Omnia*, III (Maredsous, 1942), pp. 297–323.

3. The Holy and most Blessed Bishop of Arles, Caesarius, is accounted a
native of the territory of Chalon-sur-Saône [in Burgundy]. His parents and
family stood—a great and leading example of honor and nobility—above
all their fellow citizens for their faith and virtues. . . .

4. When Caesarius had reached his eighteenth year, desirous, although
his family and parents did not know it, to attain a dwelling in the heavenly
kingdom, he threw himself at the feet of the Holy Sylvester, bishop at that
time, and begged him to tonsure him and, changing his clothes, free him for
Divine Service, and not allow his suppliant to be taken back by his parents
to his patrimony and former ties. The bishop, thanking Christ, allowed no
delay to such excellent wishes. When, with this beginning, Caesarius had
served for two years or more at Chalon, inflamed by Divine Grace, he decided to free himself more completely and become more unencumbered for
God's service, and, as the Gospel teaches, to leave not only his parents but
his country.

5. So, seizing his liberty by a profitable flight from the world's shackles,
the newly recruited Saint set out for the monastery of Lérins [off the South

coast of Gaul]. . . . He was received by the Holy Abbot Porcarius and all the elders. . . .

6. After a short time he was chosen Cellarer of the monastery. He was most careful and attentive in giving what was necessary to those who needed it, or who, for love of abstinence, demanded nothing, but to those to whom he found that what they wanted was not necessary, he would give nothing, although they asked for it. For this reason those to whom holy discernment was foreign asked the abbot to remove him from office, which was done. As soon as this task was laid aside, he so afflicted himself with what he loved, ceaseless reading, recitation of the Psalms, prayer, and vigils, that by excessive austerity he made his weak young body, which needed rather to be pampered than enfeebled, broken and bent. For instance, he lived for a week at a time on a few boiled herbs or a little gruel which he prepared each Sunday. . . .

7. Finally, his stomach giving way, he fell ill of a kind of quartan ague. . . . His holy abbot, gravely troubled by his illness, commanded and indeed forced him to go to the city of Arles to recover his health [c. 496].

8. At that time the Illustrious man Firminus, a devout Christian, and his close relation, the Most Illustrious matron Gregoria, were living in Arles; by their zeal and care for the clergy and monks, the citizens and the poor, the city was rendered more brilliant. . . . Out of compassion they took in Caesarius when he reached Arles. . . .

10. After a few days the aforesaid persons made known to the Holy Eonius, Bishop of Arles, that there was in their house a venerable and altogether praiseworthy monk, whom he ought to know and speak with in private. . . . When Caesarius had been presented to him, Bishop Eonius carefully inquired which city he came from and who his parents were. When he revealed he was from Chalon and what his family was, the bishop, greatly rejoicing, said: "My son, you are my fellow citizen and relation. . . ." He therefore began to look on the young man not as a foreigner or stranger but more closely, with the eyes of the heart.

11. The bishop soon demanded Caesarius from his Abbot, the Holy Porcarius . . . who gave him up, although unwillingly. Caesarius was ordained deacon, then presbyter. But he never gave up his monastic condition nor modified in the least the regulations of Lérins. A cleric by priesthood and functions, he remained a monk by humility, charity, obedience, and mortification. He was the first to enter the church at Matins and other hours of prayer and the last to leave. . . .

12. An abbot on an island near Arles dying, Caesarius was sent there by Eonius, so that . . . he might form the monastery in the discipline which

should be observed under an abbot. He willingly resumed the [monastic] life, . . . which he had always practiced even within the city and had always desired. He labored daily with such constancy in the monastery that God is [still] well served there today [fifty years later].

13. When he had spent a little over three years as abbot on this island, Eonius called together the clergy and [leading] citizens of Arles. He asked that when, at God's Will, he went to Christ, they should elect none other than Caesarius as his successor, so that they might rejoice when ecclesiastical discipline, which Eonius lamented had been relaxed in many ways because of his illness, might be brought back by Caesarius to its ancient state and vigor, and the work of [Caesarius as] his successor might be of some profit to [Eonius as] his predecessor, for when he left such an heir he might receive an increase of eternal blessing in the election of such a holy man. . . . [Receiving general assent to his proposal] Eonius sent messengers to the secular rulers [the Visigothic King Alaric II, to ask for ratification of his request]. All these things being arranged by Divine Providence, sure of his successor, Eonius went to the Lord.

14. When the news reached Caesarius that he would be ordained bishop, he sought out a hiding place among some tombs. But he could not be hidden, for not a sin but Grace found him out. . . . So he was compelled to receive the burden of the episcopate [503]. . . .

15. From the beginning the careful and zealous pastor of all men, he at once decreed that every day clerics should chant the Offices of Terce, Sext, and None, accompanied with hymns, in the Basilica of St. Stephen, so that if by chance some layman or penitent wished to follow these Offices he would have no excuse for not doing so every day. Caesarius himself, casting aside all care for earthly things, imitating the Apostles, calling God to witness, entrusted the administration of the Church's goods to delegates and deacons, and freed himself entirely for the Word of God, for reading, and for ceaseless preaching. . . .

16. God gave him such great grace in his speech that whatever he could see with his eyes he was able to use in the form of examples for the edification of his hearers. He so compared the chain of holy writings that he always collected the recent testimonies [from the New Testament] without losing anything of the Old [Testament]. . . .

17. When bishops or presbyters and all ranks of ministers of God or the citizens or even strangers came to see him, after greeting them and praying, for a short time he would give advice on the state of mind and welfare of his visitors or their fellow citizens. But soon, taking up the weapons of holy preaching, pointing out the uncertainty of the present, the perennity of Beatitude, he attracted some with soft speech and frightened others with

sharper words, correcting some with threats, some with charm, he drew some back from vices by love, others by severity, warning some in general terms by proverbs, reproving others more roughly and calling God to witness. With tears he threatened them with eternal punishments, to make them attend to his warnings. He put forward his teaching as he knew the manners, virtues, or vices of each man, so as to incite the good to glory and recall the bad from punishment. As a good doctor he provided different medicines for different wounds, offering not what would please each man but what would cure him, not regarding the sick man's pleasure but properly desirous of the health of the sick.

18. He used greatly to urge the bishops and other rulers of the Church not to cease to minister spiritual food to the people under their charge, saying: "Brother, you hold in Christ's Name a place in the first rank of the spiritual army. Attend with pastoral skill to the talents given you so as to restore them, doubled in value, to [God], Who lent them out on interest. Hear the prophet: 'Woe to me, for I kept silent!' (Isaiah 6:5). Hear the Apostle saying fearfully: 'Woe to me, if I do not preach the Gospel!' (1 Corinthians 9:16). Beware lest, while you occupy the episcopal throne, another may perhaps be excluded, and it may be said to you: 'They have taken the key of knowledge. They neither enter in themselves nor allow others to come in' (Luke 11:52), who could perhaps have better answered the Lord's interest." But, by the Lord's inspiration, Caesarius had this particular gift that, while he was bringing forth different things for each man, he revealed to each the course of his life, so that he who heard him not only thought him one who could read the heart but a witness to his conscience. And, as he was most severe to himself, so, for others' correction, he appeared severe to them.

19. He also added and enforced [the rule] that the laity should prepare Psalms and hymns, proses [hymns of a more popular style] and antiphons, which they should chant in a high and modulated voice, like clerics, some in Greek, some in Latin, and should not have time to waste telling stories in church. He also instituted very moving sermons, suitable for the Christian year and for Saints' festivals.

20. He took especial thought for the sick and assisted them. He chose a most spacious house in which they might listen, without any disturbance, to the Offices of the basilica. He provided beds, covers, and expenses, together with a man who could care for and treat the sick. He did not deny captives [of war] and the poor freedom to speak with him. He always instructed his minister: "See if any poor people are outside, lest, so as not to trouble us, timid and ashamed poverty may suffer injury for which we are responsible. We should not fulfill our office if we delayed to attend to the miserable or to listen to those who come to us from different provinces because of the hard-

ships they undergo." When he had freed men, as the case demanded, having taken them under the Church's protection and prayed that they should be safe, he let them go. Sighing heavily, he used to say: "Truly Christ is made a chatterer and prattler to the deaf, and yet He begs, persuades, warns, and calls all to witness." He used to add that what we advance the poor in the world we commend to Christ as surety on earth what we will receive later in Heaven. . . .

21. But adversity, that servant of the Devil, troubled the peace of this holy man, and, since no vices could be brought against him, he was accused of treason. For one of his notaries, an abandoned wretch, Licinianus by name, began to act against him the part Judas did not fear to play against Our Savior. Armed with the poison of a most brutal accusation, he suggested to King Alaric, through his counsellors, that Caesarius, since he came from [Burgundy] was seeking with all his strength to bring the territory and city of Arles under the control of the Burgundians. In reality that preeminent pastor was on his knees night and day, imploring the Lord to grant peace to the nations and quiet to the cities. For this very reason one must believe that it was the Devil who aroused barbarian ferocity to bring on the exile of the holy man. For he who prays is not acceptable or pleasing to the Enemy, for he gainsays his works. So, now, neither was the faith of innocence considered nor the truth of the accusation, but Caesarius, condemned by false and illegal accusations, was taken from Arles and relegated to Bordeaux, as if in exile [506].

22. But, that God's Grace in him might not be hidden, it happened by chance that one night [Bordeaux] was struck by a serious fire and the people, rushing to the man of God, shouted: "Holy Caesarius, by your prayers extinguish the raging flames!" When he heard this, moved by sorrow and pity, he threw himself in prayer in the path of the fire and at once stopped and repelled the masses of flames. At this sight, the voices of all present proclaimed the praise of God's Power through Caesarius. After this miracle he was so admired by all men that in Bordeaux he was seen not merely as a bishop but as an Apostle. . . .

23. He always taught, there and everywhere, that men should render to God what are God's and to Caesar what are Caesar's (see Matthew 22:21), as the Apostle teaches (see Titus 3:1), obey, indeed, kings and powers, when their orders are just, but despise the depravity of King [Alaric's] Arian belief. . . .

24. After the Saint's innocence was established, the abominable Prince [Alaric] asked him to return to Arles. . . . The King ordered that his accuser should be stoned. As the people were already rushing up, with stones in

their hands, the King's order suddenly came to Caesarius' ears. . . . He did not wish vengeance on his accuser but preferred that he should be preserved to do penance at his intercession. . . .

25. God's servant sought especially to keep [the rule] that no sinner, whether a slave or a free man under his protection, should ever receive more strokes than legitimate [ecclesiastical] discipline [prescribes], that is 39. If indeed he were found guilty of grave sin, Caesarius allowed him to be beaten again a few days later. He instructed the provosts of the church that if anyone ordered a man to be beaten more than this and he died of the beating, the man responsible would be guilty of murder.

26. When it was announced that Caesarius was returning [to Arles] and was nearing the city, every brotherhood and both sexes went out to meet him with candles and crosses, singing Psalms as they awaited the holy man's coming. And since Christ makes his faithful rejoice at His miracles and confounds the wicked by the clear light of wonders, the Lord bestowed a most plentiful rain on the ground, suffering from a very long drought. . . .

27. One day, while at the altar, after the Gospel was read, Caesarius saw some men leaving the church and disdaining first to hear his sermon. Hurrying [to the doors] he called to the people: "What are you doing, my sons? Where are you going, led by some evil idea? Stay here! Listen to the sermon for the good of your souls and listen carefully! You will not be able to do this at Judgment Day! I warn and clamor: do not be fugitives or deaf. If the soul of one of you falls under the Devil's strokes, I will not be held guilty of silence. I attest it by the force of my word." Because of this he very often ordered the doors to be closed after the Gospel. . . .

28. Caesarius, inspired by God, conceived the idea that the Church of Arles should be adorned and the city defended not only by innumerable crowds of clergy but also by choirs of virgins. . . . But diabolical envy for a time opposed these plans. For, after King Alaric had been killed by the most victorious King Clovis in battle [at Vouillé, 507], the city being under siege by Franks and Burgundians, Theodoric, King of Italy, sent an army led by his generals into Provence [508]. In this siege the monastery which Caesarius had begun to build for his sister and other virgins was largely destroyed, its beams and upper stories torn to pieces and thrown down by the barbarians' ferocity. . . .

29. Then one of the clergy, Caesarius' fellow citizen [from Chalon] and relation, terrified by fear of captivity and moved by youthful inconstancy, instigated by the Devil against the servant of God, letting himself down by a rope over the wall by night, gave himself up next day to the enemies besieging the city. When the Goths within knew this, in a rising of the people,

they rushed at the holy man, the crowd of Jews immoderately shouting and clamoring that the bishop had sent his fellow citizen by night to deliver the city to the enemy. No thought was given to faith or proof or to a clean conscience, the Jews and [Arian Gothic] heretics shouting at him without any reverence or moderation. The bishop was taken from his house and kept under close custody in the palace, so that he might either be drowned by night in the depths of the Rhône or at least held prisoner in the fortress of Ugernum. . . .

30. The church-house and the bishop's cell were filled with Arians. . . . But since the Goths could not break through the blockade of boats across the Rhône, they brought Caesarius back by night to the palace and kept him in secret, so that no Catholic knew whether he was alive.

31. While, the Devil rejoicing, this was going on to the joy of the Jews, who were giving out everywhere, without any fear of perfidy, disgraceful charges against the faithful, one night one of the Jewish band threw a letter, tied to a stone, at the enemy, as if to strike them, from the place on the city wall which the Jews were guarding. In this letter, mentioning his name and sect, he invited them to place their scaling ladders at night in the place the Jews guarded, provided that, in return for this help, no Jew within Arles should be captured or plundered. But in the morning, when the enemy had withdrawn a little from the wall, some [of the besieged] going outside the advance breastwork, among the ruined buildings . . . found the letter, brought it back, and published its contents to all men in the forum. Soon its author was found, convicted, and punished. Then indeed the savage cruelty of the Jews to God and man appeared openly. Soon our Daniel was taken out from the lions' den. . . .

32. The Goths returned to Arles with a vast number of prisoners. The holy basilicas, even the church-house, were filled with infidels. Since [the prisoners] were in great penury, Caesarius both fed and clothed them abundantly until he could free them all by purchase. When he had spent all the money Eonius his predecessor had left to the church . . . he carried the holy work to the instruments of the divine ministry; when he had given the censers, chalices, and patens of the church, he even had the ornaments of the temple sold for the redemption of the true temple of God (see 1 Corinthians 3:16). Even today the marks of axes can be seen on the pillars and screens of the sanctuary where the silver ornaments of the columns were torn off.

33. By doing this Caesarius did not deform but adorned and defended the Church. He made the bowels of their Mother open to her sons. . . . He used often to say: "I would very much like some of my Lords the bishops and other clerics to tell me what they would say (those who, by I know not what

love of superfluity, refuse to give insensible silver or gold from Christ's treasuries for men Christ owns), I would like, I say, to know what they would say if these disasters happened to *them*, whether they would wish to be freed by these insensible gifts. Would they speak of 'sacrilege' if someone delivered *them* at the price of slight objects consecrated to God? I do not believe that God will blame me for redeeming captives with what has been given for His service, Who gave Himself for man's redemption." We see some, indeed, praise the holy man's action but they do not attempt to imitate it, . . .

34. We, however, firmly believe in the Lord that it is by the compassion and faith and prayers of Blessed Caesarius that, although the city of Arles was besieged in his days, it was neither captured nor plundered. Thus, as the kingdom was then transferred from the Visigoths to the Ostrogoths, so today it is subject in Christ's Name to the rule of the Most Glorious King Childebert [511–58], as we read "They went from one nation to another, from one kingdom to another people, and," under *that* man [Caesarius], "God did not suffer" his men of Arles "to be harmed" (Psalm 105:13–14).

35. Caesarius [rebuilt] the monastery which he had begun to prepare for his sister . . . He called Caesaria from a monastery at Marseille (he had sent her there to learn what to teach and to be a disciple before being a mistress) and installed her with two or three companions in the cells he had prepared. Crowds of virgins came there in troops. Renouncing their fortunes and families . . . they longed for Caesarius as father and Caesaria as mother. . . . They were so sequestered that, to the day they died, none of them were allowed to go outside the door of the monastery. . . .

36. The Devil, raging as a savage lion against Christ's servant, by a made-up accusation again had the bishop removed from Arles and taken under guard to Ravenna in Italy [513]. . . . He reached the palace, and, with Christ as leader, approached King Theodoric. When the King saw before him the man of God, unafraid and venerable of aspect, he reverently rose to greet him, and, removing his diadem from his head, again saluted him most kindly, first questioning him on his laborious journey, then affectionately inquiring as to his Goths and the citizens of Arles. When the holy bishop had gone out, the King addressed his Court: "God will not spare those who have unnecessarily made this innocent and holy man undertake such a long and painful journey. What he is I understood when he came in: I trembled violently all over. I saw," he said, "an angelic face, an apostolic man: I consider it wicked to think any evil of a man one should venerate."

37. When Caesarius had been received in an inn, the King sent as a gift a silver dish for his table (its weight reached about 60 pounds, it contained 300 "solidi"), with the message: "Accept, Holy Bishop; your son the King

begs Your Beatitude to receive kindly this little gift and to use it in memory of him." But Caesarius, who never had silver on his table except for spoons, three days later had the dish valued and publicly sold by his ministers, and began to free many prisoners with its price. The King's servants soon informed him: "We saw your royal gift exposed for sale. With its value Caesarius is freeing crowds of prisoners. There was such a mass of the poor in his lodging and the courtyard of his house was so full that one could scarcely reach and greet him for the throng of poor men speaking to him. We also saw great troops of the unfortunate hurrying through the streets, going and returning to him."

38. When Theodoric heard of this deed he was moved to such praise and admiration that the observant Senators and nobles in his palace all rivaled each other in distributing their offerings through the Blessed Man, proclaiming they were divinely favored that they had been worthy to see such a bishop, who, in their time, by his deeds and sayings, was a true successor of the Apostles and an Apostolic Man. And, since nothing travels faster than fame, as the holy work gathered strength, the holiness of St. Caesarius at once flew to Rome, and he began to be wished for with such strength of love by the Senate and nobles, the Pope, clergy, and people, that he was taken to everyone's heart before he was seen in the body. Meanwhile he redeemed all the captives he could from across the River Durance, and especially from the city of Orange, which had been entirely reduced to captivity, part of whom he had [already] freed at Arles and soon discovered in Italy. So that their liberty might be made more complete, he paid for horses and wagons on their journey and brought them home again. . . .

42. Coming to Rome, he was presented to the then Pope, St. Symmachus [d. 514], and then to the Senators and their wives. They all returned thanks to God and King Theodoric. . . . Symmachus was so moved by Caesarius' great merits and holiness that he not only honored him as a Metropolitan [Archbishop], but gave him the special privilege of [wearing the] Pallium [a liturgical vestment to be worn at Mass]. . . .

43. Returning, Caesarius entered the city of Arles. He was received with Psalms, and, having gone away an exile, he brought with him from Italy, after redeeming the captives, 8000 "solidi". . . .

52. Who can describe how much grace appeared in his discussion of biblical questions and in elucidating obscure passages? He was greatly pleased if someone stimulated him to discuss them. He himself very often urged us on, saying: "I know you do not understand everything. Why do you not ask, so as to know? For cows do not always go to the calf, but sometimes calves to cows, to satisfy their hunger. . . . You should do the same, for in asking questions you also exercise our minds to inquire where we can find honey for your spirit. . . ."

54. He taught from memory as much as possible and always preached in a loud voice in church. When he could not preach himself, because of illness . . . he decided to instruct and place presbyters and deacons to carry out this office [instead]. Thus it would be more difficult for any bishop to suspend teaching necessary to all men on the excuse of his own incapacity. He said: "If the words of the Lord, of Prophets and Apostles, are recited by presbyters and deacons, why should they not repeat the words of Ambrose, Augustine, or any Saints, or of my own littleness? 'The servant is not greater than his Lord' (John 15:20). I think it lawful for those who are authorized to read the Gospel to recite the homilies of God's servants or expositions of canonical Scriptures in church. I discharge my responsibility by introducng this [custom]; the bishops who refuse to carry it out should know they will have to state their reasons at the Day of Judgment. For I cannot believe that anyone is so obdurate that when God says to him, 'Do not cease to call out' (Isaiah 58:1), he neither calls out himself nor allows others to do so. Let him fear the saying, 'Woe to those keeping silence about Thee, for the loquacious are dumb' (*ibid.* 6:5) and that other, 'Dumb dogs who cannot bark' (*ibid.* 56:10). The bishop will have to answer for as many souls as sheep go astray while he is silent."

55. Caesarius wrote sermons suitable to different Festivals and places but also against the evils of drunkenness and lust, discord and hatred, wrath and pride, the sacrilegious and soothsayers, against the most pagan rites of the Kalends, against augurs, tree and spring worshipers, and other vices. He had these sermons ready so that if someone came and asked for them, he not only did not refuse the request, but if he even hinted he would like them, Caesarius offered them to him and brought him them to read. He sent bishops far off in France, the Gauls, Italy, and Spain what they might have preached in their churches. . . .

56. He never ordained a deacon in his church before his thirtieth year. He never would ordain anyone, whatever his age, unless he had read the books of the Old and New Testament four times through. . . .

57. He planned and built a triple basilica in one building; the central aisle was dedicated to the higher cult of Holy Mary Virgin, one of the side aisles to St. John, the other to St. Martin. To relieve the holy virgins he had assembled from the task of burial he had monolithic chests newly cut out of great stones, very fit for human bodies, and had them spread out in close ranks over the whole floor of the basilica, so that whatever member of the congregation left the world, she would find a most holy place prepared for her tomb.

58. The monastery's Mother, Caesarius' sister, Caesaria, going to her reward in Christ, he buried her there by the episcopal throne, beside the grave

he had prepared for himself. She was succeeded by the Mother Caesaria who now rules. Her work and her companions' flourishes so that, among Psalms and fasts, vigils and reading, the virgins of Christ copy holy books beautifully, with their Mother as their teacher.

59. Caesarius continued urgent in prayer, reading, and almsgiving and in ceaseless preaching every Sunday and all Feast days. Homilies were also often read at Matins and Vespers for the sake of those present, so that no one might excuse himself on the ground of ignorance. . . .

60. Many rivals arose, indeed, who resisted his preaching of the doctrine of Grace. But O Happy Rivalry! For, through the murmuring and evil interpretations of some there arose in Gaul a wicked suspicion of Caesarius' preaching. Therefore the bishops of Christ across the Isère assembled at Valence [523]. Caesarius could not go there, as he had intended, because of illness. He sent leading men, however, bishops, presbyters, and deacons, among whom the holy Bishop Cyprian of Toulon stood out. Supporting all he said from the Bible, Cyprian demonstrated it from the writings of the most ancient Fathers. [He showed] that no one could of himself tend to Divine Perfection unless he was first called by the prevenient Grace of God. . . . Pope Boniface of blessed memory [530–32] confirmed the exposition of St. Caesarius with his apostolic authority. . . .

61. Caesarius often said in his sermons: "If you love God's Word, you will certainly hold fast in your heart what I have put there. . . . What Christ's Love has won in you you will return when you share it with others. But do not think that only the souls of your relations, friends, or clients are to be fed with our exhortation. I attest in the presence of God and His Holy Angels that you will be answerable for the damnation of your sick slaves if, when you return [from church], you do not pass on what I said to them as to your friends or relations. For know that a slave is subject to you at present by his bodily condition; he is not bound to you for eternity." And again he used to say to those he had addressed: "What did we say, brothers? What did we discuss, my sons? I ask you, what have we said up to now in this discourse? If you love [God], hold fast these things; if you remember them our speech has certainly entered your hearts." By such means he made even the unwilling anxious to retain his teaching.

62. At his table the noon meal and dinner were always accompanied with reading, so that the inner and outer man being well fed, both might doubly rejoice. I admit that in this enclosed and shut-up atmosphere the listeners were sweating and many were greatly mortified when, in front of him, they were found to have soon forgotten [what they had heard read]. What is worse, only a few were able to provide brief summaries of the story told

them. In his church-house, whether he was there or not, a meal was always prepared for his clergy or any arrivals. While he lived no man came to Arles as to a strange city but as to his own house. . . .

MONASTICISM: THE LABOR OF THE BRETHREN

Gregory of Tours, *Vitae Patrum*, XVIII, ed. B. Krusch, MGH, SRM, I, 2 (Hanover, 1885), pp. 734–35.

The Abbot Ursus [d. *c.* 500] was an inhabitant of the city of Cahors; from the beginning of his life he was very devout and full of love of God. Leaving Cahors, he came into the land of Berri, where he founded monasteries at Toiselay, Heugne, and Pontigny. Leaving them under the rule of provosts . . . he entered Touraine and came to . . . Sennevières, where he established a monastery. . . . He set up another monastery, now called Loches, on the river Indre, in the hollow of a mountain. . . . He decided not to travel anywhere else but to work there with his own hands with the whole congregation [of monks] and to gain his living from the earth in the sweat of his brow, recommending to his brethren what the Apostle Paul says: "Work with your hands that you may have to give to those in necessity" (Ephesians 4:28). And also: "For he who does not work, let him not eat" (2 Thessalonians 3:10). . . .

While he was living in this way and his brethren were grinding the wheat necessary for their food by turning the mill by hand, he had the idea of [diminishing] their labor by establishing a mill in the bed of the river Indre. Fixing rows of stakes in the river, with heaps of great stones to make dams, he collected the water in a channel and used the current to make the wheel of the machine turn with great speed. By this means he diminished the monks' work and one brother could be delegated to this task. But a Visigoth named Silarius, a great favorite of King Alaric [II, 484–507], wished to take this machine from the monastery and said to the abbot: "Give me this mill, and I will give you in return whatever you like." The abbot answered: "Our poverty has set this up with great labor and now we cannot give it away, for fear that my brethren die of hunger." He replied: "If you wish to give me it freely, I give you thanks; otherwise, I shall take it by force or make another [mill] and turn back the water by dams. I shall no longer allow your wheel to turn." The abbot replied: "You will not do what God does not permit; we will not give you our mill in any way." Then Silarius, foaming with rage, had a machine made modelled on the [monks']. When the water was turned back, it flooded up under the wheel of their machine, mounting up so that the wheel became quite idle and could not be turned as usual. The guardian came, as they say, at midnight, to the abbot, while he was keeping vigil in the oratory with the brethren, and said: "Rise up, abbot, implore the Lord, for the wheel of our mill is stopped by the flood of the new channel made by Silarius." The abbot, hearing this, at once sent a brother to each of the monasteries he had founded, saying: "Prostrate yourselves in prayer and do nothing else, until I send to you again." And he did not leave the oratory, imploring God and expecting the coming of His Mercy, for two whole days and nights. As the third day began to dawn the monk who was the guardian again approached to say that the wheel of the machine was turning as usual at great speed. The abbot, going out from the oratory with his brethren, came to the bank and seeking the mill Silarius had made he could not see it. Gazing at the river-bed, he saw no trace of it. No piece of wood or stone or iron or any other remains was visible. One could only guess that at the same place where it was built the earth opened by a divine force and hid it from men's eyes. The abbot then sent messengers to his brethren, saying: "Rest now from labor for God has avenged the injury of our brothers."

2

THE ROMAN STATE AND THE CHURCH

THE ACCESSION OF THE EMPEROR THEODOSIUS IN 379 ASSURED THE ROMAN
State's support for Catholicism against its, at times, almost victorious rival,
Arianism. This support appears in the general decree of 380 against heretics
and in other laws—including a prohibition of public discussions of religious
topics (388), which experience had shown were liable to inflame popular feel-
ings. A major attack on paganism soon followed. Earlier Christian emperors
had prohibited magical practices, astrology, and sooth-saying, but in this they
were only imitating their pagan predecessors. Theodosius was the first emperor
to prohibit the whole established pagan religion of the Roman State (392).
Despite the heavy financial penalties for offenders, the law was clearly not
entirely effective. Hence there ensued a series of later laws, culminating in the
threat of the death penalty in 435. All citizens were intended to be Catholics.
Apart from Catholicism only Judaism was recognized as a legal religion—but
Jews were isolated as far as possible from the rest of the population. As the
military situation deteriorated, the State devoted more and more attention,
as if trying to appease God, to legislating on religion. Between 429 and 439,
about 150 laws were issued defending and defining the Catholic Faith. This
massive intervention of the State against the Church's opponents was wel-

comed by the greatest theologian of the Latin Church, St. Augustine, although he tried to insist on clemency in the application of the laws against
heretics.[1]

The Church, from a persecuted minority, became an immensely rich institu-
tion, heavily endowed by the State, its clergy largely exempt from the burdens
which weighed increasingly on most of their fellow citizens. Two years after
Alaric sacked Rome, church lands were exempted from most taxes. Not only
were bishops (and by 412 all clergy) immune to trial in secular courts, but
they acquired many of the functions of the local magistrate and judge. They
became arbiters between the central government and their locality.

Equipped with all this power and privilege, was the Church able to assimi-
late and change the social life of the time, or was it only able to provide an
alternative to it in monasticism? Extreme oppression of the poor by the State
and the rich is indisputable. The Church was now *part* of the political and
social structure of the oppressive Empire. It was virtually impossible for it to
protest against such all-encompassing institutions as slavery or the normal use
of torture for judicial purposes. "Defenders" of cities were created in 368 to
defend the local populations against the rich. In 409 their appointment was
shared between bishops and the very men they were intended to control. All
the Church could do was campaign against such obvious abuses as gladiatorial
combats (only finally abolished *c.* 438), and, in general, try to mitigate the
application of a totalitarian system it could not change. The right (419) to
seek asylum in a church and permission to a bishop to visit State prisons and
help prisoners are examples of the way the Church was able to alleviate the
rigor of the laws. But, by its care for the poor through its own institutions,
especially through hospitals which it created in the East and in Rome in the
fourth century and for which no precedent existed in antiquity, the Church
did more for the ordinary man than the meager influence of Christianity on
the Theodosian Code reveals.

The last two laws selected here reflect the problem created for the State by
the crowds of monks, who (especially in the East) invaded towns and pro-
voked riots. One reason why the attempt to send them back to the deserts,
where the monastic movement began, failed so soon was—as the emperors
suggest—because they were a popular counterpoise to corrupt judges. Another
was because of the vast influence they enjoyed by 392 in Church and State.

Decree Against Heretics

Theodosian Code, XVI, 1, 2 (380), trans. Clyde Pharr, *Theodosian Code*
(Princeton, 1952), p. 440. Reprinted by permission of Princeton University
Press.

1. See, for example, Letters 86, 93, and 100 in "The Fathers of the Church," 18, trans.
Sr. M. M. Mueller (New York, 1953), pp. 11–12, 56–106, 141–43.

The Roman State and the Church

Emperors Gratian, Valentinian, and Theodosius Augustuses: An Edict to the People of the City of Constantinople.

It is Our will that all the peoples who are ruled by the administration of Our Clemency shall practice that religion which the divine Peter the Apostle transmitted to the Romans, as the religion which he introduced makes clear even unto this day. It is evident that this is the religion that is followed by the Pontiff Damasus and by Peter, Bishop of Alexandria, a man of apostolic sanctity; that is, according to the apostolic discipline and the evangelic doctrine, we shall believe in the single Deity of the Father, the Son, and the Holy Spirit, under the concept of equal majesty and of the Holy Trinity.

1. We command that those persons who follow this rule shall embrace the name of Catholic Christians. The rest, however, whom We adjudge demented and insane, shall sustain the infamy of heretical dogmas, their meeting places shall not receive the name of churches, and they shall be smitten first by divine vengeance and secondly by the retribution of Our own initiative, which We shall assume in accordance with the divine judgment.

No Public Discussion of Religion

Theodosian Code, XVI, 4, 2 (388), trans. Pharr, p. 449.

Emperors Valentinian, Theodosius, and Arcadius Augustuses to Tatianus, Praetorian Prefect.

There shall be no opportunity for any man to go out to the public and to argue about religion or to discuss it or to give any counsel. If any person hereafter, with flagrant and damnable audacity, should suppose that he may contravene any law of this kind or if he should dare to persist in his action of ruinous obstinacy, he shall be restrained with a due penalty and proper punishment.

Prohibition of All Pagan Worship

Theodosian Code, XVI, 10, 12 (392), trans. Pharr, pp. 473–74.

Emperors Theodosius, Arcadius, and Honorius Augustuses to Rufinus, Praetorian Prefect.

No person at all, of any class or order whatsoever of men or of dignities, whether he occupies a position of power or has completed such honors, whether he is powerful by the lot of birth or is humble in lineage, legal status, and fortune, shall sacrifice an innocent victim to senseless images in any place at all or in any city. He shall not, by more secret wickedness, venerate his lar with fire, his genius with wine, his penates with fragrant odors; he shall not burn lights to them, place incense before them, or suspend wreaths for them.

1. But if any man should dare to immolate a victim for the purpose of sacrifice, or to consult the quivering entrails, according to the example of a person guilty of high treason he shall be reported by an accusation which is permitted to all persons, and he shall receive the appropriate sentence, even though he has inquired nothing contrary to, or with reference to, the welfare of the Emperors. For it is sufficient to constitute an enormous crime that any person should wish to break down the very laws of nature, to investigate forbidden matters, to disclose hidden secrets, to attempt interdicted practices, to seek to know the end of another's life, to promise the hope of another person's death.

2. But if any person should venerate, by placing incense before them, images made by the work of mortals and destined to suffer the ravages of time, and if, in a ridiculous manner, he should suddenly fear the effigies which he himself has formed, or should bind a tree with fillets, or should erect an altar of turf that he has dug up, or should attempt to honor vain images with the offering of a gift, which even though it is humble, still is a complete outrage against religion, such a person, as one guilty of the violation of religion, shall be punished by the forfeiture of that house or landholding in which it is proved that he served a pagan superstition. For We decree that all places shall be annexed to Our fisc, if it is proved that they have reeked with the vapor of incense, provided, however, that such places are proved to have belonged to such incense burners.

3. But if any person should attempt to perform any such kind of sacrifice in public temples or shrines, or in the buildings or fields of others, and if it is proved that such places were usurped without the knowledge of the owner, the offender shall be compelled to pay twenty-five pounds of gold as a fine. If any person should connive at such a crime, he shall be held subject to the same penalty as that of the person who performed the sacrifice.

4. It is Our will that this regulation shall be so enforced by the judges, as well as by the defenders and decurions of the several cities, that the information learned by the defenders and decurions shall be immediately reported to the courts, and the crimes so reported shall be punished by the judges. Moreover, if the defenders and decurions should suppose that any such crime should be concealed through favoritism or overlooked through carelessness, they shall be subjected to judicial indignation. If the judges should

be advised of such crimes and should defer punishment through connivance, they shall be fined thirty pounds of gold; their office staffs also shall
be subjected to an equal penalty.

Reinforced Penalties for Pagans

Theodosian Code, XVI, 10, 25 (435), trans. Pharr, p. 476.

*Emperors Theodosius and Valentinian Augustuses to Isidorus, Praetorian
Prefect.*
We interdict all persons of criminal pagan mind from the accursed immo-
lation of victims, from damnable sacrifices, and from all other such practices
that are prohibited by the authority of the more ancient sanctions. We command that all their fanes, temples, and shrines, if even now any remain entire, shall be destroyed by the command of the magistrates, and shall be
purified by the erection of the sign of the venerable Christian religion. All
men shall know that if it should appear, by suitable proof before a competent judge, that any person has mocked this law, he shall be punished with
death.

Jews and Christians Forbidden to Intermarry

Theodosian Code, III, 7, 2 (388), trans. Pharr, p. 70.

*Emperors Valentinian, Theodosius, and Arcadius Augustuses to Cynegius,
Praetorian Prefect.*
No Jew shall receive a Christian woman in marriage, nor shall a Christian
man contract a marriage with a Jewish woman. For if any person should
commit an act of this kind, the crime of this misdeed shall be considered as
the equivalent of adultery, and freedom to bring accusation shall be granted
also to the voices of the public.

Exemption from Public Services for Clerics

Theodosian Code, XVI, 2, 2 (319), trans. Pharr, p. 441.

*Emperor Constantine Augustus to Octavianus, Governor of Lucania and of
Bruttium.*

Those persons who devote the services of religion to divine worship, that is, those who are called clerics, shall be exempt from all compulsory public services whatever, lest, through the sacrilegious malice of certain persons, they should be called away from divine services.

Exemption from Most Taxes for Church Lands

Theodosian Code, XVI, 2, 40 (412), trans. Pharr, p. 447.

Emperors Honorius and Theodosius Augustuses to Melitius, Praetorian Prefect.
We have carefully considered the tenor of a reasonable plan, and it is Our pleasure to prescribe by a strict regulation from what compulsory public services the churches of the separate cities shall be specifically held exempt.

Indeed, first of all, the contumely of that well-known usurpation must be abolished, that is, the landed estates consecrated to the uses of the heavenly mysteries shall not be vexed by the burden of compulsory public services of a menial nature. The injustice of constructing and repairing roads shall not bind any unit of taxable land which enjoys the lot of such privileges. No extraordinary burden or superindiction shall be required of such units of taxable land; no restoration of bridges, no responsibility for transportation shall arise; no gold and other such taxes shall be required. Finally, nothing in addition to the regular tax payment, which the sudden burden of extraordinary necessity may demand, shall be assessed upon the compulsory public services that are required of such land units. If any person should contravene this statute, he shall incur the severity of due punishment which must be imposed by law upon the sacrilegious, and he shall then be punished by the exile of perpetual deportation.

Bishops Not to Be Tried in the Secular Courts

Theodosian Code, XVI, 2, 12 (355), trans. Pharr, p. 442.

Emperors Constantius and Constans Augustuses to their dear friend Severus, Greetings.
By a law of Our Clemency We prohibit bishops to be accused in the courts, lest there should be an unrestrained opportunity for fanatical spirits to accuse them, while the accusers assume that they will obtain impunity by the kindness of the bishops. Therefore, if any person should lodge any com-

plaint, such complaint must unquestionably be examined before other bishops, in order that an opportune and suitable hearing may be arranged for the investigation of all concerned.

Rights Granted to the Church

Sirmondian Constitutions, 13 (419), trans. Pharr, pp. 483–84.

Title 13: persons who flee for sanctuary to the churches shall be safe within fifty paces outside the doors. unrestricted entrance shall be available to a bishop who is visiting prisons.

Emperors Honorius and Theodosius, Pious Augustuses.

It is fitting that humanity, which was known even before Our times, should temper justice. For when very many people flee from the violence of a cruel fortune and choose the protection of the defense of the churches, when they are confined therein, they suffer no less imprisonment than that which they have avoided. For at no time is an egress opened to them into the light of the vestibule. Therefore the sanctity of ecclesiastical reverence shall apply to the space of fifty paces beyond the doors of the church. If anyone should hold a person who goes forth from this place, he shall incur the criminal charge of sacrilege. For no compassion is granted to the fugitives if the free air is denied them in their affliction.

We grant to the priest the right also to enter the courts of the prison on a mission of compassion, to heal the sick, to feed the poor, and to console the innocent; when he has investigated thoroughly and has learned the case of each person, according to law he shall direct his intervention before the competent judge. For We know, and supplications have come to Us in regard to such cases in numerous audiences, that very many persons are frequently thrust into prison in order that they may be deprived of the freedom to approach a judge; and when a rather humble person once begins to suffer imprisonment before his case is known, he is compelled to suffer the penalty of outrage. The contumacious office staff shall immediately pay to Our fisc two pounds of gold if the feral doorkeeper should exclude a priest who is caring for such sacred matters.

"Defenders" of Cities: How They Are to Be Appointed

Codex Iustiniani, 1.55.8 (409), trans. P. R. Coleman-Norton, *Roman State and Christian Church*, II (London, 1966), pp. 524–25.

Emperors Honorius and Theodosius Augustuses to Caecilian, Praetorian Prefect.

We command defenders to be appointed thus, that they, imbued with the orthodox religion's sacred mystery, should be created by decree of the most reverend bishops and clergymen and distinguished men and rentiers and curials; and report concerning their appointment must be made to the most illustrious praetorian power. . . .

MONKS: A LAW SOON REPEALED

Theodosian Code, XVI, 3, 1–2, trans. Pharr, p. 449.

1 (390). Emperors Valentinian, Theodosius, and Arcadius Augustuses to Tatianus, Praetorian Prefect.

If any persons should be found in the profession of monks, they shall be ordered to seek out and to inhabit desert places and desolate solitudes.

2 (392). The same Augustuses to Tatianus. . . .

We direct that the monks to whom the municipalities had been forbidden, since they are strengthened by judicial injustices, shall be restored to their original status, and the aforesaid law [of 390] shall be repealed. Thus indeed, We revoke such a decree of Our Clemency, and We grant them free ingress into the towns.

3

THE ATTEMPT TO CONVERT THE COUNTRYSIDE

THE EFFECTS OF CONSTANTINE'S CONVERSION TOOK CENTURIES TO PENETRATE most of Western Europe. Even in 400 the Church was still largely dependent on the State for support. Maximus of Turin (d. *c.* 415) asked his city congregation (Sermon 106): "What should be said of us, who are forced to live piously, not by devotion but by terror?" At the same time Maximus admitted that the imperial laws against paganism were often not carried out.

Paganism was not an imaginary foe. There is archaeological evidence for a pagan revival in the fourth century, even under the orthodox Emperor Theodosius (379–95). In the Alpine diocese of Trent in 397 missionaries who tried to prohibit their converts taking part in the traditional rites by which the fields were blessed and their fertility assured, were murdered. In general, resistance was passive but very effective.

During the fourth century the Church organization had been extended. In 400 there were fifty bishoprics in North Italy, where there had been five or six in 300, and seventy in Gaul, compared with twenty-six a century before. But, especially in Gaul, this extension of the Church principally affected the towns, which were decreasing in population and importance. Even Martin of

Tours' energetic missions hardly went beyond the small towns of his diocese. The distribution of Christian inscriptions in Gaul confirms the literary sources and shows that there was a great difference between the relatively Christian Provence and Rhône valley and the North and West. The Barbarian Invasions, from 407 onward, disrupted the barely nascent Christian organization in the countryside and destroyed some major centers, such as Trier, almost completely.

The advance was resumed slowly. The destruction of the great forest sanctuaries of Celtic Gaul and their replacement by Christian churches often came late. Caesarius of Arles, in the most Christianized area of Gaul, is continually concerned in the sixth century with paganism and even with recently restored pagan temples.[1] If the elaborate myths of Olympus were forgotten, the old Celtic beliefs in the gods of springs and forests were fully alive in Caesarius' Gaul and in Martin of Braga's Galicia.

I include here a sermon by Maximus of Turin in North Italy and Martin of Braga's *On the Castigation of Rustics* (usually, but less correctly, termed their *Correction*). Besides being a model catechism, it shows the difficulties faced by the Church in the countryside, no doubt intensified in Galicia by the fact that there it had to contend with Priscillianist heresy—the real religion of the land from about 400 to Martin's time, *c.* 550–80—as well as with the Arianism of the Suevic invaders. That paganism was a real danger in Galicia is shown by the canons of the Second Council of Braga (572).

Maximus' sermon is addressed to the landowners of the diocese of Turin, many of whom lived in Turin the greater part of the year, away from their estates and comfortably detached from their problems. Maximus reminds them of their responsibility for the salvation of their peasants or "rustics." Here this word means not only the completely dependent farm laborers, but also the lord's bailiff; the cult Maximus attacks was not purely a private matter but was known to all the inhabitants of the estate, except perhaps its owner. Maximus' picture of pagan rites was no doubt influenced by the long tradition of Christian apologetic literature (especially in his portrait of the "seer"), but it seems close to reality.

Maximus appealed to the peasants' masters, Martin of Braga to the "rustics" themselves (here understood as all the inhabitants of the countryside). To do this, Martin, like Caesarius of Arles before him, adopts a deliberately simple style, concentrating on the main points of the argument.

Many rustics could not see why, in Martin's words, "one cannot worship God and the Devil at once." They could not see that their familiar deities, their rural shrines were as desperately evil as the Church made out. Hence the insistence with which Martin hammers home his view that idolatry originated through the Devil's instigation. This thesis makes his sermon a unified whole.

---

1. Sermon 53, trans. Sr. M. M. Mueller, "Fathers of the Church," 31 (New York, 1956), pp. 263–65.

The Attempt to Convert the Countryside

Martin knew the audience he was addressing was one of men bound in back-breaking and ceaseless labor, always uncertain in its results, and living scarcely above the famine level, once they had paid their rent and taxes. Martin paints for them (14) an understandable picture of Heaven, as the exact opposite of their daily life, together with a vivid picture of Hell. The precepts he sets out (18) are clear and concrete; he concentrates on observance of the Lord's Day. He is concerned to inculcate a few basic moral lessons with biblical texts. He was attacking much the same practices that appear in Caesarius' sermons. Like Caesarius (Sermon 6), he contrasts the "songs of the Devil" with the Creed and the Lord's Prayer, but Caesarius does not speak so clearly of rival "incantations" (16). Martin was apparently successful in extirpating locally the use of pagan names for the days of the week (8). Portuguese is the only language in Western Europe which uses simply the second, third, etc., day of the week.

Both Caesarius' and Martin's sermons were much used by later preachers. Martin's work was used by one of the first missionaries to Germany, Pirminius (d. 753), and later by Aelfric (c. 1000), in his Anglo-Saxon Homilies.

Martin is exceptional in not recommending the use of force against the recalcitrant pagan or his shrine. Caesarius did not hesitate to do so. Nor did the Church Councils of Toledo, after the Visigoths had united the Iberian Peninsula. But force was not successful, for one of the last Visigothic Councils (Toledo XVI, 693, canon 2), only twenty years before the Arabic Conquest, acknowledges the widespread existence of pagan practices, for which it prescribes very severe penalties (see also Part Two, 2). Pope Gregory the Great (590–604) is repeatedly concerned with paganism, advocating force against its adherents in Italy. A letter of 594 (*Registrum*, IV, 23) "to the Nobles and Proprietors in Sardinia" tells them—repeating less forcefully the arguments of Maximus—that they are responsible for their peasants' conversion. If they are not prepared to act, he refers them to the missionaries he had sent to the island to remedy local disinterest and sloth. Two and three hundred years after Theodosius' blanket prohibition, men still clung to their age-old rites.

1. Maximus of Turin, *Sermo CVII* (after 405), ed. A. Mutzenbecher, *CCSL*, 23 (Turnhout, 1962), pp. 420–21.

That idols should be removed from private estates.

Some days ago I admonished your charity, brethren, that, as religious and holy men, you should remove all pollution of idols from your properties and cast out the whole error of paganism from your fields. For it is not right that you, who have Christ in your hearts, should have Antichrist in your houses; that your men should honor the devil in his shrines while you pray to God in church. And let no one think he is excused by saying: "I did not order this, I did not command it." Whoever knows that sacrilege takes place on his estate and does not forbid it, in a sense orders it. By keeping silence and not reproving the man who sacrifices, he lends his consent. For the blessed Apostle states that not only those who do sinful acts are guilty, but also those who consent to the act (Romans 1:32). You, therefore, brother, when you observe your peasant sacrificing and do not forbid the offering, sin, because even if you did not assist the sacrifice yourself you gave permission for it. If your order was not behind the crime your will is still to blame. As long as you remain silent, what your peasant does pleases you: if he did not act in this way perhaps he would displease you. So the subject does not merely involve himself in sin when he sacrifices; he also involves his lord, who does not forbid him; if he had done so neither would have sinned.

Idolatry is a great evil. It pollutes those who practice it. It pollutes the inhabitants of the region. It pollutes those who look on. It penetrates its ministers, it penetrates those who know of it and those who keep silent. The peasant's offering defiles the lord of the land. He cannot *not* be polluted when he eats food gathered by sacrilegious hands, brought forth by earth stained with blood, stored in foul barns. For all things are defiled, all are abominable, where the devil dwells, whether houses, fields, or peasants. There is nothing free from evil where everything is steeped in evil. If you entered a rustic shrine you would find there bleaching sods [the remains of a turf altar] and dead coals—a worthy devil's sacrifice when a dead god is worshiped with dead things. And if you went into the fields you would see wooden altars and stone images, suitable to a rite in which insensible gods are served at moldering altars. If you woke up earlier [than you usually do] you would see a rustic reeling with wine. You ought to know that he is what they call either a devotee of Diana [that is, an epileptic or one who is moon-mad] or a soothsayer. For a god who makes mad usually has a frantic priest. Such a priest prepares himself with wine for his goddess' blows, so that, being drunk, the wretch may not feel his punishment. They do this not only out of intemperance but by design, so that, buoyed up by wine, they may feel less pain. The seer who thinks piety is intensified by cruelty is wholly useless. How merciful this god [must be] to others who is so cruel to his priests! To sketch briefly this seer's dress. He has a shaggy head with long hair. His breast is bare, he has a cloth half round his loins and, like a gladiator prepared for combat, he brandishes a weapon in his hand. But he is worse than a gladiator, for *he* is forced to fight against another man, whereas this fellow has to fight against himself. The gladiator strikes at other's guts, this man tears his own limbs to pieces, and, if one can say this, as his trainer works on the gladiator, so his god urges this man on to self-flagellation. Wrapped in this dress, bloody with his self-slaughter, judge for yourselves whether he is a gladiator or a priest! As the public outrage of gladiators has been removed by the religious piety of our princes, these gladiators of insanity should be removed by Christians from their own dwellings.

2. Martin of Braga, *On the Castigation of Rustics* (*c.* 574), ed. C. W. Barlow, *Martini episcopi Bracarensis Opera Omnia*, Papers and Monographs of the American Academy in Rome, 12 (New Haven: Yale University Press, 1950), pp. 183–203, with corrections by A. F. Kurfess, in *Aevum*, 29 (Milan, 1955), pp. 181–86.

To the Most Holy and to me Most Beloved Brother in Christ, Bishop Polemius, Bishop Martin.

1. I received the letter of Your Holy Charity, in which you write me that, for the castigation of rustics, who, still living in the primitive superstition of pagans, worship demons rather than God, I should send you some work, however brief, on the origin of idols and their abominations. But since it is necessary to offer them a short notice of things from the beginning of the world, such as will suit their taste, I was obliged to touch the vast forest of past times and actions in a slight compendium, and to season food for rustics with rustic speech. So, God helping you, thus shall your sermon begin:

2. We wish, dearest brethren, to announce to you, in the name of the Lord, those things which you have either not heard, or, having heard, have perhaps forgotten. We ask your charity, therefore, to listen carefully to what is said for your salvation. Long, indeed, is the account set out in the Holy Scriptures, but, so that you may remember a little of it, we commend to you these few [points] out of many.

3. When God in the beginning made heaven and earth, He made spiritual creatures, angels, in that heavenly dwelling, who might stand in His Sight and praise Him. One of these, who was made the first Archangel, seeing himself in such glory, did not honor God His Creator, but held he was like unto Him, and, for this pride, with many other angels who agreed with him, he was hurled down from that heavenly seat into this air which is under heaven. And he, who was the first Archangel, having lost the light of his glory, was made the dark and horrid Devil. So too those other angels who, agreeing with him, were thrown out with him from heaven, the splendor of their glory lost, were made demons. But the remaining angels, who continued subject to God in the glory of His Brightness, in the Sight of the Lord, are called holy angels. For those who were cast down with their Prince, Satan, for their pride, are called fugitive angels and demons.

4. After this ruin of the angels it pleased God to form man of the dust of the earth, whom He placed in paradise. And He said to him that, if he kept

the precept of the Lord, he might succeed, without death, to that heavenly place whence those fugitive angels fell, but if he disregarded God's commandment, he should die. The Devil, seeing, therefore, that man was made so that he might ascend to the Kingdom of God in the place whence he had fallen, seized by envy, persuaded man to transgress the commands of God. For this offense man was cast out from paradise to the exile of this world, where he might undergo many labors and sorrows.

5. Now the first man was called Adam, and his wife, whom God created from his very flesh, was called Eve. From these two the whole human race was propagated. But they, having forgotten God their Creator, committing many crimes, roused God to anger. Wherefore, God sent the Flood and drowned them all, except one just man, Noah by name, whom He preserved with his children for the restoration of the human race. Therefore, from the first man, Adam, until the Flood, there passed by 2242 years.

6. After the Flood the human race was again saved by the three sons of Noah, preserved with their wives. And when an increasing multitude began to fill the world, men, again forgetting God their Creator, began to worship creatures. Some adored the sun, others the moon and stars, others fire, others deep water or springs of waters, believing all these things not to be made by God for the use of men but to be gods arisen of themselves.

7. Then the Devil or his ministers, demons, who were thrown down from heaven, seeing ignorant men . . . wandering after creatures, began to show themselves in different forms to men and to speak with them and to seek that men should offer them sacrifices on high mountains and in shady groves and worship them as God. They took on themselves the names of evil men who passed their lives in every crime and wicked deed. So one said he was Jove, who was a magician and so incestuous in his many adulteries that he had his sister as his wife, who was called Juno; that he corrupted his daughters, Minerva and Venus, and filthily defiled his nieces and all his relations. Another demon called himself Mars, who was a perpetrator of strife and discord. Then another demon chose to call himself Mercury, who was the wretched inventor of all theft and fraud, to whom, as to the god of gain, greedy men, as they pass crossroads, fling stones, offering heaps of stones as a sacrifice. Another demon took the name of Saturn, who, basking in cruelty, even devoured his sons at birth. Another demon feigned to be Venus, who was a whore. She did not only whore with innumerable adulterers but even with her father Jove and her brother Mars.

8. See what these abandoned men were when they lived, whom ignorant rustics most wrongly honored for their discoveries. The demons took their names so that [the rustics] might worship them as gods and offer them sacri-

fices and imitate the deeds of those whose names they invoked. The demons also persuaded men to build them temples, to place there images or statues of wicked men and to set up altars to them, on which they might pour out the blood not only of animals but even of men. Besides, many demons, expelled from heaven, also preside either in the sea or in rivers or springs or forests; men ignorant of God also worship them as gods and sacrifice to them. They call on Neptune in the sea, on Lamiae in the rivers, on Nymphs in springs, on Dianas in woods, who are all malignant demons and wicked spirits, who deceive unbelieving men, who are ignorant of the Sign of the Cross, and vex them. However, not without God's permission do they do harm, for [the rustics] have angered God and do not believe with their whole heart in the Faith of Christ, but are so inconstant that they apply the very names of demons to each day and speak of the "days" of Mars, Mercury, Jove, Venus, and Saturn, who made no *day*, but were the worst villains of the Greek race.

9. For When Omnipotent God made heaven and earth, He then created light, which alternated with the darkness seven times during the period of his labors. For on the first day He made the light which was called Day; on the second the firmament of heaven was made; on the third the earth was divided from the sea; on the fourth the sun and moon and stars were made; on the fifth four-footed, flying, and swimming things; on the sixth man was formed. The seventh day, when all the world and its adornment were finished, God called rest. Therefore the one light, which was made first of the works of God, being divided into seven parts after the division of God's works, was called the week. Therefore what madness is it for a man baptized in the Faith of Christ not to honor the Lord's Day, on which Christ rose again, and to say he honors the "days" of Jove, Mercury, Venus, and Saturn, who have no day, but were adulterers, magicians, and evil men and died evil deaths in their land! But, as we said, under the appearance of these names, men show absurd veneration and honor to demons.

10. Error, too, so deceives the ignorant, that they think the Kalends [1st] of January is the beginning of the year, which is entirely false. For, as Holy Scripture says, the eighth day before the Kalends of April [March 25], at the equinox, was constituted the beginning of the first year. For so we read: "And God divided the light and the darkness" (Genesis 1:4). For every division entails equality, and so on [March 25] the day has as many hours as the night. And so it is false that the Kalends [1st] of January is the beginning of the year.

11. Now what is to be sorrowfully said of that most foolish error whereby [rustics] observe the "days" of moths and mice and (if it can be said) a Christian venerates mice and moths instead of God? For if bread or cloth is not

protected from them in a cask or box, they will in no way spare what they find because of the special feasts offered them. But in vain does wretched man make these calculations on the future, as that if, in the beginning of the year, he is glutted and joyful in every way, so it will be the whole year through. All these observances of pagans are sought out by the devices of demons. But woe to that man who shall not have had God as his friend and who has not received from *Him* satiety of bread and security of life! See how you perform these vain superstitions, either secretly or openly, and never cease from these sacrifices of demons. Why do they not provide for you, so that you are always glutted, safe, and happy? Why, when God grows angry, do vain sacrifices not defend you from locusts, mice, and many other tribulations which God sends you in His Wrath?

12. Do you not clearly understand that the demons lie to you in these observances, which you vainly cling to, and often trick you in the auguries which you practice? For, as the most wise Solomon says: "Divinations and auguries are vain" (Ecclesiasticus 34:5), and as a man fears them so shall his heart be deceived. "Do not give your heart to them, for they have led many astray" (*ibid.* 6–7). Behold Holy Scripture states this and thus it is most certainly, for the demons seduce unhappy men by the cries of birds until, through frivolous and vain things, they both lose the Faith of Christ, and themselves rush unprepared upon death. God did not command man to know the future but that, always living in fear of it, he should seek from Him the governance and sustenance of his life. It is only for God to know something before it occurs, but demons delude vain men with diverse arguments until they lead them into an offence against God and draw their souls with them into Hell, lest man enter the Kingdom of Heaven, from which [the demons] were thrown down.

13. For that very reason, when God saw wretched men so tricked by the Devil and his evil angels, that, forgetting their Creator, they adored demons as God, He sent His Son, His Wisdom and Word, to lead them back from diabolical error to the worship of the true God. And, because the Divinity of the Son of God could not be seen by men, He received human flesh from the womb of Mary Virgin, not conceived by union with a man but of the Holy Spirit. The Son of God, therefore, born in human flesh, the invisible God concealed within but outwardly a man, preached to men and taught them to abandon idols and evil deeds, to go out from the power of the Devil and return to the worship of their Creator. After He taught He willed to die Himself for the human race. He suffered death freely, not unwilling. He was crucified by the Jews, Pontius Pilate being judge. . . . Taken down from the Cross, He was placed in a tomb. The third day He rose alive from the dead

and lived with His twelve disciples for forty days, and, so that He might show that His True Flesh had risen again, He ate after His Resurrection before His disciples. When forty days were over, He commanded His disciples to announce to all peoples the Resurrection of the Son of God, and to baptize them in the Name of the Father, of the Son, and of the Holy Spirit in forgiveness of sins, and to teach those who had been baptized to depart from evil (that is, diabolical) works, from murder, theft, perjury, fornication, drunkenness, and adultery. And after He commanded these things, in the sight of His disciples, He ascended into Heaven and sits there at the Right Hand of the Father, and from there will come at the end of the world in the very Flesh which He bore into Heaven.

14. But when the end of the world shall come, all peoples and all men, who descend from those first men, Adam and Eve, will rise again, both good and evil. And will come before the Judgment of Christ, and then they who lived well will be separated from the wicked and will enter into the Kingdom of God with the holy angels, and their souls, united with their bodies, will be in eternal rest, never to die again. There will be no toil or pain there, no sadness, no hunger or thirst, no heat or cold, no darkness or night, but, always happy and wanting nothing, in light and glory, they will be like the angels of God, for they have merited to enter into that place whence the Devil with the angels of his party fell. There, then, all who were faithful to God remain forever. For those who were unbelieving, or unbaptized, or if they were baptized, after their Baptism were flung down to idols and murders or adulteries, or to perjuries and other evils, and died without penitence, all who were found thus are damned with the Devil and with all the demons they worshiped and are sent in the flesh into eternal fire, where that inextinguishable fire lives forever, and that flesh, once it has risen again, will forever groan in torment. It desires to die again that it may not feel the pain, but this is not permitted, that it may feel eternal tortures. This is what the Law [of Moses] states, the prophets announce this, the Gospel of Christ, the Apostles, all Holy Scripture attests these things which we have said to you now, plainly, a few things from among many. It is for you henceforth, dearest sons, to remember what we have said, and either, by acting well, to hope for future rest in the Kingdom of God, or (God forbid!), by acting wickedly to expect unending future fire. For eternal life and eternal death are both placed in man's will. What each chooses for himself, this he shall have.

15. You faithful, therefore, who have come to Christ's Baptism in the Name of the Father, the Son, and the Holy Spirit, think what pact you made with God in that very Baptism. For when you each gave your name at the font, Peter or John, for instance, or whatever name, you were thus questioned by

the bishop: "How are you called?" You replied—if you were already able to reply—or certainly he who promised for you and received you from the font said, for instance: "He is called John." And the bishop asked: "John, do you renounce the Devil and his angels, his worship and idols, his thefts and frauds, his fornications and drunkenness, and all his evil works?" And you replied: "I renounce." After this abjuration of the Devil you were again asked: "Do you believe in God the Father Omnipotent?" You replied: "I believe." "And in Jesus Christ, His Only Son, Our Lord, who was born of the Holy Spirit from Mary Virgin, suffered under Pontius Pilate, was crucified, dead, and buried; the third day rose alive from the dead, ascended to the heavens, sits on the Right Hand of God the Father, shall come thence to judge the living and the dead?" And you replied: "I believe." And again you were asked: "Do you believe in the Holy Spirit, the Holy Catholic Church, the forgiveness of all sins, the resurrection of the flesh, and eternal life?" And you replied: "I believe." So consider the pact you made with God in Baptism. You promised to renounce the Devil and his angels and all his evil works. And you confessed you believed in Father, Son, and Holy Spirit, and hoped, at the end of the age, for the resurrection of the flesh and eternal life.

16. See what a bond and confession God holds from you! And how can any of you, who has renounced the Devil and his angels and his evil works, now return again to the worship of the Devil? For to burn candles at stones and trees and springs, and where three roads meet, what is it but the worship of the Devil? To observe divinations and auguries and the days of idols, what is it but the worship of the Devil? To observe the "days" of Vulcan [August 23] and the first days of each month, to adorn tables and hang up laurels, to watch the foot, and to pour out fruit and wine over a log in the hearth, and to put bread in a spring, what is it but the worship of the Devil? For women to invoke Minerva in their weaving, to keep weddings for the "day" of Venus [Friday], and to consider which day one should set out on a journey, what is it but the worship of the Devil? To mutter spells over herbs and invoke the names of demons in incantations, what is it but the worship of the Devil? And many other things which it takes too long to say. And you do all these things *after* renouncing the Devil, after Baptism, and, returning to the worship of demons and to their evil works, you have betrayed your Faith and broken the pact you made with God. You have abandoned the Sign of the Cross you received in Baptism, and you give heed to signs of the Devil by little birds and sneezing and many other things. Why does no augury harm me or any other upright Christian? Because, where the Sign of the Cross has gone before, the sign of the Devil is nothing. Why does it harm *you*? Because you despise the Sign of the Cross and fear the sign you made for your-

selves. Likewise you have abandoned the Holy Incantation, that is the Creed you received in Baptism, and the Lord's Prayer, and you cling to diabolical incantations and chants. Whoever, therefore, having despised the Sign of the Cross of Christ, turns to other signs, has lost the Sign of the Cross which he received in Baptism. So, too, he who has other incantations invented by magicians and enchanters, has lost the Creed and the Lord's Prayer, which he received in the Faith of Christ, and has trampled underfoot the Faith of Christ, for one cannot worship God and the Devil at once.

17. If, therefore, beloved sons, you acknowledge that all the things we have said are true, if a man knows he has done these things after Baptism, and has broken the Faith of Christ, let him not despair of himself, nor say in his heart, "Since I have done such great evil after Baptism, perhaps God will not forgive me my sins." Do not doubt the mercy of God. Only make such a pact in your heart with God that, from now onward, you will no longer worship demons, nor adore anything except the God of Heaven, nor commit murder, nor adultery nor fornication, nor steal nor perjure yourself. And when you have promised this to God of your whole heart, and, further, have ceased to commit these sins, trust in God's pardon, for thus says the Lord by the prophet: "In whatever day the unjust shall forget his iniquities and do justice, I also will forget all his iniquities" (Ezekiel 18:21). God, therefore, waits for repentance. But that repentance is true when a man no longer does the evil he did but both asks for pardon for his past [sins] and bewares lest he return again to them in the future, and, on the other hand, practices good, both providing alms for the hungry poor, refreshing the tired guest, and, whatever he does not wish another should do to him, not doing to another, for in this word the commandments of God are fulfilled.

18. We beg you, therefore, dearest brethren, to remember these precepts of God, which God deigns to give you by our humble and unworthy [person], and consider how you may save your souls, so that you think not only of this present life and the passing good of this world, but rather recall what you promised in the Creed you believed, that is the resurrection of the flesh and eternal life. If, therefore, you have believed and still believe that the resurrection of the flesh and eternal life, in the Kingdom of Heaven among God's angels, will come to be . . . then think most of all on [saving your souls] and not always on the troubles of the world. Prepare your way by good works. Often visit the church or the shrines of the saints to pray to God. Do not despise the Lord's Day, which is called the Lord's because the Son of God, Our Lord Jesus Christ, rose that day from the dead, but treat it with reverence. Do no servile work on the Lord's Day, that is in the field, meadow, vineyard, or other heavy work other than cooking food necessary to refresh

the body. One may journey to nearby places on the Lord's Day, not, however, for evil reasons but for good, that is either to visit holy places or a brother or friend, or to console the sick, or to lend counsel or help to the suffering. Thus, then, should a Christian man venerate the Lord's Day. For it is evil and shameful enough that those who are pagans and ignorant of the Faith of Christ, adoring the idols of demons, should reverence the "day" of Jove or of any demon, and abstain from work [then], when certainly the demons nei-ther created nor control any day. And we, who worship the true God and believe the Son of God has risen from the dead, shall we not reverence the day of His Resurrection, that is the Lord's Day? Refuse, therefore, to injure the Lord's Resurrection but treat it with reverence, for the hope we have in it. For as He, Our Lord Jesus Christ, the Son of God, who is our Head, the third day rose in His Flesh from the dead, so we, who are His members, hope we shall rise again in our flesh at the end of the age, so that each shall receive either eternal rest or eternal pain, according as he acted in his body in this age.

19. And so we, with God as witness and that of the holy angels who hear us, have performed our duty to Your Charity, and, as we were commanded, have imparted to you the Lord's money. It is now for you to consider and to see how each shall render what he has received with interest, when the Lord comes in the Day of Judgment (see Matthew 25:27). But we pray the mercy of the same Lord, that He may guard you from all evil and make you worthy companions of His angels in His Kingdom, Who lives and reigns through the ages of ages. Amen.

4

THE CHURCH AND THE BARBARIANS

A. Different Attitudes to the Barbarians

"FROM THE END OF THE FOURTH CENTURY THE CHRISTIAN CHURCH WAS asked not only to exorcise the devils [of paganism] but to tame the barbarians" (Momigliano). The danger of a barbarian takeover of the Roman world was increasingly obvious. Barbarians already filled the élite corps of the army and most of the posts of command. From the death of the Emperor Theodosius in 395 the effective military rulers of the Western Empire were either barbarians or reliant on barbarians. In 407 there came the invasion of Gaul, in 409 of Spain, in 410 the sack of Rome by the Visigoths. In 429 the Vandals crossed from Spain to North Africa, the richest province of the West. By 439 its capital, Carthage, had fallen. Gaul and Spain were largely occupied by Visigoths, Sueves, and Burgundians. Italy maintained a precarious independence under puppet emperors. In 476 it also fell under a barbarian, King Odovacar. In 490 it was to pass to the Ostrogoths under Theodoric.

The sequence of events by which province after province passed to barbarian control until the Western Empire disappeared is naturally clearer to us than it was to contemporaries.

In 400 the Catholic Church was largely identified with the Roman State.

St. Ambrose of Milan (c. 339–97) is usually represented as an independent exponent of Christian morality who did not hesitate to excommunicate Theodosius for the massacre of Thessalonica until he did public penance. There was another side to him: he was a Roman patriot whose *De officiis* is an attempt to create for the clergy a Christian version of Cicero's guide to Roman statesmen.

Paulinus of Nola, like Ambrose a Roman aristocrat, had, like him, held high office in the State, but his retirement from the world was more absolute than that of Ambrose and his interests somewhat different. Ambrose was concerned with the whole Empire, Paulinus with the monastic movement in the West (see p. 18) and the shrine of his local Saint Felix. His patriotism consisted in imploring the saints' aid against Alaric, already threatening Rome in 402. This common reliance on the saints was satirized by Claudian, a nominal Christian from Egypt but basically a court poet of unusual gifts.

St. Jerome (c. 347–419) had lived in Bethlehem since 386 but followed, through his ceaseless correspondence, every rumor from his native Latin West. Despite his renunciation of both the world and classical literature in favor of the vocation of monk and translator of the Bible, his lamentation for Rome's fall in 410 is perhaps the most impassioned that exists. His own words failing he resorts to the Bible. Rome, the unclean or even accursed city in Christian tradition, is transmuted into Jerusalem the Holy. Virgil is blended with the Psalms, as they are blended in Augustine's *Confessions* and *City of God*.

Paulinus of Béziers and Orientius react directly to the devastation of the hitherto safe provinces of Gaul and Spain. They attempt to use the tragedy to deepen the spiritual life of their readers. In Orientius, exaltation of ascetics as the only true Christians (p. 17) shows that, for him, retirement from the world was the only answer to the crisis.

There were more ambitious attempts to explain what was happening. It required explanation. The Christian Empire was undergoing worse disasters, within twenty years of the prohibition of pagan worship in 392, than had befallen Rome for many centuries. And this was at the hands of barbarians who generally adhered to the Arian heresy (finally condemned in the Empire in 381). Arians seemed to Catholics to destroy the full divinity of Christ and of the Holy Spirit—by making them less than God the Father—and so to be almost worse than pagans.

St. Augustine of Hippo was as moved as Jerome by the disaster to the Roman world but he sought to map out an explanation in *The City of God* (413–26). For Augustine, the disaster was a crucial test for the Christian. "Now," he wrote, "the world is like an olive press at work. If you are lees you will spill away in the gutters; if you are fine oil you will be treasured up in jars" for Christ.[1]

Augustine's disciple, Orosius, elaborated a subsidiary point of his master's

---

1. *Miscellanea Agostiniana*, I, ed. G. Morin (Rome, 1930), p. 151.

explanation in 417.[2] Worse things had happened before Rome became Christian. Therefore Christianity was not responsible for the present ills of Rome. In any case things were improving fast.

In about 440 the monk Salvian of Marseille wrote his *On the Government of God*.[3] He held the torments of Rome were deserved by the Romans' sins. He took an extremely favorable view of the barbarians, excusing them for being Arians on the ground of ignorance and pointing out very acutely the evils of the Roman State.

To the Catholics persecuted by the barbarians the optimism of Orosius, and especially of Salvian, must have seemed premature. C. Courtois, *Les Vandales et l'Afrique* (Paris, 1955), argues that the identification of the Catholic Church in North Africa with the Roman landed proprietors (expropriated by the Vandals) explains the fierceness of the Vandal persecution. He does not deny the historicity of the episode translated here from Victor of Vita. Persecution returned under Thrasamund (496–523). The leading Catholic bishop, Fulgentius of Ruspe, replied by his verses, intended to be sung by Catholics. Their "vulgar style" was meant for the people. Augustine had adopted a similar style for the same reason in his *Psalm Against the Donatists*, a popular schismatic movement in North Africa. Like Augustine's writings earlier, those of Fulgentius were rapidly carried to all the countries of the Latin West. Catholics everywhere, living under Arian rulers, would have been comforted by his verses as they were inspired by Victor of Vita's description of North Africa's heroic endurance of Arian barbarian persecution.

Roman Patriotism

1. The providential role of the Roman Empire.
Ambrose of Milan, *On Psalm 45.21* (*c.* 394), *PL*, 14, col. 1143B.

In the beginning of the Church God diffused the power of the Roman Empire throughout the whole world, and brought together in His peace minds in discord and divided lands. Living under one earthly empire all men learnt to confess, by Faith, the rule of One Omnipotent God.

2. One must defend one's country.
Ambrose, *De officiis*, I, 27, 129 (389), *PL*, 16, col. 61B.

Therefore, granted that these and other things connected with them are virtues, so too is Fortitude full of Justice, which defends the Fatherland in

2. *Seven Books of History Against the Pagans*, trans. I. W. Raymond (New York, 1936).
3. *On the Government of God*, trans. E. M. Sanford (New York, 1930).

war from barbarians, or at home defends the sick, or defends one's companions against robbers. . . .

Ibid., III, 3, 23, PL, 16, col. 151C.

But what is so against Nature as to injure another for your own profit, when natural affection teaches us to undergo troubles and undertake toil for the protection of the community, and it is reckoned a glory to any man if he seeks the quiet of all men at his own risk? Every man thinks it much more delightful to repel disaster to the Fatherland than danger to himself, and much more distinguished to expend his labor for his country than to pass his life in ease and pleasures.

3. May the Saints defend the Empire! (Against the Visigoths, 402).
Paulinus of Nola, Carmen, 26, vv. 246–59, 425–29, ed. W. von Hartel, CSEL, 30 (Vienna, 1894), pp. 255, 261.

Address to St. Felix of Nola

Implore, I beg, Christ to come to our aid. For Your God is He by Whom Joshua the strong ordered the sun and moon to stand still for his triumphs (see Joshua 10). And since the Lord has given you the prosperity of the Roman Empire, Felix, order your servants the elements to serve our good; that the stars may stand so that the day may be longer and the sun and moon remain motionless at your order, suspending the constellations' course so that the Roman victory may be complete. As in Assyria, at Babylon, Daniel conquered the lions by his prayers, so may wild barbarism be broken by Christ and conquered by you, Felix, and your captives lie around your feet as the lions once lay round the prophet. . . . The warlike flood of battle approaches; turn it away from our land; may the impious hand of warriors abstain from this sacred soil, which has Your Grace for rampart! May the enemy fear your church as demons fear it! May blood not soil what flames and floods have fled!

4. A Roman general who relied too much on the Saints (401?).
Claudian, Carmina minora, 50 (77), ed. T. Birt, MGH, AA, X (Berlin, 1892), p. 340.

Against James, Commander of the Cavalry

By the ashes of St. Paul, by the threshold of Venerable St. Peter, General James, do not tear my verses to pieces! So may St. Thomas act as shield for your breast and St. Bartholomew accompany you to war; so that by the

Saints' help the Barbarian may not cross the Alps. May St. Susanna lend you her strength; so that, should any savage enemy try to cross the frozen Danube he will be swallowed up as the rapid coursers of Pharaoh; may the avenging sword strike the Gothic hordes and the hand of St. Thecla grant success to the Roman forces! So may your dead-drunk boon companion yield you a signal triumph and casks pour out in floods their wine to quench your thirst! May your right hand never be stained with enemy blood! Do not, General James, tear my verses to pieces.

REACTIONS TO THE BARBARIAN INVASIONS

1. To the sack of Rome by the Visigoths (410).
Jerome, Letter 127, 12, ed. I. Hilberg, *CSEL*, 56 (Vienna, 1918), pp. 154–55.

A terrible rumor has arrived from the West. Rome is besieged; the lives of the citizens have been redeemed by gold. Despoiled, they are again encircled, and are losing their lives after they have lost their riches. My voice cannot continue, sobs interrupt my dictation. The City is taken which took the whole world. It had perished of famine before it died by the sword, and only a few captives were found. The fury of the hungry sought out horrible food; men tore each other to pieces; a mother did not spare her infant at the breast and ate what she had brought forth a little before. "By night Moab was taken, its walls fell by night" (Isaiah 15:1). "O God, the heathen have come into Thy inheritance, they have defiled Thy holy temple. They have made of Jerusalem a shed for an orchard keeper. They have given the bodies of Thy servants as food to the birds of the air, the flesh of Thy Saints to the beasts of the earth; they have poured out their blood as water round about Jerusalem, and there was no man to bury them" (Psalm 79: 1–3).

What tongue can tell the slaughter of that night?
What eyes can weep the sorrows and affright?
An ancient and imperial city falls:
The streets are filled with frequent funerals;
And grisly Death in sundry shapes appears.
    (Virgil, *Aeneid*, II, 361–65, 369, trans. Dryden)

2. To the invasion of Gaul and Spain (407–9).

a. Paulinus, Bishop of Béziers, *Epigramma*, vv. 8–21, 26–41, 87–95, ed. C. Schenkl, *CSEL*, 16 (Vienna, 1888), pp. 503–5, 507.

Tell us then, Salmon, what has become of you, what is the state of your Fatherland, what pleases you in it? For the first time the Barbarian, violating the treaty of peace, throws himself on the fields, the wealth of the inhabitants and their "coloni." Neither country houses built of solid marble nor the cliff-like blocks employed for useless theaters serve today to prolong our life. An inner plague, a deep laid struggle has long worn us out . . . the enemy is all the more dangerous that he is more hidden. But if the Sarmatian lays waste the land, if the Vandal burns it with fire and the swift Alan plunders it, we try, for a dubious result and at the price of painful toil, to restore all to its earlier state. . . . It is more urgent to clear a vineyard, to root up thorns, to replace a door wrenched off its hinges or a broken window, than to till the wide fields of our soul and to raise up the ruined honor of our captive spirit.

Neither the enemy, nor famine, nor plague has touched us; we are what we always were, subject to the same vices as ever. He who used to dine until nightfall still joins one day to the next, drinking by lamplight. Pedius was an adulterer; he is an adulterer still. . . . Polio was envious, he is so still. Albus used to be out for [official] honors: in the ruins of the world is he to be less ambitious? Nothing is sacred to us except profit: honesty is defined by utility; we give vices the names of virtues and the miser is called frugal. . . .

Our enemy [the Devil] rages everywhere. It is not surprising if men subject to him are conquered by the terror of war. If we returned to a sane state of mind, if our soul, freed and purified from the dark mists [of error], opened itself to Christ, if we applied the sickle of the Word to our heart and were willing to cut the knots of our old vices, [then] no force could prevail against the servants of Christ; the bow of the Alan would not strike us down; the war, which enslaves us, would not overwhelm us entirely, and the enemy, which now riots with pride at our overthrow [would cause us no fear].

b. Orientius, *Commonitorium*, II, vv. 165–192, 257–60, ed. R. Ellis, *CSEL*, 16 (Vienna, 1888), pp. 234–35, 237.

See with what suddenness death has weighed on the whole world, how many peoples the violence of war has struck down. Neither dense and savage forests nor high mountains, not rivers rushing down through swift rapids, not citadels on remote heights nor cities protected by their walls, not the barrier of the sea nor the sad solitude of the desert, not holes in the ground nor caves under forbidding cliffs could escape from the barbarians' raids.

Many were victims of false friendship, many of perjury, many of civic treason. Plots and popular violence have done much evil. Those not conquered by force have been overcome by famine. The unhappy mother fell with her children and her husband; the master shared slavery with his slaves. Some lay as food for dogs. . . . In villages and great villas, through the countryside, at crossroads, in every district, all along the roads, there is death, suffering, destruction, fire, and mourning. All Gaul reeked in one funeral pyre.

But why should I recount the deaths of a world which is dying by the law of all that perishes? Why should I repeat the number of those dying in the world when you yourself see your last day is hurrying on? I pass over how many die by the sword, how many by falling buildings, by fire, by poison, by flood, how many war, famine, and plague carry away. Death, by different ways, is the same for all. . . . Blessed is he who, awaiting God's solemn judgment on cities and nations, can do so with a constant mind, calmly sure of the innocence of his life. . . .

c. A Spanish inscription referring to destruction by the Vandals (409–429), ed. G. B. de Rossi, *Inscriptiones christianae urbis Romae*, II.1 (Rome, 1888), p. 296.

May our peace glorify those the enemy despised, and honor be [the Martyrs'] rather than the shock of destruction. We gave this abode to the Saints with perennial glory. You [the Martyrs] draw your servants into the lot of the future kingdom.

CATHOLICS IN NORTH AFRICA UNDER THE ARIAN VANDALS

1. Persecution (483).
Victor, Bishop of Vita, *Historia persecutionis africanae provinciae*, II, 31–33, ed. M. Petschenig, *CSEL*, 7 (Vienna, 1881), pp. 35–36 (describing a stage on a forced march of 4966 Catholic clergy and laity, who were being sent into exile).

The enemy searches out the most confined and foul quarters to shut up the army of God. They are not allowed even the consolation of receiving visitors: sentinels are placed at the doors. . . . The confessors of Christ are heaped up, one on top of the other, like a swarm of locusts, or, to speak more exactly, as grains of the most precious bread. In this mass of men there was no way of drawing aside to satisfy the needs of nature. They were forced to defecate and urinate there. The appalling stench was worse than any kind of torment. By bribing the Moorish guards with large sums we were sometimes allowed secretly in to them while the Vandals were asleep. At the entrance we were plunged up to our knees in an abyss of filth. Then we saw the fulfillment of the prophecy of Jeremiah: "Those who were brought up in the purple have embraced their own dung" (Lamentations 4:5). Finally, the Moors, shouting at them from every direction, ordered them to prepare for the rest of their journey. They went out, then, on a Sunday, with their clothes and faces covered in excrement but, in spite of the Moors' cruel threats, they exultingly sang a hymn to the Lord: "Behold the glory reserved to His Saints" (Psalm 149:9).

2. Catholic popular propaganda (about 515).
Fulgentius, Bishop of Ruspe, *Abecedarium* (against the Arians), vv. 234–43, 290–300, ed. C. Lambot, *Revue bénédictine*, 48 (1936), pp. 232, 233.

They pursue the faithful of Christ with malice. They threaten the wretched with death in two forms. They seduce those they can with gifts and break others with terror. We may know there dwells in them he who is called lion and dragon for his evil. They give forth smooth words to deprave men and promise riches to the poor. They receive criminals and honor them, and give altars to [that is, ordain] the incestuous and polluted, that they may do what evil they will without fear. . . .

We should not fear the faithless Arians, who are now placed in power over the world, and who afflict Catholics persevering in the Faith. Rather let us rejoice in all tribulation. For the rest, brothers, keep yourselves carefully. Never enter their churches to pray. They are not the churches of God but caves of robbers, a shop for souls, and the entrance of Hell. Therefore all sons of God who want to be His heirs should pray to their Father within the bosom of their Mother, and not go to this stepmother, who seeks to kill them all.

B. *The Case of Clovis*

The conquest of the Roman West by a very small number of barbarians— perhaps 5 percent of the total population of the provinces they ruled—created many problems. The inevitable tension between the conquerors and their far more civilized and numerous subjects was greatly heightened by differences of religion. The Sueves in Northwest Spain, the Visigoths in Spain and Gaul, the Burgundians in Gaul, Odovacar (476–89), and later the Ostrogoths in

The Church and the Barbarians

Italy, and the Vandals in North Africa were all Arian Christians and, as such, separated from their Roman subjects, all of whom were officially—and their ruling classes convinced—Catholics. The pagan Franks were in somewhat the same position in Gaul.

In the end this situation could be resolved in one of two ways, either by reconquest by the unconquered Roman (or Byzantine) East, or by the peaceful assimilation of the barbarians by the Catholic majority. Reconquest took place in North Africa and Italy, assimilation in Gaul with the Franks, and in Spain with the Visigoths. (The Sueves and Burgundians also became Catholics but too late to save themselves from the more powerful Visigoths and Franks.)

In North Africa tension between the Arian rulers and their subjects was acute since the Vandal conquest of 429–39 and periods of persecution more frequent than of respite. Appeals for help to the Emperor in Constantinople were eventually heard by Justinian (527–65), who claimed to be actuated by religious motives in undertaking the successful (and popular) reconquest of North Africa in 533.

In Italy the Ostrogoth King Theodoric (490–526) had tried to rule so as to content the Catholic majority. The Church's privileges, granted by Roman rulers, were continued and increased, as we can see from the *Variae*, a collection of letters written by the Roman senator Cassiodorus in the name of Theodoric and his successors.[1] Theodoric could be generous to Caesarius of Arles (p. 39). But at the end of his reign, suspecting intrigues with the Emperor in Constantinople, Theodoric executed several senators and imprisoned Pope John I, who soon died. Romano-Gothic co-existence was revealed as hollow and the way was open for Justinian's invasion of Italy (535). In the long struggle with the Ostrogoths that followed Justinian's surest allies were the Italian Church and the senatorial nobility.

The Vandal and Ostrogoth kingdoms perished, at least in part, because of the religious division between the Arian barbarians and their Roman subjects. The Visigoths barely saved themselves from the same danger. It was after the Byzantines had occupied the Southeast of Spain (552) and exploited a Catholic pretender to the throne (580–84) that King Recared became a Catholic in 587 (Part II, One). In 507 the Visigoths had already lost almost all Gaul to the Franks, led by Clovis, a convert from paganism to Catholicism.

The conversion of the Franks holds a central place in that of Western Europe. They were the first Germanic people to prefer Catholicism to Arianism. In this way they chose assimilation rather than continued separation—leading eventually to the destruction which overtook the Vandals and Ostrogoths. Fusion with the local population was only to be had—as the Visigoths and also the Lombards found later—through entry into the Catholic Church.

The conversion of Clovis was necessary to enable that of his people to be-

1. *Variae*, trans. T. Hodgkin (London, 1886).

From the Roman to the Barbarian World

gin. It is also worth studying because the considerations that appear to have influenced him may reasonably be thought to have influenced other men of the time.

The standard account of Clovis' conversion in Gregory of Tours is not entirely clear and was written almost a century after the event. I have collected here the key documents. They are in chronological order, with Gregory's account coming last. Apart from Clovis' letter these documents were all written by leading Gallo-Roman bishops. They show how such men dealt with a pagan prince and how they conceived of Clovis' conversion.

Clovis succeeded his father Childeric in 481 or 482 as King of the Franks settled round Tournai. He was only fifteen at the time, only one of a number of rival Frankish kings in modern Belgium, Northern Gaul, and the Rhineland. These facts help to explain the tone of the letter Clovis soon received from Bishop Remigius of Reims, the Metropolitan (presiding bishop) of his ecclesiastical province. As Tessier remarks, the letter's tone "bears witness to the pre-eminent situation acquired by the episcopate" and to Clovis' need to have it on his side. Remigius, although in the sphere of influence of Clovis' rival, Syagrius, a Roman general who had become the independent "King of Soissons," had no hesitation in entering into correspondence with Clovis. By now the Roman State in the West was dead and the Church had replaced it in dealing with the barbarians. It constituted the one possible bridge between Rome and the Germanic world.

In 486 Clovis overthrew Syagrius and extended his kingdom south to Soissons and Reims. As he took over more former Roman territory, he necessarily became even more aware of the importance of the Church. He did not have enough warriors to occupy Gaul in depth or to disregard the leaders of the local population. The letter of Bishop Avitus of Vienne—who held the same position in Burgundian territory that Remigius held in Northern Gaul— shows that Clovis adopted a deferential tone to the Church long before he became a Catholic. At the same time Clovis was in touch with Arian kings— the Visigoths, who ruled most of Gaul south of the Loire—the Burgundians, and Theodoric in Italy. Avitus' letter, together with Cassiodorus' *Variae*, show the Arians trying to draw Clovis into their fold.

Sought after by both churches, Clovis wished to give his choice of Catholicism the greatest possible publicity. He apparently sent messengers to invite Avitus (the principal Catholic bishop of an Arian king) to attend the ceremony. Avitus, conscious of the moment, contrasts Clovis' courage in taking this step—in giving up his past, his pagan *Fortuna*—with the hesitations of his own ruler, King Gundobad.

If the end of Avitus' letter, with its date, had been preserved, scholars would have been spared much controversy as to the date of Clovis' conversion. The traditional date is 496–97 but some have suggested 506, immediately before the decisive encounter with the Visigoths. It seems impossible to decide this controversy, though it is difficult to suppose that Clovis waited until 506 to bring the Church's influence definitely on to his side. Clovis' letter on campaign (the only document we have from him) shows him anxious to propitiate the bishops of what had been Visigothic Gaul by making clear his respect for the Church's officers, servants, and possessions. It was important for Clovis to do this at once. In the very uncertain situation after his victory at Vouillé in 507, when Theodoric was intervening in the South—where he succeeded in taking Provence and in saving the Visigothic kingdom from complete destruction—Clovis needed all the help he could get. See the *Life of Caesarius of Arles*, Chaps. 28–34 (see pp. 37–39).

Not all was political calculation in Clovis. Nicetius of Trier's letter and Gregory of Tours (*History*, II, 27) agree that Clovis was much impressed by the miraculous powers possessed by St. Martin of Tours and other saints and would not have wished to anger them by despoiling the possessions of their churches.

Nicetius wrote about fifty years after Clovis' death in 511 but he could have been well informed of the tradition in Clovis' family. His view of Clovis' conversion supplements Gregory's. Nicetius cites Clovis' wife, the Catholic princess Clotilde—partly, no doubt, because he is writing to her granddaughter, another Catholic princess married to a non-Catholic. But Nicetius sees Clovis' conversion as influenced by the miracles at Tours. This view is psychologically very probable (see p. 32): Gregory tells us (*History*, IX, 15) that the same admiration for Catholic miracles influenced the Visigothic Recared's conversion in 587. Nicetius' letter was to the point. He was right in discerning greatness for Clotsinda's husband, the Lombard King Alboin, the future conqueror of much of Italy. Nor was the possible conversion of the Lombards a remote parallel to that of the Franks—though in fact it did not take place until the seventh century—for most Lombards were pagans when Nicetius wrote, only the king and some nobles being Arians.

Gregory of Tours collects and juxtaposes different traditions as to Clovis' conversion. If he stresses Clotilde's influence, he also has Clovis appeal to Christ for aid in a battle. That this scene recalls the well-known story of Constantine's conversion after the victory of the Milvian Bridge does not mean that it is inauthentic. The Alamans were the most serious threat to Clovis from across the Rhine. Their defeat was a crucial event in his life and he may well have seen himself as a new Constantine. As Mr. J. M. Wallace-Hadrill remarks, Clovis' wife and Bishop Remigius were there to remind Clovis of the first Christian emperor, "if he needed reminding." Gregory's account of the actual Baptism shows Remigius making clear to Clovis (as Avitus had done) the total break he must endure with his past.

From Clovis' time the extension of Catholicism in Western Europe was bound up with the rise of Frankish hegemony. Avitus' idea of using the Franks as missionaries to pagan peoples, of linking their military dominance with the advance of Catholicism, had a long future ahead of it.

Clovis' conversion also meant, however, that the Church now had a ruler who was liable to interfere in its internal affairs. One has only to contrast

Remigius' letter to the young pagan king in 481 with his reference to him in 512, a year after his death, to see what Remigius had been prepared to do at Clovis' bidding. (See also p. 99.)

Clovis Appears on the Scene

Bishop Remigius of Reims to Clovis (c. 481), ed. W. Gundlach, CCSL, 117 (Turnhout, 1957), pp. 408–9.

To the celebrated and rightly magnificent Lord, King Clovis, Bishop Remigius.
A strong report has come to us that you have taken over the administration of the Second Belgic Province. There is nothing new in that you now begin to be what your parents always were. First of all, you should act so that God's Judgment may not abandon you and that your merits should maintain you at the height where you have arrived by your humility. For, as the proverb says, man's acts are judged. You ought to associate with yourself counselors who are able to do honor to your reputation. Your deeds should be chaste and honest. You should defer to your bishops and always have recourse to their advice. If you are on good terms with them your province will be better able to stand firm. Encourage your people, relieve the afflicted, protect widows, nourish orphans, so shine forth that all may love and fear you. May justice proceed from your mouth. Ask nothing of the poor or of strangers, do not allow yourself to receive gifts from them. Let your tribunal be open to all men, so that no man may leave it with the sorrow [of not having been heard]. You possess the riches your father left you. Use them to ransom captives and free them from servitude. If someone is admitted to your presence let him not feel he is a stranger. Amuse yourself with young men, deliberate with the old. If you wish to reign, show yourself worthy to do so.

The Conversion of Clovis: Its Significance Recognized

Bishop Avitus of Vienne to Clovis (c. 496), ed. R. Peiper, MGH, AA, VI.2 (Berlin, 1883), pp. 75–76.

Bishop Avitus to King Clovis.
The followers of [Arian] error have in vain, by a cloud of contradictory and untrue opinions, sought to conceal from your extreme subtlety the glory

of the Christian name. While we committed these questions to eternity and trusted that the truth of each man's belief would appear at the Future Judgment, the ray of truth has shone forth even among present shadows. Divine Providence has found the arbiter of our age. Your choice is a general sentence. Your Faith is our victory. Many others, in this matter, when their bishops or friends exhort them to adhere to the True Faith, are accustomed to oppose the traditions of their race and respect for their ancestral cult; thus they culpably prefer a false shame to their salvation. While they observe a futile reverence for their parents [by continuing to share their] unbelief, they confess that they do not know what they should choose to do. After this marvelous deed guilty shame can no longer shelter behind this excuse. Of all your ancient genealogy you have chosen to keep only your own nobility, and you have willed that your race should derive from you all the glories which adorn high birth. Your ancestors have prepared a great destiny for you; you willed to prepare better things [for those who will follow you]. You follow your ancestors in reigning in this world; you have opened the way to your descendants to a heavenly reign. Let Greece indeed rejoice it has elected an emperor who shares our Faith; it is no longer alone in deserving such a favor. Your sphere also burns with its own brilliance, and, in the person of a king, the light of a rising sun shines over the Western lands. It is right that this light began at the Nativity of Our Redeemer, so that the waters of rebirth have brought you forth to salvation the very day that the world received the birth of its Redemption, the Lord of Heaven. The day celebrated as the Lord's Nativity is also yours, in which you have been born to Christ, as Christ to the world, in which you have consecrated your soul to God, your life to your contemporaries, your glory to posterity.

What should be said of the glorious solemnity of your regeneration? If I could not assist in person among the ministers [of the rite] I shared in its joy. Thanks to God, our land took part in the thanksgiving, for, before your Baptism, a messenger of Your Most Subtle Humility informed us that you were a "competens" [that is, to be baptized within forty days]. Therefore the sacred night [of Christmas] found us sure of what you would do. We saw (with the eyes of the spirit) that great sight, when a crowd of bishops around you, in the ardor of their holy ministry, poured over your royal limbs the waters of life; when that head feared by the peoples bowed down before the servants of God; when your royal locks, hidden under a helmet, were steeped in holy oil; when your breast, relieved of its cuirass, shone with the same whiteness as your baptismal robes. Do not doubt, most flourishing of kings, that this soft clothing will give more force to your arms: whatever Fortune has given up to now, this Sanctity will bestow.

I would wish to add some exhortations to your praises if anything escaped either your knowledge or your attention. Should we preach the Faith to the convert who perceived it without a preacher; or humility, which you have long shown toward us [bishops], although you only owe it to us now, after your profession of Faith; or mercy, attested, in tears and joy to God and men, by a people once captive, now freed by you? One wish remains for me to express. Since God, thanks to you, will make of your people His own possession, offer a part of the treasure of Faith which fills your heart to the peoples living beyond you, who, still living in natural ignorance, have not been corrupted by the seeds of perverse doctrines [that is, Arianism]. Do not fear to send them envoys and to plead with them the cause of God, who has done so much for your cause. So that the other pagan peoples, at first being subject to your empire for the sake of religion, while they still seem to have another ruler, may be distinguished rather by their race than by their prince. [End of letter missing.]

CLOVIS ON CAMPAIGN: TO THE CHURCH IN SOUTHERN GAUL

To the Bishops of Aquitaine (507–8), ed. A. Boretius, pp. 1–2.

To the Holy Lords, most worthy of an apostolic see, King Clovis.

Rumor reporting what was done or ordered to all our army before We entered the land of the Goths, it could not be passed over [in writing to] Your Holiness.

First of all, We ordered, as regards the ministry of the churches, that no one should attempt to steal anything from them, nor from the holy women and widows who are approved as devout in the religion of the Lord. Similar orders were given with regard to clerics or sons of clerics or of widows, who were living with their parents, also with respect to the slaves of churches, who were proved to be such by bishops' oaths, so that none of these should suffer any violence or harm. If any of them has been captured, either in churches or outside, We order that they should be set free without delay. With regard to the other lay prisoners taken during the war, your apostolic letters [of protection] are to be honored. For, of those who were plundered within Our Peace, whether clerics or laymen, if you truly acknowledge your letters sealed with your ring, write to Us that, on Our part, you may know Our Precept is confirmed. . . .

Pray for me, Holy Lords, most worthy of an apostolic see.

CLOVIS AND THE INTERNAL AFFAIRS OF THE CHURCH

Bishop Remigius of Reims to Bishops Heraclius (of Paris or Sens), Leo, and Theodosius (of Auxerre), 512, ed. Gundlach, CCSL, 117, pp. 409–10.

Paul the Apostle in his Letter says: "Charity never fails" (1 Corinthians 13:8). That you could send me such letters shows that charity does not dwell in you. As for Claudius, who, you write, is not a presbyter, I only asked you to reveal the cause of your indignation. I do not deny that he has sinned gravely but you should have respected my age, if not my merits. . . . For fifty-three years I have been a bishop and no one has addressed me so impudently. You say: "It would have been better had you [Remigius] not been born. . . ." I made Claudius a presbyter, not corrupted by gold but on the testimony of the very excellent King [Clovis], who not only strongly asserted but defended the Catholic Faith. You write: "What he ordered was not canonical. . . ." The ruler of the country, the guardian of the fatherland, the conqueror of nations enjoined this. . . .

CLOVIS AS EXAMPLE TO OTHER BARBARIAN KINGS

Bishop Nicetius of Trier to Clotsinda, Queen of the Lombards (563–65), ed. Gundlach, CCSL, 117, pp. 419, 421–23.

To the most clement Lady, daughter in Christ, Queen Clotsinda, Nicetius a sinner. . . .

I conjure you, Lady Clotsinda, by the tremendous Day of Judgment, that you both read this letter carefully and often try to expound it to your husband [King Alboin]. . . .

[Arguments from the Bible in favor of the Catholic doctrine of the Trinity and against the Arian view.]

Let us come to the twelve disciples of Christ, for the very [Arian] Goths today venerate them and their relics, but furtively. . . . Why is it that they do not enter the basilicas where the bodies [of the Apostles] are venerated? Why is it that when King Alboin sends his faithful there and leads them to the thresholds of the Lords Peter, Paul, John or of other Saints, that they do not dare to undertake anything there, except furtively, as dogs, from outside, that they may deceive souls? They consult about celebrating Masses there but they do not dare [do so] because they are clearly not the disciples of the Lord Peter and they are proved to be the enemies of Christ; these unhappy men are known to destroy [men] He redeemed by the Cross. And so such a king and such an age recognizes their poison.

If the King chooses let him send his men to [Gaul], to the Lord Martin [at Tours], at his feast, which is the 11th of November, and, if they dare, let them venture to do something there, where every day we see the blind receive their sight, the deaf their hearing, and the dumb their speech. What shall I say of lepers or of many others, who, no matter with what sickness they are afflicted, are healed there year after year? Perhaps they will say: "They feign to be blind!" What do they say when they have been blind from birth, when we see them receive sight there by God's Grace, returning healed to their own place? What shall I say of the [shrines of the] Lord Bishops Germanus [of Auxerre], Hilary [of Poitiers], or Lupus [of Troyes], where so many wonders occur every day, so great that I cannot express them in words: where the afflicted (those having demons) are suspended and whirled round in the air and confess the [power of the] Lords I have named? Do these things happen in Arian churches? They do not, because the demons do not feel that God and the Holy Lords dwell there: a demon does not drive out a demon (see Mark 3:23). But no demon is permitted to rove where the Saints dwell. So it is that the place where God is found is made clear. What of the Lord Bishops Remigius [of Reims] and Medard [of Noyon], whom I believe you have seen? We cannot set out how many wonders we see God do by them.

You have heard how your grandmother, Lady Clotilde of good memory, came into France, how she led the Lord Clovis to the Catholic Law, and how, since he was a most astute man, he was unwilling to agree to it until he knew it was true. When he saw that the things I have spoken of were proved he humbly prostrated himself at the threshold of the Lord Martin [at Tours] and promised to be baptized without delay. You have heard what he did when he was baptized to the heretical Kings Alaric [II, of the Visigoths] and Gundobad [of Burgundy]. You are not ignorant of what riches he and his sons possessed in the world.

Such an admirable man as King Alboin is said to be, when the world offers him such glory, why is he not converted, or why does he come late to ask for the way of salvation? O Good God, who art the Glory of the Saints and all men's salvation, enter his mind. And you, Lady Clotsinda, when you send word, give us comfort, that we may all rejoice at such a star, such a jewel. . . . I beg that you not be idle; clamor without ceasing, do not cease to sing. You have heard the saying: "The unfaithful husband shall be saved by the faithful wife" (1 Corinthians 7:14). You know that salvation will be granted first to those who convert a sinner from his sin. Watch, keep vigil, for God is propitious to you. I pray that you so act that you both make the Lombard people strong over their enemies and allow us to rejoice at your salvation and at that of your husband.

The Conversion of Clovis in Gregory of Tours

Gregory of Tours, *History of the Franks*, II, 20–22 (begun 576–80), trans. O. M. Dalton (Oxford, 1927), pp. 67–70.

20(29). Of Queen Clotild the king had a firstborn son whom the mother wished to be baptized; she therefore persistently urged Clovis to permit it, saying: "The gods whom ye worship are naught; they cannot aid either themselves or others, seeing that they are images carved of wood or stone, or metal. Moreover the names which ye have given them are the names of men and not of gods. Saturn was a man, fabled to have escaped by flight from his son to avoid being thrust from his kingdom; Jupiter also, the lewdest practicer of all debaucheries and of unnatural vice, the abuser of the women of his own family, who could not even abstain from intercourse with his own sister, as she herself admitted in the words 'sister and spouse of Jove.' What power had Mars and Mercury? They may have been endowed with magical arts; they never had the power of the divine name. But ye should rather serve Him, who at His word created out of nothing the heaven and earth, the sea and all therein; who made the sun to shine and adorned the heaven with stars; who filled the waters with fish, the earth with animals, the air with birds; at whose nod the lands are made fair with fruits, the trees with apples, the vines with grapes; by whose hand the race of man was created; by whose largess every creature was made to render homage and service to the man whom he created." Though the queen ever argued thus, the king's mind was nowise moved towards belief, but he replied: "It is by command of our gods that all things are created and come forth; it is manifest that thy god availeth in nothing; nay more, he is not even proven to belong to the race of gods." But the queen, true to her faith, presented her son for baptism; she ordered the church to be adorned with hangings and curtains, that the king, whom no preaching could influence, might by this ceremony be persuaded to belief. The boy was baptized and named Ingomer, but died while yet clothed in the white raiment of his regeneration. Thereupon the king was moved to bitter wrath, nor was he slow to reproach the queen saying: "If the child had been dedicated in the name of my gods, surely he would have survived, but now, baptized in the name of thy God, he could not live a day." The queen replied: "I render thanks to Almighty God, Creator of all things, who hath not judged me all unworthy, and deigneth to take into His kingdom this child born of my womb. My mind is untouched by grief at this event, since I know that they which be called from this world in the white robes of baptism shall be nurtured in the sight of God." Afterwards she bore another son, who was baptized with the name of Chlodomer. When he too began to ail, the king said: "It cannot but befall that this infant like his brother shall straightway die, being baptized in the name of thy Christ." But the mother prayed, and God ordained that the child should recover.

21(30). Now the queen without ceasing urged the king to confess the true God, and forsake his idols; but in no wise could she move him to this belief, until at length he made war upon a time against the Alamanni, when he was driven of necessity to confess what of his free will he had denied. It befell that when the two hosts joined battle there was grievous slaughter, and the army of Clovis was being swept to utter ruin. When the king saw this he lifted up his eyes to heaven, and knew compunction in his heart, and, moved to tears, cried aloud: "Jesus Christ, Thou that art proclaimed by Clotild Son of the living God, Thou that art said to give aid to those in stress, and to grant victory to those that hope in Thee, I entreat from a devout heart the glory of Thy succor. If Thou grant me victory over these enemies, and experience confirm that power which the people dedicated to Thy name claimeth to have proved, then will I also believe on Thee and be baptized in Thy name. I have called upon mine own gods, but here is proof that they have withdrawn themselves from helping me; wherefore I believe that they have no power, since they come not to the succor of their servants. Thee do I now invoke, on Thee am I fain to believe, if but I may be plucked out of the hands of mine adversaries." And as he said this, lo, the Alamanni turned their backs, and began to flee. And when they saw that their king was slain, they yielded themselves to Clovis, saying: "No longer, we entreat thee, let the people perish; we are now thy men." Then the king put an end to the war, and having admonished the people, returned in peace, relating to the queen how he had called upon the name of Christ and had been found worthy to obtain the victory. This happened in the fifteenth year of his reign.

22(31). Then the queen commanded the holy Remigius, bishop of Reims, to be summoned secretly, entreating him to impart the word of salvation to the king. The bishop, calling the king to him in privity, began to instill into him faith in the true God, Maker of heaven and earth, and urged him to forsake his idols, which were unable to help either himself or others. But

Clovis replied: "I myself, most holy father, will gladly hearken to thee; but one thing yet remaineth. The people that followeth me will not suffer it that I forsake their gods; yet will I go, and reason with them according to thy word." But when he came before the assembled people, or ever he opened his mouth, the divine power had gone forth before him, and all the people cried with one voice: "O gracious king, we drive forth our gods that perish, and are ready to follow that immortal God whom Remigius preacheth." News of this was brought to the bishop, who was filled with great joy, and commanded the font to be prepared. The streets were overshadowed with colored hangings, the churches adorned with white hangings, the baptistery was set in order, smoke of incense spread in clouds, perfumed tapers gleamed, the whole church about the place of baptism was filled with the divine fragrance. And now the king first demanded to be baptized by the bishop. Like a new Constantine, he moved forward to the water, to blot out the former leprosy, to wash away in his new stream the foul stains borne from old days. As he entered to be baptized the saint of God spoke these words with eloquent lips: "Meekly bow thy proud head, Sicamber; adore that which thou hast burned, burn that which thou hast adored." For the holy Remigius, the bishop, was of excellent learning, and above all skilled in the art of rhetoric, and so exemplary in holiness that his miracles were equal to those of the holy Silvester; there is preserved to us a book of his life, in which it is related how he raised a man from the dead. The king therefore, confessing Almighty God, three in one, was baptized in the name of the Father, the Son, and the Holy Ghost, and anointed with holy chrism, with the sign of the Cross of Christ. Of his army were baptized more than three thousand; and his sister Albofled, who not long after was taken to the Lord, was likewise baptized. And when the king was sorrowing for her death, the holy Remigius sent him a letter of consolation, beginning after this fashion: "The cause of thy sadness doth afflict me with a great affliction, for that thy sister of fair memory hath passed away. But this shall console us, that she hath in such wise left the world as that we should rather lift up our eyes to her than mourn her." And another of his sisters was converted, by name Lanthechild, who had fallen into the heresy of the Arians; she also received the holy chrism, having confessed the Son and the Holy Ghost equal to the Father.

PART TWO

Christianity in a Non-Roman World

The conversion of Clovis is a great turning point. It made possible the shift from a Mediterranean-centered Christianity to one whose capital was situated by 800 at Aachen and whose spiritual centers were in England, North France (as Gaul was becoming), and Germany. This shift greatly accentuated the cultural—as yet not formal ecclesiastical—break with the Byzantine East, still centered at Constantinople.

The Western Church again had Catholic rulers who were as determined as Christian Roman emperors had been to have their way in the wide areas in dispute between the secular and spiritual domains. But they were not as likely to prevail. Their administration was more rudimentary, their sources of income less certain, their prestige less absolute than the administration, income, and prestige of the Church. There was tension as well as fusion between Church and barbarian monarchy yet the Church could not do without a strong king, for that meant anarchy, and royal as well as conciliar legislation was necessary to enforce Christianity on the largely pagan population. In many ways Clovis' descendants, the Merovingians, anticipate the Carolingians in their role as patrons and promoters of the slow advance of Christianity, though their work has received far less recognition. *Methods* of conversion will be discussed more fully later. Here I wish to indicate some main differences between Christianity in Western Europe in about 400 and some three centuries later.

In the early Church the Liturgy was the common action of all present. The relation between the priest at the altar and the people was close. As more and more of the rural population, with very little Latin, entered the Church, the situation changed. While the Liturgy continued to be important (see 4, below), other ways had to be found to assist the clergy to reach men's minds.

At the same time the Bible had become inaccessible. Caesarius of Arles (d. 543) and Pope Gregory the Great (d. 604) continued to preach *on* the Bible. They invited the people to read it, or, if unlettered, to have it read to them. But, even in Romanized Provence or in Rome itself, they were fighting a rearguard action. In general the laity, even if literate, knew only the Psalms and depended for the rest on preaching. And after the sixth century sermons were rarely devoted to biblical themes. Bede translated the Gospel of St. John not for the laity of Northumbria but for the clergy lacking Latin. He even had to translate the Creed and the Lord's Prayer for them (see p. 161). Things were scarcely better in France. When addressing the laity preachers preferred stories from the Lives of the Saints or Acts of Martyrs. These were also read in church. Gregory the Great wrote his most popular work—popular in its style as well as content—the *Dialogues*, on the lives of the saints of Italy and on visions of the future life.[1] The type of exhortation found in Martin's sermon (p. 63) recurs in later preachers. Simple morality was stressed more than adherence to a Divine Mystery. The examples chosen from the Bible were taken especially from the Book of Proverbs. Boniface, in Germany, used Caesarius' sermons on morality, not those on the Bible.

God and Christ became more remote from men. A Merovingian prayer for victory over rebels began: "O Lord God, Creator of all things, terrible and strong." For Gregory the Great God was One who did miracles, who was strong above all, who conquered, who could strike offenders against His Majesty blind in a moment (see, for example, *Dialogues*, III, 29). In men's minds Christ, too, was being approximated to this representation of God. His full Divinity had been so strenuously upheld against the Arians that His Humanity was obscured. He is mentioned alone as God in the prologue to the Salic Law (p. 93). Churches were dedicated "In the Name of our God Jesus Christ," without mention of God the Father. A gravestone of the Frankish period near Bonn shows Christ as King of Heaven, with a lance in his right hand, towering over the conquered Serpent. This All Powerful King of Heaven, God of battles, evidently appealed to an ordinary Frank as He did to Clovis (in Gregory of Tours).

In the monastic *Rule* of St. Benedict, which was gaining ground throughout these centuries and was to conquer the Christian West with the Carolingians, Christ is above all a King and God a Judge. This transformation of the Christian God into a ruler whose actions were conceived very much like those of the despotic emperors of the time can be seen in art, in the church Liturgy, and in the constant insistence of sermons on the Divine Judgment.

Inevitably, mediators were needed between the increasingly terrifying and remote Christ as Judge and King and miserable humanity. These mediators existed in the martyrs and saints whose shrines flourished throughout the West, and in the living ascetics and saintly bishops who castigated and governed their flocks as accepted representatives on earth of the Supreme Judge in Heaven.

F. J. E. Raby remarked of Pope Gregory the Great that "his world was a world 'without any order,' in which natural law was unknown, a world of de-

---

1. *Dialogues*, trans. O. J. Zimmerman, "Fathers of the Church," 39 (New York, 1959).

mons and witchcraft, of miracles and wonders, and over it all was spread the
horror of that day,

When, shrivelling like a parchèd scroll,
The flaming heavens together roll."

Part of the fascination of the sixth and seventh centuries is the simultaneous
existence of this "world picture," which certainly dominated all but a few
minds, and the steadfastness with which Christian statesmen and administrators, of whom Gregory is an outstanding example, maintained what order
could be saved from the Roman past, instilled what Christian principles they
could into their people, and even, as Gregory did, helped to advance the
frontiers of Christianity in Northern Europe. Yet the insistence on instilling
into men "the constant terror of an angry Judge" (E. I. Watkin) had its effect.
The Church acquired a military and legal stamp in these centuries—when its
hierarchy was modeled after the militarized hierarchy of the Late Roman Empire and its God after that Empire's despotic ruler and his lesser imitators, the
barbarian kings—that is not yet effaced.

1

FUSION OF CHURCH AND
MONARCHY

THE RULER WORSHIP OF THE ANCIENT WORLD DID NOT CEASE WITH CON-
stantine's conversion. It was transmuted into the liturgical homage the Church
accorded Christian emperors. If Christ became an Emperor, emperors and
kings were invested with Divine Grace. There was no clear separation of the
divine and human spheres.

The mediating role of Visigothic Spain in the introduction of the idea of the
Divine Christian ruler into barbarian Western Europe seems clear. The Visigothic rulers were deeply influenced by the East Roman or Byzantine Empire,
where Christian ruler worship had been systematized since the fifth century,
and where there was little doubt that the emperor controlled the Church.
Recared (586–601) certainly saw himself as a new Constantine, as continuing
the "Apostolic" struggle against Arianism that Constantine began at Nicaea.
The *Laudes* the bishops gave Recared at Toledo are an act of homage, of
ruler worship. In Spain, as in Byzantium, the king was supreme Judge of the
Church, condemning heresy and ending schism. Through Spain, these ideas
reached Charlemagne, "King and Priest," and, through him, the Ottonian
emperors. Spain also made its own contributions. Visigothic kings, certainly
from 672, possibly from Recared, were the first Christian rulers to be anointed

with holy oil at their coronation, a ceremony certainly taken from the Old Testament kings of Israel. In the eighth century it was adopted by Anglo-Saxons and Franks. Like the Franks later, Visigothic kings saw themselves as leaders of a chosen people, the new Israel of God, and as endowed with all the supernatural sanction the kings of Israel had possessed.

With this strain of thought are combined, in Carolingian France, the ideas represented by the prologue to the Salic Law, where Christ is "almost a national God." The formula "Long live Christ!" is strikingly unorthodox. The orthodox formula was "Christ *lives*." The implication of the prologue is that the Christ who *will* live is He who "loves the Franks."

Recared's speech and the prologue are signs of the beginning of the long growth of the great myths of religious nationalism which reappear, in Spain in the Reconquista of the country from Islam and in the Conquest of the New World, in France in the Crusades and in Joan of Arc. Spanish and French writers of the reigns of Philip II and Louis XIV looked back for the religious sanction their rulers claimed to Recared and to Clovis.

The Church blessed the arms of these princes as—forgetting its early aversion to the profession of war—it had blessed those of Roman emperors from Constantine onward. The Spanish Church Order translated here is not exceptional. Still more space was given in the Frankish rituals to blessing weapons, banners, the army and its commander.

Visigothic Spain: The Most Catholic King

"Tome of the Most Holy Faith" presented by King Recared to the Third Council of Toledo (589), "in which the Arian heresy was condemned in Spain," and the official conversion of the Visigoths to Catholicism was celebrated, *PL*, 84, col. 342–45.

"Although Omnipotent God has given Us charge of the kingdom for the profit of its peoples, and has entrusted the rule of not a few races to Our Royal Care, however We remember Our mortal condition, and that We cannot merit future Beatitude unless We devote Ourselves to the cult of the True Faith and please Our Creator at least with the confession which He deserves. As We are raised in Royal Glory far above Our subjects, by so much We should provide for those things which are God's, and increase Our Hope and take care of the races God has given Us. For the rest, what can We give the Divine Omnipotence for such great benefits, when all things are His and He needs nothing that we have, except that we believe in Him with the devotion with which, according to the Sacred Scriptures, He Himself wished to be understood and commanded to be believed?"

[Trinitarian Creed]

"You also, Bishops of God, should recall how many troubles the Catholic Church of God in Spain suffered until now from the adversary. When the Catholics sustained and defended the unyielding truth of their Faith, and the heretics supported with pertinacious animosity their own perfidy, I also— as you see by the results—set on fire by warmth of Faith, have been impelled by the Lord, that, putting aside the obstinacy of infidelity and the fury of discord, I might lead this people, which served error under the name of religion, to the knowledge of the Faith and to the fellowship of the Catholic Church.

All the famous race of Goths is present, known to almost all peoples for its manhood. Although it was until now separated from the Faith and from the unity of the Catholic Church by the depravity of its teachers, now, however, united with me, it shares in the communion of that Church which welcomes a multitude of different races in its maternal bosom and nourishes them at its loving breasts, of which the prophet said: 'My house shall be called a house of prayer for all peoples' (Matthew 21:13). Not the conversion of the Goths alone is among the favors We have received; more still, the infinite number of the Suevic race, which, with the help of heaven, We have subjected to Our kingdom. Although they were led into heresy by another's fault, We have brought them back to the fount of truth. And so, Most Holy Fathers, I offer to the Eternal God by your hands, as a holy and acceptable sacrifice, these most noble races, which by Our Diligence have been gained for the Lord. For I shall enjoy an unfading crown and the retribution of the just if these peoples, which, by Our Care, hastened to the unity of the Church, remain firm and constant within her. And, as by Divine Disposition, We were charged to bring these peoples to the unity of the Church of Christ, so it is for you to instruct them in Catholic dogmas, so that, completely prepared in the knowledge of truth, they may know how to reject the error of pernicious heresy and to keep by charity the road of the True Faith, embracing ever more fervently the communion of the Catholic Church.

For the rest, as I trust that this most famous race has easily attained pardon for having sinned only through ignorance, so I do not doubt that it would be much more serious if, knowing the Truth, it should embrace it halfheartedly, or (may this never happen!) turn its eyes from the blaze of light. For this reason I considered it to be necessary to call Your Beatitudes together, trusting in the sentence of the Lord in which He says: 'Where two or three are gathered together in My Name, there I will be in the midst of them' (Matthew 18:20). I believe, then, that the Blessed Divinity of the Holy Trinity is present at this Holy Council, and so I declared my Faith among you, as in the sight of God, aware of the Divine sentence which says: 'I have not hidden Your Mercy and Truth from before the multitude' (Psalm

40:10). I have heard the Apostle St. Paul commanding his disciple Timothy: 'Fight the good fight of faith, lay hold on eternal life to which you were
called, proclaiming a good confession [of Faith] before many witnesses'
(1 Timothy 6:12). . . ."

[Recared states his adherence to the four first General Councils of the
Church and anathematizes the heretics they condemned.]

"Let Your Reverences, then, hasten to add Our Faith to the canonical testimonies, and to hear from the bishops, religious, and first men of Our race
the Faith which they wisely confessed to God in the Catholic Church. Preserve all this, noted in detail and confirmed by their signatures, as a testimony of God and men for times to come, that [men may know that] those
peoples at whose head We are in God's Name in the Royal Power, abjuring
their former error, received the Spirit, the Paraclete, in God's Church, by
the unction of the most holy chrism and the imposition of hands. They confessed the same Spirit as One and Equal with the Father and the Son, and by
His Gift they have been established in the bosom of the Holy Catholic
Church. If some of them refuse to believe in this Our true and holy confession, may they experience the Wrath of God with eternal anathema, and
may their perdition be joy to the faithful and an example to the unfaithful.
To this My confession I have joined the Holy Constitutions of the aforesaid
Councils and I have signed them with all simplicity of heart, having God as
My Witness."

[The Creeds of the Councils of Nicaea (325), Constantinople I (381),
and Chalcedon (451).]

Signature of King Recared. "I King Recared signed with my right hand,
under God's Protection, this holy and true confession, which the One Catholic Church confesses throughout the whole world, holding it fast in my heart
and affirming it by word of mouth."

"I, the Glorious Queen Baddo, signed with my hand and of my whole
heart this Faith which I believed and have received."

Then the whole Council broke into praises to God and honoring the
King.

I. "Glory to God, Father and Son and Holy Spirit, to Whom it belongs to
care for the peace and unity of His Holy Catholic Church!" II. "Glory to
Our Lord Jesus Christ, Who, at the price of His Blood, gathered together
the Catholic Church out of all races!" III. "Glory to Our Lord Jesus Christ,
Who has joined such an illustrious race to the unity of the True Faith and
has created one flock and one shepherd!" IV. "And to whom has God
conceded eternal merit unless to the Truly Catholic King Recared?" V. "To
whom the eternal crown, unless to the Truly Orthodox King Recared?" VI.
"To whom present and eternal glory unless to the true lover of God, King

Recared?" VII. "He is the conqueror of new peoples for the Catholic Church!" VIII. "He truly deserves the reward of an apostle who has fulfilled the apostolic office! May he be pleasing to God and men who has so marvelously glorified God on earth! With the aid of the Lord Jesus Christ, Who lives and reigns in the Unity of the Holy Spirit, through the ages of ages. Amen."

THE FRANKS: THE MOST CHRISTIAN RACE

Longer prologue to the Salic Law (8th century), ed. K. A. Eckhardt, *Lex Salica, 100 Titel-Text*, Germanenrechte N. F. (Weimar, 1953), pp. 82–84, 86–90.

The famous race of Franks, whose Founder is God, strong in arms, true to its alliances, deep in counsel, noble in body, untouched in sincerity, beautiful in form, daring, swift, and fierce, now converted to the Catholic Faith, free from heresy; while still held in a barbaric [rite], by God's inspiration, according to the quality of its customs, sought after the key of knowledge, desiring justice, keeping piety. . . .

But when, by God's favor, Clovis, King of the Franks, powerful, glorious, and famous, first received Catholic Baptism, what was held less suitable in the pact was lucidly emended by the blows of Kings Clovis, Childebert, and Lothar.

Long live Christ who loves the Franks! May He guard their kingdom, fill their leaders with the light of His Grace, protect their army, accord them the defense of the Faith! May the Lord of Lords concede them, of His Mercy, the joys of peace and days full of happiness! For this is the race which, brave and valiant, threw off in battle from their necks the most hard Roman yoke, and it is the Franks who, after Baptism, have enclosed in gold and precious stones the bodies of the Holy Martyrs, whom the Romans had burnt by fire, mutilated by the sword, or thrown to wild beasts!

A CHRISTIAN KING GOES OUT TO BATTLE

Ordo quando rex cum exercitu ad prelium egreditur (Spain, 7th century), ed. M. Férotin, *Le Liber Ordinum*, Monumenta ecclesiae liturgica, V (Paris, 1904), col. 149–53.

When the king arrives at the door of the church two deacons clothed in albs offer him incense. All the clergy, in albs, remain in the choir, except for those who will precede the king with the cross. When the king enters the church, and has prostrated himself in prayer, when he rises up the verse shall be sung:

"May God be in your journey and His angel accompany you."

Then this prayer is said:

"O Lord of Hosts, the strength of virtues and virtue of the strong, the champion against the enemy, the victory of the humble, the achiever of victories, the height of kings, the ruler of kingdoms, be present to our religious prince, with the peoples subject to him, as leader of the saving way, the way of peace, the inspirer of right decision. May the king have, by Thy Grace, O Lord, strong armies, faithful generals, minds in concord, by which he may overcome the adversary and defend his own. Give him, O Lord, of Thy Spirit, to think of what are needful and to perform them, so that, fortified by Thy Protection, marching with his subject people and going out from this present church of Thy Apostles Peter and Paul with angel guardians, he may valiantly carry out the acts of war, so that, always adhering to Thee, he may triumph over his enemies and, returning, restore to us who beseech Thee the height of saving joy."

Blessing:

"May the Spirit of the Good God lead us by the ineffable grace of Divinity into the right road. Amen.

May He be your guide on the way who willed to be our way of salvation. Amen.

So that you who have vowed your conscience to God may, protected by His aid, unroll the way of your saving journey. With the aid of the mercy of our God. . . ."

The deacon goes to the altar and raises the golden cross, in which wood of the Holy Cross is enclosed, which always goes with the king in the army, and bears it to the bishop. Then the bishop, having washed his hands, hands it to the king, and the king to the priest, who will bear it before him. As the cross is placed in the king's hand, the bishop begins this antiphon, which is chanted with these verses:

"Accept from the Hand of the Lord certain judgment as a helmet, and may God's creature be armed for the punishment of thy enemies. Take up the inexpugnable shield of equity. For the punishment [of thy enemies].

For power is given you from the Lord and virtue from the Most High. For the punishment [of thy enemies]."

After the second verse all shall go up and receive their standards from the priest behind the altar and shall go forth immediately, the clergy in the choir chanting the same antiphon, with these verses:

"Blessed be Israel! Who is like unto thee, O People saved by the Lord? The shield of thy aid, the sword of thy glory. For the punishment. . . .

Thy enemies shall deny thee and thou shalt break their necks. For the punishment. . . .

Thy foot shalt not be moved nor shall He slumber who guards thee. For the punishment. . . .

Behold He shall not slumber nor sleep who guards Israel. For the punishment. . . .

The Lord shall protect thee, the Lord is thy protection upon thy right hand. For the punishment. . . .

By day the sun shall not burn thee nor the moon by night. For the punishment. . . .

The Lord shall guard thee from all evil: the Lord shall guard thy soul. For the punishment. . . ."

After all raise their standards and go outside the door of the church at once "Glory to the Father" shall be sung. . . . Then the deacon saying: "Humble yourselves for the blessing," this blessing shall be said by the bishop:

"The Saving Sign of Wood and Nail, which thou, Sacred Prince, hast received with pious hands, may it be for thy salvation and an increase of perpetual blessing. May thy egress be in peace and may the Cross of Christ always be present on the way to your armies. May it give you religious counsel and prepare strong means for your expedition. May this Wood, by which Christ despoiled Principalities and Powers, triumphing over them in Himself, become the means of your gaining singular glory in victory. Amen. So that, by the victory of the Holy Cross, you may complete your journey, begun here, happily, and bring back to us flourishing titles of your triumphs. Amen. As we bid you farewell with the kiss of peace we shall receive you on your happier return here with praises of victory. Amen. By the Grace of Our Lord Jesus Christ."

After this blessing the deacon says: "In the Name of Our Lord Jesus Christ, go in peace." "Thanks be to God."

And so the king bids farewell to the bishop and at once this antiphon [is begun] by those who march before the king with the Cross:

"O Lord God, the strength of my salvation, cover my head in the day of battle."

And they sing before the king until he has gone outside the door of the church. But the priest or deacon who has taken the Cross from the king shall always go before him until he has mounted. And so they begin the journey.

THE KING AS GOD'S VICAR

Edict of Guntramn (585), ed. Boretius, pp. 11–12.

Guntramn, King of the Franks, to all bishops and judges in our kingdom.

We believe that the Author of Supernal Majesty, by whose rule all things are governed, is pleased if the rules of justice are observed among our people, and that He, Pious Father and Lord, who has always preserved human frailty by His aid, will deign to grant the needs of those whom He knows keep His commandments. Therefore, while we deliberate for the stability of our kingdom and the salvation of our people, we know that every crime which is punished by canons and laws for fear of God is perpetrated within our kingdoms by the instigation of the adversary of good, and, without doubt because of this, by the wrath of heaven men and beasts are known to perish by different calamities or die of disease or the sword when divine judgments are not dreaded. So it is that many perish by committing forbidden things through ignorance and not only lose the present life sooner [than they might do] but sustain the tortures of Hell.

Therefore to you, most holy bishops, to whom the paternal clemency of God has given your office, our speech is first addressed, in the hope that you will study to correct the people Divine Providence gave you by frequent preaching and rule them with pastoral care, so that, when all men, loving justice, try to live honestly, celestial kindness may concede tranquillity and the salvation of all men. And, although the cause of preaching is particularly yours without any admonition from us, still we believe you share in the sins of others if you do not assiduously correct the faults of your sons but pass them over in silence. For neither can we, to whom the authority of the Supreme King has given the power to reign, evade His Wrath, if we do not care for the people subject to us.

Therefore we have decreed in this general statute that on all Lord's Days, on which we honor the mystery of the Holy Resurrection, and on other feasts when the whole people is customarily assembled in church, no bodily work should be done, apart from what is necessary to prepare food, and no lawsuits should be heard.

But you, apostolic bishops, joining with you your fellow priests, the elder sons of the Church and the local judges, and whoever you know whose honesty of life commends them, correct the people with constant preaching so that mystical exhortation may move the good and pastoral correction may lead those who stray to the right road, so that all may together strive to live laudably and preserve unity and justice, and that the Holy Church may receive Christians free from all filth of sin. Whoever, priest or layman, being often admonished, shall fail to amend, shall—depending on the degree of his fault and his personal rank—be either corrected by canonical severity or by legal penalty, for the innocent cannot be free and secure until a certain punishment for crimes attains the criminal, nor is it less pious to crush the wanton than to raise up the oppressed. It is fitting, therefore, that justice and equity should be enforced in all things, and that the legal punishment of judges should fall on those the canonical preaching of bishops has not corrected. When past crimes are cut off no one will dare to commit future offences and thus curbs may keep all who stray to the path of discipline and in all our land the rules of peace and concord may advance.

All judges shall strive to give just judgments, pleasing to God, for there is no doubt that our sentence will condemn more sharply those who have not judged according to equity. Judges shall not presume to commission or send out deputies over the region committed to them who may exercise venal justice or plunder those under them.

When clerics transgress, as greater reverence is due them for the love of God, so they should be more sharply restrained. If holy pastors or judges (which God forbid!) try to hide the crimes of their subjects rather than restrain them they may know that they are themselves the more guilty.

Those things which we have decreed in this edict we wish to be perpetually observed, for in the holy synod of Mâcon, as you know, we sought to define what we now publish by the present declaration.

2

LEGISLATION

A. The Church's Legislation

THE COUNCIL OF ORLÉANS WAS HELD AFTER CLOVIS' VICTORY OVER THE VISI-goths in 507. Although much of Gaul was still outside Clovis' rule, Orléans could be called the first Gallic "national" Church Council. Clovis was respon-sible for the Council's meeting. Canons 4–7 and probably also 1–3 and 8–10 are an answer to the royal questionnaire. It was to the Church's as well as the King's interest to have questions concerning the right of asylum and the clergy's recruitment settled—though they arose again before long (pp. 106–107). The Council regulated the problem of the Arian clergy and churches of the South (10), but hardly dealt with paganism. It made some liturgical decisions (24, 26–27), insisted on the authority of diocesan bishops (7, 14, 15, 17, 23) while trying to make them use their position properly (5, 6, 16), regulated the clergy's life (9, 13, 29) and that of monks (19–22). It was less concerned with penitents (11–12) and the laity (18).

Church Councils helped to maintain church discipline; their comparative rarity in seventh-century Gaul is one of the signs of the decline of the Gallic Church. The only diocesan synod preserved from Merovingian Gaul is that of Auxerre. The inevitable gap between conciliar prescriptions and real life is

smaller here than in a national Council. The canons cover superstitions (Auxerre was a large rural diocese), the Liturgy, diocesan organization, the clergy,
monks, laity, ritual sins (8, 36, 37, 42), suicide, adultery, incest, and idolatry.
(I have translated all but the purely liturgical canons.)

A NATIONAL CHURCH COUNCIL: ORLÉANS, 511

C. de Clercq, ed., *CCSL*, 148A (Turnhout, 1963), pp. 4–12.

Letter [from the bishops] to King [Clovis].
To their Lord, the son of the Catholic Church, the Most Glorious King
Clovis, all the bishops whom you have ordered to be present at the Council.
Since so great a care for our glorious Faith excited you to the service of
the Catholic Religion, that in the zeal of a priestly soul you have commanded the bishops to meet together to treat in common of necessary affairs, we, in conformity with this will and [following the] headings you have
given us, have replied by the decisions which seemed to us just. If what we
have decided is approved by your judgment, the consent of so great a King
and Lord will increase the authority of the resolutions taken by so many
prelates.
When, by God's doing, by the summoning of the Most Glorious King
Clovis, the Council of high priests was gathered together in the city of Orléans, by discussion in common it was agreed that what they decided by
word should be also strengthened by the testimony of writing.
1. Of murderers, adulterers, and thieves, if they fly to a church, we have
decided that what the ecclesiastical canons have decreed and the Roman
Law has laid down should be observed; it should not be permitted to drag
them from the church or the church-house or the bishop's house; they should
not be handed over except with oaths sworn on the Gospels that they may
be safe from death, from mutilation, and from all nature of punishment,
provided that the guilty party agree with him against whom they have acted
on the satisfaction due. If a man is shown to have violated his oath [and
harms the man who had sought asylum], as guilty of perjury he shall be separated not only from the communion of the Church and of all clerics but also
from the life of Catholics. If the guilty man shall refuse to make composition
with the man he has wronged and shall, through fear, leave the church, he
shall not be sought for by the Church or by clerics.
2. We have decreed that the following is to be done with regard to abduc-
tors. If an abductor flees to a church with the girl he has abducted and it

appears that the woman has suffered violence, she shall at once be freed from the power of her ravisher, and he, granted impunity from death or serious bodily harm, shall either be subjected to servitude or have freedom to redeem himself. But if she who was abducted has a father and the girl has given her consent to the ravisher, either before or after the abduction, she shall be returned pardoned to the power of her father, and the ravisher shall be obliged to satisfy the father under the aforesaid conditions.

3. The slave who has fled to the church for whatever fault, if he has received oaths from his lord on his confession of fault, shall at once be forced to return to the service of the lord, but if, after these oaths have been sworn by the lord and [the slave] has been handed over, he shall be proved to have suffered some punishment for the fault for which he was pardoned, [the lord], as was stated above [canon 1], for his contempt of the Church and denial of his [sworn] faith, shall be held a stranger to the communion and converse of Catholics. But if indeed the slave, defended by the Church, shall, by the insistence of clerics, have received the oaths of his lord for impunity for his fault, and shall refuse to leave [the church], he may be seized by his lord.

4. We have decreed, with regard to the ordination of clerics, that no layman shall presume to the clerical office, unless either by command of the King, or with the consent of the [local] judge, [but] the sons of clerics, that is, the sons, grandsons, and great-grandsons, who are bound to follow the order of their parents, shall be in the power and control of bishops.

5. Of the offerings or lands which our Lord the King has deigned to confer as a gift to the churches, or . . . may confer by God's inspiration, with the immunity [from taxation] of these lands or of clerics, we have decided it is most just that whatever God shall deign to give as their produce shall be expended in reparation of churches, in alms given to priests and the poor, or in the redemption of captives, and that clerics should be forced to assist the work of the Church. If any bishop shall stand out as less solicitous and devoted to this work he shall be publicly reprimanded by the other bishops of the province. But if he shall not improve even under such a rebuke he shall be held unworthy of the communion of his brethren until he amend his error.

6. If someone believes he has some claim against a bishop, either on behalf of the church or on his own account, if he does not bring forward either insults or calumnies, he may not be removed from the Church's communion simply for bringing the charge.

7. No abbots, presbyters or any clergy or those living in the profession of religion may come to the King without the knowledge and commendation of their bishop to ask for favors. If any one dare to do so, he shall be deprived

of the honor of his rank and of communion, until his bishop receive his reparation through full penance.

8. If a slave is ordained either deacon or presbyter in the absence or ignorance of his lord, and the bishop knowing that he is a slave, he shall remain in the clerical office, [but] the bishop shall give his lord double compensation. But if the bishop did not know he was a slave, those who bore testimony, or asked for him to be ordained, shall be bound to [pay] the same recompense.

9. If a presbyter or a deacon shall commit a capital crime he shall at the same time be expelled from office and from communion.

10. We have decreed that this is to be observed regarding heretical clerics, who come to the Catholic Faith in full faith, and the basilicas which the Goths have hitherto held in their perversity. If the clerics are truly converted and entirely accept the Catholic Faith and display a worthy life, they shall receive the office of which the bishop judges them worthy, with the laying on of hands. [Their] churches shall be consecrated by the rite which we use for ours.

11. Those who, having once received penance, forgetful of their religious profession, relapse into lay life, shall be suspended from communion and separated from the converse of all Catholics. If, after this interdict, anyone presume to eat with them he also shall be deprived of communion.

12. If a deacon or presbyter, for any offence, shall depart from the altar under the profession of penitence, and if other [ministers] are lacking and the necessity arises, one asking for Baptism may be baptized [by them].

13. If any widow of a presbyter or deacon join herself in a second marriage to any man, they shall either be punished and separated, or, if they persist in their criminal intent, they shall both be punished by excommunication.

14. Going through the ancient canons we thought earlier statutes should be renewed, so that of the offerings of the faithful on the altar [of city churches] the bishop shall claim half for himself and the second rank of clergy shall receive half, all estates remaining in the power of the bishop.

15. . . . Of the things which any of the faithful offers to parishes, in lands, vines, slaves, and property, all shall be in the power of the bishop; however, of those things offered on the altar [of a country church] a third shall faithfully be handed over to the bishop.

16. The bishop shall distribute, as far as his means allow, clothes and food to the poor or sick, who, because of their weakness, cannot work with their hands.

17. . . . All basilicas, wherever built or built today, shall be in the power of the bishop in whose territory they are situated.

18. No surviving brother shall marry his brother's widow; none shall dare

to wed his dead wife's sister. If they do this they shall be punished by ecclesiastical penalties.

19. Abbots, because of the humility of religion, shall be under the control of bishops, and if they do something outside their Rule, they shall be corrected by bishops. Every year they shall gather at the bishop's summons in the place he chooses. But monks shall be subject to their abbots in all obedience. If one of them is contumacious or wanders around or presumes to have something of his own, all he may have acquired shall be taken from him by his abbots, according to the Rule, for the profit of his monastery. But those who wander around where they are found, shall be brought, as fugitives, with the bishop's aid, under guard, and the abbot who in future does not discipline such persons with correct punishment, or who receives an alien monk, shall know he is guilty.

20. No monk may use a stole in the monastery or may possess rings with gems.

21. If it is proved that a monk has lived in a monastery or received the habit and later marries a wife, one guilty of such a deception shall never ascend to ecclesiastical office.

22. No monk who has abandoned the monastic congregation, impelled by ambition and vanity, shall presume to build a cell of his own will, without permission of his bishop and abbot.

23. If a bishop, out of human kindness, grants small vineyards or plots of land to clerics or monks to cultivate, or to hold for a time, even if a long space of years shall elapse, the church shall suffer no prejudice, nor shall the prescription of secular law be opposed to the church, to prevent it [recovering the land].

24. It is decreed . . . that not fifty but forty days' [fast] be observed before the Feast of Easter.

25. No town dweller may celebrate the Feasts of Easter, the Lord's Nativity, or Pentecost in his villa [country house] unless he is proved to be kept there by illness.

26. When men are gathered to celebrate Mass in God's Name, the people is not to leave until the Solemnity of Mass is completed and, where a bishop is present, his blessing has been given.

27. Rogations, that is litanies, are to be celebrated by all churches before the Ascension of the Lord, so that the preceding three days' fast shall end in the Lord's Ascension. In these three days slaves and handmaids shall be excused all work, so that the whole people may more easily come together. In these three days let everyone abstain and live on Lenten food.

28. The clerics who neglect to be present at this holy work shall receive discipline according to the will of their bishop.

29. Let bishops, presbyters, and deacons keep the rules of past canons on the [prohibition of] intimacy with women.

30. If any cleric, monk, or layman shall think he should observe divination or auguries or casting the lots, which they lyingly say are "of the Saints," to whomever they should believe they should make them known, they are to be expelled from the Church's communion with those who believed in them.

31. A bishop, unless impeded by infirmity, may not fail to be present on the Lord's Day at the nearest church.

[Subscriptions of thirty-two bishops.]

A DIOCESAN COUNCIL: AUXERRE, 561–605

C. de Clercq, pp. 265–70.

1. It is not permitted to dress up as a calf or as a stag on the Kalends [1st] of January or to present diabolical gifts; on that day all favors shall be granted as on other days.

3. It is forbidden to make offerings or keep vigils of the Saints' festivals in private houses, or to discharge vows among woods or at sacred trees or at springs, but, whoever has a vow, let him keep vigil in the church and fulfill his vow [by giving] to the servants of the church or to the poor. Nor let anyone dare to make feet or images of men out of wood.

4. It is forbidden to turn to soothsayers or to augurs, or to those who pretend to know the future, or to look at what they call "the lots of the Saints," or those they make of wood or bread. But, whatever a man wishes to do, let him do it in the Name of God.

5. Forbid especially, in every way, these observances on the vigils which are kept in honor of St. Martin.

7. At the middle of May all presbyters shall come to the synod in the city, and on the [1st] of November all the abbots shall meet at the council.

8. It is forbidden to offer "mellita," which is called "mulsa" [a mixture of wine and honey] at the altar in the Divine Sacrifice, or any potion other than wine mixed with water. Great sin and crime belong to the presbyter who dares to offer any drink other than wine in the consecration of the Blood of Christ.

9. It is forbidden for choirs of laymen or girls to sing songs or prepare banquets in the church, for it is written: "My house shall be called a house of prayer" (Isaiah 56:7).

12. It is forbidden to give the Eucharist or the kiss [of peace] to the dead, or to wrap their bodies in veils or palls [ecclesiastical vestments].

15. One dead body may not be placed on top of another.

16. On the Lord's Day it is forbidden to harness oxen or to do other work.

17. Whoever, of his own will, either throws himself into water or hangs himself or throws himself from a tree, or pierces himself with iron, or in any way chooses to kill himself, Sacrifice shall not be offered for him.

20. If (which is sinful to say) a presbyter, deacon, or subdeacon shall after ordination procreate children or commit adultery, and the archpriest shall not bring this to the notice of the bishop or archdeacon, he shall be excommunicated for a full year.

21. A presbyter, after ordination, may not sleep in one bed with his wife, nor commit carnal sin with her. [The same is decreed] for deacons and subdeacons.

23. If a monk shall commit adultery in a monastery or dare to have private possessions or commit a theft, and his abbot shall not correct this himself, or shall not inform the bishop or archdeacon, he shall be enclosed in another monastery to do penance.

24. No abbot or monk may be present at a wedding.

25. No abbot or monk may act as godfather.

26. If an abbot permits a woman to enter his monastery or commands that she assist at some festivals there, he shall be enclosed for three months in another monastery and be content with bread and water.

27. No man may marry his stepmother.

28. No man may marry his stepdaughter.

29. No man may marry his brother's widow.

30. No man may marry his dead wife's sister.

31. No man may marry the daughter of his brother or sister, nor may the children of two brothers or sisters marry.

32. A nephew may not marry his uncle's wife.

33. No presbyter or deacon may be present at the place where criminals are tortured.

34. No presbyter may sit in judgment [in a case] where a man may be condemned to death.

35. No presbyter or deacon or any cleric may hand over his fellow cleric to a secular judge for any cause.

36. A woman may not receive the Eucharist with her bare hand.

37. A woman may not place her hand on an [ecclesiastical] pall.

38. One may not communicate with the excommunicate nor take food with him.

39. If a presbyter or any member of the clergy or people knowingly receives one who has been excommunicated, without the consent of he who excommunicated him, or takes food or holds converse with him, he shall be subject to the same sentence.

40. A presbyter may not sing or dance at a banquet.

41. No presbyter or deacon may cite anyone before a secular judge, but, if he has a cause, he shall ask his brother or some layman [to act] in his stead.

42. Each woman, when she communicates, shall have her veil [to put over her hand]. If she does not have it she shall not communicate until another Lord's Day [see canon 36].

43. Whatever judge or layman shall dare to injure any presbyter or deacon or any of the clergy, including the younger members, without recourse to the court of the bishop, or archdeacon, or archpresbyter, shall be held a stranger from all Christians for a year.

44. If any layman shall contumaciously delay to hear the admonition of his archpresbyter, he shall be held a stranger from the thresholds of the Holy Church until he fulfill this saving command. Furthermore, he shall sustain the many penalties which the Most Glorious Lord King commanded in his precept.

[Subscribed by the bishop, thirty-four presbyters, three deacons, seven abbots.]

B. Legislation of the Barbarian Monarchies

The Church's legislation needed ratification by royal authority. The same problems existed in Spain, France, and Italy; tension existed everywhere between king and church. "The world," Pope Gregory the Great declared in 591, "is full of priests," but, he went on, "priests are intent on secular affairs." The Frankish King Chilperic, Gregory's contemporary, spoke of his office "passing" to the bishops of his kingdom. Although bishops never held royal or municipal office in Merovingian times, their unofficial position made them all the more powerful since royal authority—as rapacious and less impressive than that of Rome—was hated and despised. Bishops had taxes removed, secured loans from the king, and themselves financed public works. Their courts were more popular than royal courts. They protected freedmen, the poor, widows, and orphans. All this apart from their special claim to direct men's consciences and regulate much of their daily lives.

The Church's claims clashed with the monarchies'. All kings thought themselves God's Vicars. Merovingian legislation shows that Clovis' successors, whatever their private lives, felt themselves no less responsible for their subjects than Visigothic or Lombard rulers. Guntramn, in 585, saw it as much his duty to make his bishops preach as to make his judges do justice. King Ratchis prologue to his laws sees law as gradually progressing under Christian influence. (See the prologue to the Salic Law, p. 93 and also p. 96.)

Actual legislation reveals the limitations of the Church's influence. In Spain the Jewish minority preoccupied Church and State throughout the seventh century but all attempts to bring about their genuine conversion failed. However, Visigothic legislation as to the nominal Christians—Jews forcibly baptized—formed a very important precedent for the Spanish Inquisition's action against the "*conversos*" in the fifteenth and sixteenth centuries. Jews, although not persecuted elsewhere as in Spain, were sharply discriminated against (see Lothar II's Edict, 10). Persecution of paganism, particularly of magical practices, in whose efficacy everyone believed, continued.

The Church's privileges were more extensive than in Roman times: monastic vows were enforced; penalties were prescribed for offenders against Sunday rest; the Church's influence is clear in laws on marriage, where the degrees of relationship within which marriage was prohibited were considerably extended. The Visigothic law against sodomy was based on the XVI Council of Toledo, chap. 3. Liutprand's determination to reform the Lombard Laws under papal guidance is striking. He went beyond Roman Law in forcing those guilty of magic to carry out the Church's penalties as well as his own.

The most convinced Christian king was limited in what he could do; see Liutprand's edict on the duel. *Conflict* between Church and king could arise over many issues, including the right of asylum in church, the status of slaves and freedmen, lay courts' right to try clerics, and the question of church appointments.

The Roman State had granted the right of asylum. Visigothic Law, even under the Arians, endorsed this, as did Lothar I (d. 561) in France and Anglo-Saxon and Frisian Laws. Imbert holds that "in the law of asylum Christian influence marked most strongly the *public* law of the West." In an age of comparative anarchy asylum "was perhaps the best obstacle to unlimited exercise of private vengeance."

The Council of Orléans not only gave slaves asylum in church but defended their ordination as clerics. (Roman Law declared a master could recover a slave, even when ordained.) In 549 freeing slaves in church was described as a "national custom" in France. It is not clear whether the monarchy accepted the Church's position.

Roman Law gave the clergy the right to be tried in their own courts. This right was not conceded by the barbarian kingdoms without a struggle (see Lothar II's Edict, 4). Most strikingly, bishops, both in France and Spain, were asked to revise lay judges' decisions.

In 614 Lothar II, the first king to rule all France since 561, issued an Edict immediately after a Church Council at Paris. Comparison between the Edict and the Acts of the Council shows the tension that still existed between Church and king.

Continual reiteration of the same prohibitions does not mean that they had no effect, even if "the prohibition is really a record." Christian influence is clear, even if imperfectly accepted, in the concepts of law and of monarchy, of the human person, marriage, and the family.

LOMBARD ITALY: A LINE OF CHRISTIAN LEGISLATORS

Prologue of King Ratchis to his laws (after 746), ed. F. Beyerle, *Leges*, pp. 185–86.

It behoves Us to fulfill carefully the precepts of Christ Jesus Our Savior, by whose Providence We have arrived at the summit of power. With the aid of His Mercy We have foreseen those things to be decreed which are suitable to the race committed to Us, that is the Lombards, Catholic and beloved by God. For the Most Glorious and High King Rothari, the ruler of this race of Lombards, instituted laws by divine inspiration and cut off all dissensions of evil men by royal zeal. He indeed decreed that his successors should mould to gentleness and piety what God should teach them was hard and rough [in his laws]. Then his successor, the Most Excellent King Grimoald, while he carefully and vigilantly considered the needs of all men, added those things which pleased him, to exalt the cause of salvation and to diminish evil. After him the Most Glorious and Orthodox Upholder of the Faith and ruler of this race, and Our bringer-up by the Mercy of Almighty God, the High and Excellent and Most Wise Prince Liutprand, persevering in the works of God and in daily vigils, adorned with all chastity and sobriety, drew out all things in decent order by God's inspiration and confirmed it in his edict with his Lombards and Judges.

And so, by the Providence of Our Redeemer, I, by divine aid, Ratchis, the Most Excellent and Distinguished Prince, in the second year of my reign, on the Kalends of March, in the fourteenth indiction, with the Judges of Our, the Lombard, race have carefully considered what were decreed by Our predecessors and found some things to be just and some needing to be purified.

Judaizing Christians in Spain

Lex Visigothorum, XII, 2, 16 (642–52), trans. Scott, *Visigothic Code*, pp. 376–77 (revised).

As the crime of pretended belief in Christ should be deplored by all Christians, for the same reason it should be evident that no person, under any circumstances, is deserving of pardon, who is proved to have renounced a good religion for a bad one. Therefore, because a cruel and astounding act of presumption should be extirpated by a still more cruel punishment, We declare, by the following edict: that, whenever it has been proved or shall be proved that a Christian, of either sex, and especially one born of Christian parents, has practiced circumcision, or any other Jewish rite (may God avert this!), he shall be put to an ignominious death by the zeal and co-operation of Catholics, under the most ingenious and excruciating tortures that can be inflicted, [that he may learn] how horrible and detestable that offence is, which he has so infamously perpetrated. All the property of such a person shall be confiscated for the benefit of the royal treasury, if this error has contaminated his heirs and relations who have consented to it.

Against Paganism

France: Precept of King Childebert I (*c.* 533–58), ed. Boretius, pp. 2–3. (The only existing copy of this document is mutilated and incomplete.)

We believe that, God favoring Us, it belongs to Our Grace and the salvation of the people, if the Christian people, having given up the worship of idols, shall serve God, to Whom we promised complete loyalty, purely, as He shall teach us. And since it is necessary that the people, which does not keep the precepts of bishops as it should, should be corrected also by Our rule, We have decreed that this letter should be sent out everywhere. We order that any men who, once admonished, shall not at once cast out images and idols, dedicated to the devil, made by men, from their fields, or shall prevent bishops from destroying them, shall not be free, once they have given sureties, until they appear in Our Presence.

It is for Us to see how the offence against God shall be vindicated against the sacrilegious, in accordance with our faith, as the bishop pronounces from the altar what is declared in the Gospel, the prophets, or the (letter of the) Apostle, to the limit of Our understanding. Complaint is made to Us that many sacrileges are performed among the people. From this God is in-

jured and the people through sin go down to death, passing nights in drunkenness and scurrilous songs, even on the holy days of Easter, of the Lord's
Nativity, and the other [Church] feasts, or dancing on the Lord's Day through
towns. We absolutely forbid all these things from which God is known to be
injured. Whoever, after the admonition of the bishops and Our Precept,
shall dare to perpetrate these sacrileges, if he is of servile rank, We order he
shall receive a hundred blows, if he is free or of honorable status [the rest
is lost].

AGAINST MAGICAL PRACTICES

1. Spain: *Lex Visigothorum*, VI, 2, 4 (642–52), trans. Scott, *The Visigothic Code*, p. 204 (revised).

Magicians and invokers of tempests, who, by their incantations, bring
hail-storms upon vineyards and fields of grain; or those who disturb the
minds of men by the invocation of demons, or celebrate nocturnal sacrifices
to devils, summoning them to their presence by infamous rites; all such persons detected, or found guilty of such offences by any judge, agent, or super-
intendent of the locality where these acts were committed, shall be publicly
scourged with two hundred lashes; shall be scalped; and shall be dragged by
force through ten villages of the neighborhood, as a warning to others. And
the judge, lest, hereafter, the aforesaid persons may again indulge in such
practices, shall place them in confinement, and see that they are provided
with clothing and food, to deprive them of an opportunity of inflicting further injury; or he may send them to the king, to be disposed of at his royal
pleasure. Those who are convicted of having consulted such persons, shall
each receive two hundred lashes in the assembly of the people, in order that
all who are guilty of such a crime may not go unpunished.

2. Lombard Italy: Liutprand 84. I (727), ed. Beyerle, *Leges*, pp. 139–40.

If some one, forgetful of the fear of God, shall go to a soothsayer, male or
female, for divination, or to receive any answers from them, he shall pay
half his price in the Sacred Palace, according as he is valued . . . and he
shall also do penance according to the [Church] canons. In the same way he
who worships at a tree which the rustics call holy and at springs, or performs
sacrilege or incantation, shall similarly pay half his price. . . . And if someone, knowing of a male or female soothsayer, shall not denounce them or
shall conceal those who go to them, he shall suffer the same penalty. Who-

ever sends his servant or handmaid to see these soothsayers to get some answer from them, if it is proved, they shall pay the above penalty. But if the
servant or maid goes to the soothsayer without the consent of his lord, for
the same reason, then his lord must sell him outside the province. And if
the lord fails to do this, he shall suffer the foresaid penalty.

France: Rights Granted to the Church

Precept of King Lothar I (558–61), ed. Boretius, p. 19 (translated in part).

6. If a judge unjustly condemns anyone against the law, in Our absence he
shall be punished by the bishops, so that what he wrongly decided he shall,
after reconsideration and discussion, amend.

7. No one, by Our Authority, shall dare to marry a widow or virgin without their consent, nor shall they be unjustly and surreptitiously carried off.

8. No one shall dare to marry a nun.

10. The offerings of the dead to churches shall not be carried off by
anyone.

11. Out of Our zeal for the Faith, We concede that no agent or tax collec-
tor shall enter the possessions of the Church, its fields or pastures, or take a
tenth on its herds of swine. Public officials shall not require any assistance
from the Church or from clerics who have received immunity from Our father or grandfather.

12. Whatever has been given to the Church or to clerics or to any persons
by the munificence of the aforesaid princes of glorious memory shall remain
theirs.

13. Whatever a church, clerics, or Our provincials [that is, non-Franks]
shall be shown to have owned, unchallenged, for thirty years, shall (given a
just beginning to their ownership) remain theirs, nor shall any suit be re-
vived after so many years. . . .

Spain: Bishops Are to Revise Sentences by Unjust Judges

Lex Visigothorum, II, 1, 30 (680–87), trans. Scott, The Visigothic Code, p. 35
(revised).

We direct the bishops of God, to whom the Divine Authority has been
committed to remedy the misfortunes of oppression and poverty, that they

admonish, with paternal piety, such judges as oppress the people with unjust decrees, by which means such wrongs may be remedied. But if those invested with judicial functions, have either decided unjustly, or have imposed a wrongful sentence upon any one, then the bishop, in whose diocese this has been done, shall summon the judge who is alleged to have acted unjustly, and shall render a just decision, sitting along with him, in the presence of ecclesiastics, or other persons of respectability. But if the judge, moved by perversity, refuses to correct the iniquitous judgment given by him, after the bishop has exhorted him to do so, then the bishop shall have the privilege of rendering judgment alone; and the wrongful decision of the judge, subsequently set aside by him [the bishop], as well as his own decision, shall be committed to writing, and be deposited among the records of the court. The bishop shall inform Us of his judgment on the case of the oppressed party, so that the cause which appears to be right may be confirmed by Us. If the judge should prevent the party whom he has oppressed from appearing before the bishop, he shall forfeit two pounds of gold to Our Glory.

ASYLUM IN CHURCHES

Visigothic Spain: *Lex Visigothorum*, IX, 3, 1–3 (probably all 5th or 6th century), trans. Scott, *The Visigothic Code*, pp. 331–32 (revised).

1. No one shall dare to remove, by force, any person who has sought sanctuary in a church unless said person should attempt to defend himself with arms.

2. Where anyone takes refuge at the door of a church, and does not lay down his arms, and is killed; the person who struck him shall be liable to no penalty or reproach therefor.

3. Where anyone violently removes his slave or a debtor from the altars where he sought sanctuary, without the consent of a priest, or of the custodians of the church; as soon as the fact has been brought to the notice of the judge, if he is a person of high rank, the offender shall be compelled to pay a hundred "solidi" to the altar which sustained the injury. A person of inferior station shall pay thirty "solidi," and if he should not have the means to do so, he shall be arrested by the judge, and receive a hundred lashes in public. The master shall then regain possession of his slave, and the debtor shall be surrendered to his creditor but pardoned [for their fault].

CHRISTIAN MARRIAGE

1. France: Decree of Childebert II (594), ed. Boretius, p. 15.

We decree that no one may enter on an incestuous marriage, that is, with his brother's wife or his wife's sister or his uncle's wife or that of a close blood relation. If he takes his father's wife he shall incur danger of death. As for the foresaid marriages, which appear to be incestuous, We order that they be amended by the preaching of the bishops. He, indeed, who refuses to hear his bishop and is excommunicated, shall sustain eternal condemnation before God and shall be wholly banished from Our Palace, and shall lose all his possessions to his legitimate relations, since he refused to receive the remedies of his priest.

2. Lombard Italy: Liutprand 33. IV (723), ed. Beyerle, *Leges*, p. 118.

We decree, by God's command, that henceforth no man dare to marry the widow of his first cousin or of the latter's son. If he does this illicit act he shall lose his possessions. And those born of such a marriage shall be replaced as legitimate heirs by close relations. If there are no close relations the royal fisc shall inherit. We have added this [law] because the Bishop of the Roman City, who is head of the churches and priests of God throughout the world, exhorted Us by a letter not in any way to permit such a marriage.

AGAINST SODOMY

Lex Visigothorum, III, 5, 7 (693–701), trans. Scott, *The Visigothic Code*, p. 111 (revised).

The doctrine of Orthodox Faith requires Us to place Our censure upon vicious practices, and to restrain those who are addicted to carnal offences. For We counsel well for the benefit of Our race and Our Country, when We take measures to utterly extirpate the crimes of wicked men, and put an end to the evil deeds of vice. For this reason we shall attempt to abolish the horrible crime by which men do not fear to defile men by filthy debauchery, which is as contrary to Divine Precept as it is to chastity. And although the authority of the Holy Scriptures, and the censure of earthly laws, alike, prohibit offences of this kind, it is nevertheless necessary to condemn them by a new decree; lest if timely correction be deferred, still greater vices may arise. Therefore, We establish by this law, that if any man whosoever, of any age, or race, whether he belongs to the clergy, or to the laity, should be convicted, by competent evidence, of the commission of the crime of sodomy, he shall, by order of the king, or of any judge, not only suffer emasculation, but also the penalty prescribed by ecclesiastical decree for such offences, and promulgated in the third year of Our reign.

DIFFICULTY OF ERADICATING UN-CHRISTIAN CUSTOMS: THE JUDICIAL DUEL

Italy: Liutprand 118. II (731), ed. Beyerle, *Leges*, pp. 155–56.

We recall that We decreed with Our judges that he who killed a free man should lose all his substance. Now, truly, when they accuse a man, whom they were perhaps treating with some severity, of killing his kinsman (who died in bed), by poison, and when he wished to seek the truth by combat, as was the ancient custom, it seemed a serious matter to Us that a man should lose all his substance by a duel. And so We provide that henceforth, if such a case is brought forward, he who wishes to vindicate the death of his relation by combat against him who killed him by poison, must observe those things which We decreed in an earlier edict. He must swear on the Gospels that he does not raise the matter deceitfully but because he has a definite suspicion. Then he may seek the truth by combat, as the ancient custom was. And if he [who is accused] is slain he shall not lose all his possessions to his accuser, or to *his* champion, who fought against him, but shall make a composition according to his rank, as the law decreed before. For We are uncertain of the Judgment of God and We have heard that many have unjustly lost their cause by a duel. But because of the custom of Our Lombard race We cannot prohibit this law.

THE FRANKISH MONARCHY AND THE CHURCH

Edict of Lothar II (October 18, 614), ed. Boretius, pp. 20–23 (compared with the canons of the Council of Paris of 614, subscribed by seventy-four bishops from France, held a week before, ed. C. de Clercq, *CCSL*, 148A [Turnhout, 1963], pp. 275–80).

The Acts or Constitutions of the Illustrious Prince, King Lothar, for the whole people in the gathering of bishops assembled at the Synod of Paris. . . .

There is no doubt that the happiness of Our kingdom should increase, by Divine aid, most of all if We study to preserve inviolate in Our time what has been well done, decreed, and constituted. What has been done against reason or may happen from now on (may God avert this!) We have sought, with Christ as Ruler, to amend by Our Edict.

1. Therefore We have decreed that the canons [of the Church] shall be observed in all things, and that what has been passed over shall be always observed from now onward, so that, at the death of a bishop, a man shall be elected in his place who should be ordained by the Metropolitan, with the bishops of the province. If he is worthy he shall be ordained by the choice of the Prince. Certainly, if he is chosen from the [royal] palace he shall be ordained for the merit of his person and doctrine.

[Compare the Council of Paris, canon 2:

When a bishop dies a man propitious to Christ should be ordained in his place, whom the Metropolitan, by whom he is to be ordained, shall elect with the bishops of the province, the clergy and people of the city, without any transfer of money. But if, either by the intervention of a [civil] power, or by some negligence, someone is introduced into a church without the election of the Metropolitan and the consent of clergy and people, his ordination shall be held as null, according to the statutes of the Fathers.]

2. No bishop is to elect his successor but one may be substituted for him when he is so affected that he can neither rule his church nor his clergy. Also no one, while a bishop is alive, shall presume to take his place. If he ask for it it shall least of all be given to him.

[Based on Council of Paris, canon 3.]

3. If a cleric, drawn by some honor, despising or passing over his bishop, goes to the King or to some powerful persons or chooses a patron, he shall not be received [by the Church], unless he seems to ask for pardon. If, for some reason, he goes to the King and returns to his bishop with the King's Letter, he shall be forgiven. He who presumes to keep him after an admonition from his bishop shall be deprived of holy communion.

[This is identical with canon 5 of the Council, with the important exception of the second sentence in the Edict, which is not in the canon.]

4. No judge shall dare to detain or condemn a cleric of any rank for a civil case (he may for a criminal), unless he is manifestly convicted. [This does not apply] to presbyters and deacons [who are apparently not to be detained even then]. Clerics convicted of a capital crime shall be detained according to the canons and tried by the bishops [sitting with the civil judges?].

[Compare canon 6 of the Council:

No judge shall dare to detain or condemn either presbyter or deacon or cleric or the junior [members of] the Church [those in minor orders] without the knowledge of the bishop. If he does this he shall be separated from the Church which he sought to injure until he recognizes and amends his fault.]

5. If there is a suit between a public official and the men of the Church, the provosts of the Church and the public judge shall judge them in a public audience.

6. If any person die intestate his relations shall succeed to his possessions, according to the laws, without contradiction from the judges.

[Compare canons 8–10 and 12, which protect legacies to the Church.]

7. The freedman of any free men shall be defended by bishops, according to the text of his charter of freedom, and shall not be judged or called back to the royal fisc unless the bishop or provost of the Church is present.

[Compare canon 7 of the Council of Paris:

The freedmen of all free men shall be defended by bishops and not called back to the royal fisc. If anyone wishes to enslave them or to call them back to the fisc and neglects, when admonished by the bishop, to come to his audience, or delays to amend what he has done, he shall be excommunicated.]

8. Wherever a new tax has impiously been imposed and the people protest against it the matter shall be mercifully amended by inquiry.

10. Jews ought not to hold public office over Christians. Whoever dares to associate himself with such an action [reading dubious in the original] shall incur a most severe sentence from the canons.

[This refers to canon 17 of the Council:

No Jew shall dare either to ask the Prince for any authority over Christians or to exercise it. If he attempts this he, with all his family, shall receive the grace of Baptism from the bishop of the city where he acted against the statutes of the canons.]

11. Peace and order shall, by Christ's aid, reign forever in Our kingdom and rebels and the insolence of evil men shall be most severely punished.

14. . . . The possessions of churches, priests, and the poor, who cannot defend themselves, shall be defended by public judges until the suit is heard. [This is] apart from the immunity [from public jurisdiction] granted by Our predecessors, which they gave to the Church or to powerful men, in order to insure peace and order.

15. If the men of the Church, or of powerful men, are accused of criminal offences, and their agents are required by public officials to appear in public and refuse to do so, they shall be detained [the document is illegible here].

18. As for the girls or religious widows or nuns who have vowed them-

selves to God, those living in their own houses as well as those in monasteries, no one, even by Our precept, shall remove them nor dare to marry them. If any use a precept it shall be of no effect. If anyone, either by force or by some order, dare to take them or marry them, he shall suffer a capital sentence. And if they marry in church and the ravished girl seems to agree to this they shall be separated and exiled and their property shall pass to their nearest heirs.

[This endorses canons 14–16 of the Council of Paris.]

20. The agents of bishops or of powerful men shall not force men to aid them nor dare to use violence against anyone.

21. The herders of the royal swine shall not presume to enter the woods of churches or of private men without the consent of the possessor.

22. Neither a free man nor a slave, who is not taken with something stolen, may be killed unheard by the judges or by anyone.

24. He who dares to infringe this deliberation, which We draw up with the bishops and great men [of the Court] and Our faithful in the Synod, shall be awarded a capital sentence so that others may not do the same. . . .

Lothar, King in Christ's Name, subscribed this decree.

3

CHRISTIANITY IN THE NORTH

A. *Ireland*

IF WE WANT TO UNDERSTAND THE CHRISTIANIZATION OF NON-ROMAN EUROPE
the best place to begin is Ireland. Since Ireland was never politically or cultur-
ally subject to Rome, Christianity was forced to evolve there in ways distinct
from those it had naturally assumed within the Roman Empire. What happened in Ireland in some respects provided a model for later developments in
the Low Countries, England, and Germany. In all these countries Latin culture
was introduced—or re-introduced after it had been abandoned—as an accom-
paniment to Christianity. This foreign Latin culture proved doubly attractive
because it was inseparable from the Christianity with which it arrived. Like
Christianity it had the appeal of novelty. For the Irish the Bible was not only
the sacred book of their new religion. It was also an endless series of new
puzzles, which could only be deciphered with the help of equally new Latin
grammatical and logical tools. At the same time Ireland—unlike Western
Europe—possessed a living culture of its own, expressed in a vernacular literature that had not been obliterated by a Roman overlay. With the coming of
Christianity—preeminently the religion of a book—the existing oral tradition
of learning in Irish developed a written form which paralleled Hiberno-Latin,

as that gradually came into being. The existence within the same country of two native literatures in different languages is an unusual phenomenon. It is found first in Ireland and only later (as Christianization advanced there) in Anglo-Saxon England and in Germany. There is no parallel development in Latin Europe until well past the year 1000. The existence of these two literatures is not only of philological interest. As even the two short texts translated here may indicate, Old Irish texts can shed a different light on contemporary society than anything available from Latin records.

Both the lack of a Roman political framework, within which Christian missionaries could establish themselves, and the strength of the earlier native tradition deeply affected the way Christianity evolved in Ireland. There were certainly Christian communities in south-east Ireland before the coming of St. Patrick. But, whether we date his mission as beginning in about 432 or some thirty years later, it is clear that when Patrick died the conversion of the country as a whole was far from complete. An ecclesiastical source, known as "The First Synod of Patrick," later than his time and probably dating, at the earliest, from the mid-sixth century, shows that at that time paganism was still a force in society. The traditions of troubled Christian-pagan relations concerning the pagan center of Tara lead one to suppose that the establishment of the main early Christian shrines in Ireland, such as Armagh or Kildare, near or on the sites of pagan sanctuaries, could only have been a gradual and difficult process.

The first phase of evangelization appears to have been carried out by a number of individual saints, only a few of whom are likely to have been bishops. The later tradition sees these early figures not connected with Patrick as holy men who lived a life which alternated periods as hermits with periods as wandering preachers. In some ways they resembled St. Martin of Tours (see p. 18 above) in the earlier part of his career. It is only well into the sixth century that one finds large communities of monks established in Ireland. This development was probably inspired by contacts with South Wales but also with South-Western France, Spain, and the Mediterranean world in general. In this period travel by sea was far easier than by land. Direct trade between the Mediterranean and a number of Celtic monastic and secular sites (in Cornwall, South Wales, and Ireland) is documented by archaeological finds. It is reasonable to think that the ships that brought oil and wine also transported books and ideas.[1]

By the seventh century the Irish Church had come to differ in a number of ways from the rest of Western Christendom. In a pastoral, non-urban society, the Church's main centers were not episcopal cities but rural monasteries. While bishops, in Ireland as elsewhere, continued to exercise their normal

1. E. G. Bowen, "The Geography of Early Monasticism in Ireland," *Studia Celtica*, 7 (1972), pp. 30–44.

Christianity in the North

liturgical role (see 4, below), they were overshadowed as administrators and, usually, as spiritual leaders, by powerful abbots, whose monasteries were linked in groups or *paruchiae*, some of them scattered over larger areas than the dioceses of Western Europe. One of the main *paruchiae* was that founded by St. Columb Cille (Columba), who died in 597. While its chief monastery was Iona in the Inner Hebrides, off the West coast of Scotland, the group as a whole included other houses in Scotland and Ireland, and, for a time, also in England. St. Columban (Columbanus), who died in 615, came from Bangor in northern Ireland but he set up houses in France and North Italy. In the late seventh century the bishopric of Armagh (in modern Ulster), linked by tradition to Patrick, and that of Kildare, in Leinster, with the shrine of Brigit, imitated the great monastic *paruchiae* and tried to set up confederations of churches for themselves. This overriding importance of monasteries was related to two central institutions in Ireland, kinship and the clan, and the existence of over-kings, who acted as overlords of a number of petty kings. The abbots of Iona, while celibate, were normally succeeded by other members of the family of the founder of the *paruchia*, Columb Cille. Columb Cille was born a member of a princely family in Ireland. The position of monastic overlord of a number of monasteries which he attained can be seen as parallel to that of an over-king in Ireland. His influence, which was inherited by his successors at Iona, in the selection of the Dál Riata kings who ruled the Irish settlers occupying South-West Scotland, had much to do with his family connections. In turn, his role in politics must have assisted the spread of his *paruchia*.

The seventh-century Irish Church can be seen as divided into two main parties—"Romans" and "Irish"—by a controversy which came to dominate all other issues of church polity in the period. The "Romans," with their main centers in southern Ireland, were in closer intellectual touch with the continent than the "Irish," further to the north. The earlier adherence of the "Romans" to the continental dating of Easter appears to have been motivated by their general desire to conform to the standards of the Western Church rather than follow older local traditions.[2] While, on the question of Easter, they gradually won over the rest of the Irish Church, in other respects native traditions prevailed.

It is possible that in the past overmuch stress has been laid on differences between Irish Christianity and that of the continent, and notably between the secular laws which governed the country and the ecclesiastical legislation which was standard outside Ireland. It has been argued recently that in Christian Ireland only one learned class existed and that the early written laws (in Irish), and perhaps also Old Irish poetry, were produced by the same type of

2. Pádraig Ó Neill, "*Romani* Influences on Seventh-Century Hiberno-Latin Literature," *Irland und Europa* (1984), pp. 280–90.

scholar who was responsible for the Latin ecclesiastical code of early eighth-century Ireland.[3] It remains true that Irish secular legislation continued to justify polygamy (admittedly by an ingenious reference to the patriarchs of the Old Testament). While Irish Christian society was far from permissive (there were, for instance, severe penalties for adultery), it was legally polygamous. In this it differed fundamentally from the rest of Christendom. The Irish Church was unable to change this. While in Ireland the Church triumphed over paganism it did so largely by its fusion with older traditions. As with the election of abbots for monasteries, so with intermarriage between first cousins (prohibited in ecclesiastical law) and with legacies to the Church, the interests of the kin were protected. Legacies to which the kin objected were invalid even in church law. It would be difficult to find a parallel to this major concession on the continent.[4]

If one turns to the literature produced in Irish—much of it probably in monasteries—one finds that the heroes of the pagan past continued to be revered in a way which would, again, be hard to parallel elsewhere in Western Christendom. The pagan gods had their attributes transferred to Christian saints. Saints such as Columb Cille, who were deeply involved in aristocratic feuds and battles, proved excellent substitutes for the old Celtic war-gods.[5] The pagan goddess Brigid became conflated with a fairly shadowy Christian saint. At Kildare the two cults merged.[6] The Old Irish poem *Hail Brigit*, probably written in the eighth century (included here in translation), illustrates a number of the distinctive features of Irish Christianity. While the poem celebrates Brigit's presiding at Kildare over her great double monastery (of monks and nuns) and notes that her fame "has outshone the fame of the king," the poet is mainly concerned to record a long list of the kings and warriors of the past. He seems more interested in lamenting the departed glories of the now "deserted" Alenn, the memory of its victory-feasts with their gold and silver trophies, the drinking of mead and wine and recitation of poems, "the ardor of its men," and "the beauty of its women," than he is in singing the triumph of Christianity. The reference to auguries (14) seems to show that they had not entirely vanished from the scene. Not the least of Brigit's merits, in the poet's eyes, is her descent from King Bresal Brec, who is seen as once ruling over Ireland (13, 26).

3. Donnchadh Ó Corráin, "The Old Testament and Early Irish Law," paper given to the III International Colloquium on Ireland and Europe in the Early Middle Ages (Dublin, 1984). For another view see D. A. Binchy, *The Linguistic and Historical Value of the Early Irish Law Tracts* (Dublin, n. d.), pp. 100f.

4. Ó Corráin, "Irish Law and Canon Law," *Irland und Europa*, pp. 157–66.

5. Alfred P. Smyth, *Warlords and Holy Men* (London, 1984), p. 96 (the whole chapter on Columb Cille is of interest).

6. Kim McCone, "Brigit in the Seventh Century: A Saint with Three Lives?", *Peritia*, 1 (1982), pp. 107–45. See also R. Sharpe, "St. Patrick and the See of Armagh," *Cambridge Medieval Celtic Studies*, 4 (1982), pp. 33–59.

We have the good fortune to possess a *Life* of Columb Cille written by Adomnán (d. 704), one of his successors as abbot of Iona, which is one of the most remarkable accounts of any saint written in this period.[7] Based on the living Iona tradition, it is an extraordinary blend of much undoubtedly historical information with folklore. Behind the miracles, prophecies, and visions the *Life* recounts, there is the real portrait of an exceptional man. Columb Cille's foundation of Iona, the monastic life lived there, and the saint's mission to the Picts of Scotland are all convincingly described, the more so that the success of this mission is not exaggerated. Columb Cille very soon became a general hero. He is celebrated in praise poems in Old Irish which may be earlier in date than Adomnán's *Life*. They catch—at times even better than does Adomnán—the danger of the sea-voyages undertaken by Columb Cille and other Irish monks whom "the wind swept over the sea in boats" (probably in the frail wickerwork boats covered in hides in use at the time). "It was not," says the poet, "on soft beds he undertook elaborate prayers, he crucified—it was not for crimes—his body on the green waves."[8]

Columb Cille died in 597, thirty-four years after his emigration from Ireland to Scotland. He left behind him not only great fame but a solidly established and well-organized network of monasteries subordinated to Iona. It was on this foundation that his successors were to build. By the late seventh century Columban monasteries were spread throughout Pictland. Missionaries from Iona, invited by an exiled Anglo-Saxon prince on his return as king, carried Christianity to Northumbria, founding the bishopric and monastery of Lindisfarne which remained subordinate to Iona until 664 (see 3, C, below). Long after this date Iona remained a leading intellectual center, producing what may have been the earliest annals composed in the Celtic world, and, as is now thought, the marvelous illumination of the *Book of Kells*. In Adomnán (abbot 679–704), it possessed one of the most remarkable figures of the age.

The *Life* of Columb Cille was only one of Adomnán's achievements. He also used a direct account given him by a Frankish bishop as the basis for an excellent description of the Christian East which included not only the Holy Land but also Alexandria and Constantinople.[9] Adomnán's successful diplomatic missions to Northumbria are evidence of the extent to which he (and Iona) were still respected there. Perhaps his most remarkable achievement, however, was the promulgation of the *Cáin Adomnáin* or "Law of the Innocents" (most of which is included here) at the Synod of Birr in Ireland in 697. The description at the beginning of the work of the lot of women before the Law clearly exaggerates when it extends the condition of female slaves to women in Ire-

---

7. *Adomnan's Life of Columba*, edited with translation by A. O. Anderson and M. O. Anderson (London, 1961).

8. These poems are edited with translations by Fergus Kelly, in *Ériu*, 24 (1973), pp. 1–34, and 26 (1975), pp. 66–98. I quote from 24 (1973), pp. 9, 17.

9. Adomnán, *De locis sanctis*, ed. and trans. D. Meehan (Dublin, 1958).

land in general. But the intention of the Law, to protect the clergy, women and children, churches and their property, represents a novel attempt to apply Christian standards to society and one which was well ahead of the time. The closest parallel in Western Europe, the Peace and Truce of God, only spread through France and Catalonia in the late tenth century. Recent scholarship sees the list of ninety-one abbots, bishops, kings, and tribal lords who ratified the Law as contemporary with the document itself.[10] The list is important evidence for the widespread acceptance of the Law, which was meant to apply to Ireland and Britain (that is to the Celtic areas of North Britain). The kings of the Scots of Dál Riata and of the Picts joined the kings of Ireland in ratifying the Law. A system of sanctions was established, administered by the monasteries dependent on Iona, to ensure it was enforced.

The respect for women evident in the Law is probably related to and perhaps even inspired by the exaltation of female sanctity found in some Old Irish poems of the eighth century. A long poem addressed to the Virgin Mary represents a new type of emotional religion, one found somewhat earlier in Spain and which may ultimately derive from further East, perhaps from Syriac sources.[11] The poem to Brigit, already cited, is further evidence for this new view of women. (It is worth noting that the legal right of women to take possession of land was seen as an innovation directly attributed to Brigit.)

At the same time as Columb Cille was establishing his monastery at Iona other monks were leaving Ireland for the continent of Europe. The greatest Irish missionary on the continent, St. Columban (d. 615), spent twenty-five years preaching and founding monasteries, first in Eastern France, then in North Italy. He and other Irish missionaries brought with them *Penitentials*, essentially guides for confessors, tabulating clearly penances for different sins, which could be adapted to local customs. The introduction of private penance was a major innovation. Up to now penance had been a public ceremony, witnessed by the whole local church. It could normally only be undergone once in a lifetime and so was usually put off until a man's deathbed (as Baptism had often been in the early Church). If a dying person underwent penance and later recovered he was obliged to withdraw entirely from public life. In 680 a Visigothic king who had received penance had to abdicate. A system that introduced private penance (which could be repeated) was bound to prove successful. The lists of penances for different sins, of which the *Peniten-*

10. Máirin Ní Dhonnchadha, "The Guarantor List of Cáin Adomnáin, 697," *Peritia*, 1 (1982), pp. 178–215.

11. Francis J. Byrne, "The Cult of the Blessed Virgin Mary in the Early Irish Church," paper given to the Colloquium cited in n.3, above, citing *The Poems of Blathmac, son of Cú Brettan*, ed. and trans. James Carney (Irish Texts Society, 47) (Dublin, 1964). For Syriac and Spanish connections see Edmund Bishop, *Liturgica Historica* (Oxford, 1918), pp. 161–63, 175–78 and, more generally, J. N. Hillgarth, "Ireland and Spain in the Seventh Century," *Peritia*, 3 (1984), pp. 1–16.

tial of Columbanus (translated here) is an early example, may seem very severe (some other Penitentials were less so) but the main aim was to provide "medicine for souls." The individual confessor was expected to take into account the circumstances of each case. While the main aim was to cure the sinner, the penance also had the community in mind. Penances did not only consist of fasts and the infliction of blows. They also entailed the obligation to compensate the kin of the injured party, a principle some modern legal reformers look on with favor. Here again the new ecclesiastical law is related to Irish secular laws which are built on the principle of compensation.

While the Celtic Church, in Ireland and Britain, may not have invented the practice embodied in the Penitentials, it certainly popularized it. By so doing it brought about a basic change in the religion of Western Christians, one which has affected the Latin Church down to the present day.

EULOGY OF ST. BRIGIT

Hail Brigit, an Old Irish Poem on the Hill of Alenn, ed. and trans. Kuno Meyer (Dublin, 1912), pp. 13–19.

1. Sit thou safely enthroned, triumphant Brigit, upon the side of Liffey[1] far as the strand of the ebbing sea! Thou art the sovereign lady with banded hosts[2] that presides over the Children of Catháir the Great.

2. God's counsel at every time concerning virgin Erin is greater than can be told: though glittering Liffey is thine to-day, it has been the land of others in their turn.

3. When from its side I gaze upon the fair Curragh . . . . the lot that has fallen to every king causes awe at each wreck.

4. Loegaire was king as far as the sea,—Ailill Áne, a mighty fate: the Curragh with its glitter remains—none of the kings remains that lived thereon.

5. Perfect Labraid Longsech lives no more, having trodden under foot his fair thirty years: since in Dinn Ríg—'twas a wonted abode—he dealt doom to Cobthach the Slender.

6. Lorc's grandson, Oengus of Róiriu, seized the rule of Erin . . . sway; Maistiu of the freckled neck, son of Mug Airt, threw princes across their graves.

7. Far-famed Alenn! delightful knowledge! many a prince is under its

1. I.e. the Plain of the Liffey, which included the town of Kildare.
2. I.e. the monks and nuns of Kildare.

girth: it is greater than can be fathomed when Crimthan the Victorious was seen in its bosom.

8. The shout of triumph heard there after each victory around a shock of swords, a mettlesome mass; the strength of its warrior-bands against the dark-blue battle-array: the sound of its horns above hundreds of heads.

9. The tuneful ring of its even-coloured bent anvils, the sound of songs heard there from the tongues of bards; the ardour of its men at the glorious contest; the beauty of its women at the stately gathering.

10. Drinking of mead there in every home-stead; its noble steeds, many tribes; the jingle of chains unto kings of men under blades of five-edged bloody spears.

11. The sweet strains heard there at every hour; its wine-barque upon the purple flood; its shower of silver of great splendour: its torques of gold from the lands of the Gaul.

12. Far as the sea of Britain the high renown of each king has sped like a meteor: delightful Alenn with its might has made sport of every law.

13. Bresal Brec was king over Elg,[3] Fiachra Fobrec with a fierce band of warriors; Fergus of the Sea, Finn son of Roth, they loved to dwell in lofty Alenn.

14. Worship of auguries is not worth listening to, nor of spells and auspices that betoken death; all is vain when it is probed, since Alenn is a deserted doon.

15. Bright is the smile that smiles on you from the plain . . . of Corc's land; of each generation which it reared in turn Liffey of Lorc has made ashes.

16. The Curragh of Liffey to the brink of the main, the Curragh of Sétna, a land of peace as far as the sea,—many is the king whom the Curragh of Carbre Nia-fer has overthrown.

17. Catháir the Great—he was the choicest of shapes—ruled Erin of many hues: though you cry upon him at his rath, his prowess of many weapons has vanished.

18. Fiachna of Fomuin, glorious Bresal ruled the sea with showers of spears: thirty great kings to the edge of the sea seized land around Tara of Bregia.

19. The Peaks of Iuchna, delightful place, around which many graves have settled—behold in lofty Allen the abode of Tadg, son of Nuadu Necht!

20. The apparel of Feradach—a goodly diadem—around whom crested bands would move; his blue-speckled helmet, his shining mantle,—many a king he overthrew.

3. A poetic name for Ireland.

21. Dunlang of Fornochta, he was generous, a prince who routed battles against the sons of Niall: though one were to tell the tale to all, this is not the world that was once.

22. Illann with his tribe launched thirty battles against every king, Enna's grandson, a rock against terror, it was not a host without a king's rule.

23. Ailill was a king that would bestow favour, against whom a fierce blood-dark battle-host would rise; Cormac, Carbre, Colman the Great, Brandub, a barque in which were hosts.

24. Faelan the Fair was a track of princeship, Fianamail with . . . Bran, son of Conall with many deeds, he was the wave over every cliff.

25. Oh Brigit whose land I behold, on which each one in turn has moved about, thy fame has outshone the fame of the king—thou art over them all.

26. Thou hast everlasting rule with the king apart from the land wherein is thy cemetery. Grand-child of Bresal son of Dian, sit thou safely enthroned, triumphant Brigit!

THE LAW OF THE INNOCENTS

Cáin Adamnáin, an Old-Irish Treatise on the Law of Adamnan, ed. and trans. Kuno Meyer (Oxford, 1905), pp. 3f., 15f., 21–33.

1. Five ages before the birth of Christ, to wit, from Adam to the Flood, from the Flood to Abraham, from Abraham to David, from David to the captivity in Babylon, from the Babylonian Captivity to the birth of Christ. During that time women were in bondage and in slavery, until Adamnan, son of Ronan, son of Tinne, son of Aed, son of Colum, son of Lugaid, son of Setne, son of Fergus, son of Conall, son of Niall, came.

2. *Cumalach*[1] was a name for women till Adamnan came to free them. And this was the *cumalach*, a woman for whom a hole was dug at the end of the door so that it came over her nakedness. The end of the great spit was placed upon her till the cooking of the portion was ended. After she had come out of that earth-pit she had to dip a candle four men's hands in length in a plate of butter or lard; that candle to be on her palm until division of food and distribution of liquor and making of beds, in the houses of kings and chieftains, had ended. That woman had no share in bag nor in basket, nor in the company of the house-master; but she dwelt in a hut outside the enclosure, lest bane from sea or land should come to her chief.

1. A derivative from *cumal*, "a female slave, bondmaid."

3. The work which the best of women had to do, was to go to battle and battlefield, encounter and camping, fighting and hosting, wounding and slaying. On one side of her she would carry her bag of provisions, on the other her babe. Her wooden pole upon her back. Thirty feet long it was, and had at one end an iron hook, which she would thrust into the tress of some woman in the opposite battalion. Her husband behind her, carrying a fence-stake in his hand, and flogging her on to battle. For[2] at that time it was the head of a woman, or her two breasts, which were taken as trophies.

4. Now, after the coming of Adamnan no woman is deprived of her testimony, if it be bound in righteous deeds. For a mother is a venerable treasure, a mother is a goodly treasure, the mother of saints and bishops and righteous men, an increase of the Kingdom of Heaven, a propagation on earth.

5. Adamnan suffered much hardship for your sake, O women, so that ever since Adamnan's time one half of your house is yours, and there is a place for your chair in the other half; so that your contract and your safeguard are free; and the first law made in Heaven and on earth for women is Adamnan's Law.

28. This is the enactment of the Law of Adamnan of Hi. At Birr this enactment was enjoined on the men of Ireland and Britain as a perpetual law by order of their nobles, clerics, and laymen, both their chiefs and ollaves [poet advisers] and bishops, and sages and confessors [a list of 91 names follows] and the intercession of all the men of Ireland, both laymen and clerics.

29. All then, both laymen and clerics, have sworn to fulfill the whole Law of Adamnan till Doom. They have offered up the full *eric* [honor price] of their female stock to Adamnan, and to every coarb [abbot] who will be in his seat till Doom, nor does Adamnan take away fines from chieftains and church and family to whom they are due.

30. Now, all the holy churches of Ireland together with Adamnan have besought the unity of the Godhead of the Father, and of the Son, and of the Holy Spirit, and the heavenly hosts, and the saints of the earth, that whoever fulfills this Law, both as to claim and levy and fulfillment and *eric*, may have a long and prosperous life, and may be honored in the eyes of God and of men, may be exalted in Heaven and on earth.

31. The holy churches of Ireland, together with Adamnan, have also besought God with the orders of Heaven and the saints of the earth, that who-

---

2. The use of "for" seems to imply that these trophies were to be put upon the stake which the man carried.

ever shall break the Law of Adamnan, both laymen and clerics, whoever shall not claim it, and shall not fulfill it to the best of his power, and shall not levy it from every one, both chieftain and church,—his life may be short with suffering and dishonor, without any of their offspring attaining Heaven or earth.

32. Adamnan has also set down an order of malediction for them, to wit, a psalm for every day up to twenty days, and an apostle or a noble saint for every day to be invoked with it, to wit, "*Quare*" and Peter, "*Domine quid multiplicati*" and John, "*Verba mea*" and Philip, "*Domine deus meus*" and Bartholomew, "*Dixit insipiens*" and Thomas, "*Deus, deus meus respice*" and Matthew, "*Iudica me Domine innocentium*" and Jacob, "*Dixit iniustus*" and Simon, "*Domine ne in furore*" and Thaddeus, "*Dixi custodiam*" and Matthias, "*Deus deorum*" and Mark, "*Quid gloriaris*" and Luke, "*Dixit insipiens*" and Stephen, "*Exurgat deus*" and Ambrose, "*Salvum me*" and Gregory of Rome, "*Deus, venerunt gentes*" and Martin, "*Deus, quis similis*" and old Paul, "*Deus laudem*" and George. "*Audite caeli quae loquor*," "*Non nobis, Domine, non nobis, sed nomini tuo*," &c.

33. Here begins the speech of the angel to Adamnan:—

After fourteen years Adamnan obtained this Law of God, and this is the cause. On Pentecost eve a holy angel of the Lord came to him, and again at Pentecost after a year, and seized a staff, and struck his side, and said to him: "Go forth into Ireland, and make a law in it that women be not in any manner killed by men, through slaughter or any other death, either by poison, or in water, or in fire, or by any beast, or in a pit, or by dogs, but that they shall die in their lawful bed. Thou shalt establish a law in Ireland and Britain for the sake of the mother of each one, because a mother has borne each one, and for the sake of Mary mother of Jesus Christ, through whom all are. Mary besought her Son on behalf of Adamnan about this Law. For whoever slays a woman shall be condemned to a twofold punishment, that is, his right hand and his left foot shall be cut off before death, and then he shall die, and his kindred shall pay seven full *cumals* [the value of 21 cows], and one-seventh part of the penance. If, instead of life and amputation, a fine has been imposed, the penance is fourteen years, and fourteen *cumals* shall be paid. But if a host has done it, every fifth man up to three hundred shall be condemned to that punishment; if few, they shall be divided into three parts. The first part of them shall be put to death by lot, hand and foot having first been cut off; the second part shall pay fourteen full *cumals*; the third shall be cast into exile beyond the sea, under the rule of hard regimen; for the sin is great when any one slays the mother and the sister of Christ's mother and the mother of Christ, and her who carries the spindle and who clothes every one. But he who from this day forward shall put a woman to death and does not do penance according to the Law, shall not only perish in eternity, and be cursed for God and Adamnan, but all shall be cursed that have heard it and do not curse him, and do not chastise him according to the judgment of this Law."

This is the speech of the angel to Adamnan.

34. This is the enactment of Adamnan's Law in Ireland and Britain: exemption of the Church of God with her people and her emblems and her sanctuaries and all her property, live and dead, and her law-abiding laymen with their lawful wives who are obedient to Adamnan and to a lawful, wise and pious confessor. The enactment of this Law of Adamnan is a perpetual law on behalf of clerics and women and innocent children until they are capable of slaying a man, and until they take their place in the tribe, and their (first) expedition is known.

35. Whoever wounds or slays a young clerical student or an innocent child under the ordinance of Adamnan's Law, eight *cumals* for it for every hand (engaged), with eight years of penance, up to three hundred *cumals*; and one year of penance for it for each one from three hundred to one thousand or an indefinite number; and it is the same fine for him who commits the deed and for him who sees it and does not save to the best of his ability. If there is neglect or ignorance, half the fine for it, and. . . . that it is neglect and that it is ignorance.

36. A further enactment of this Law: full due to every Church which is in good behavior; half-due to her for her *termon* [lands] outside the green; full due to her for every degree, both for wounding and theft and burning; half-due for her sanctuaries; half-due for merely touching the hair (?) of clerics without wounding or theft. It is full due to every church for violating her emblems wherever it is done.

37. These are the judges of Adamnan's law in every church and in every tribe, to wit, the clerics whom the community of Adamnan chooses and to whom they commit the enactment of the Law.

38. These are the pledges of this Law: one-third of the pledge in bronze or silver, according to the estimation of every territory, out of the property of every case. The pledge (to be redeemed) on the third day, judgment on the fifth day, payment on the tenth in all other cases; in this case the pledge (is to be redeemed) at once (?), judgment on the third day, payment on the fifth.

39. A further enactment of the Law, that in every suit a hostage is to be adjudged (?) both for the ranks of the laity and those of the church, within

territories inside and outside, for small and large dues, in obedience to Adamnan or his communities. There is legal notice and impounding, and the Law of Adamnan or his communities shall not become extinct.

40. A further enactment of the Law: If innocent children or clerics are slain, it is to their tombs of burial their dues come, and their *urradas*-dues [under native law] to their chiefs within their kindred.

41. A further enactment of the Law, that payment in full fines is to be made to Adamnan for every woman that has been slain, whether a man has a share in it, or cattle or a hound or fire or a ditch or a building,—for everything that is made is liable in the Law, both ditch and pit and bridge and fire-place and (door-)step and pools and kilns, and every other danger, except the woman deserves it. But one-third is left to be kept. If it is a witless person, the other two-thirds shall die. The one-third is his who has the right to it.

42. Whatever violent death a woman dies, except it be (by) the hand of God, or (in consequence of) rightful lawful cohabitation, it is paid in full fines to Adamnan, both slaying and drowning and burning and poison and breaking and perishing in a quagmire and death by tame beasts and pigs and cattle. If, however, it is a first crime. . . . or on the part of the pigs or hounds, they shall be killed at once, and half the due of a human hand for it; if it is not a first crime, full due is paid.

43. There shall be no cross-case or balancing of guilt in Adamnan's Law, but each one pays for his crimes for his own hand. Every trespass which is committed in Adamnan's Law, the communities of Adamnan are entitled to a . . . of it, apart from women, whether it be innocents, or clerics, or any one to whom they commit it, viz. a *cumal forbaich* [super levy] to the community of Hi where seven *cumals* are paid, and half a *cumal* from seven half-*cumals*. Six *séts* on thirty *séts*, three *séts* on five *séts*.[3]

44. One-eighth of everything small and great to the community of Adamnan from the slaying of clerics or innocent children. If it be a life-wound any one inflicts on a woman or a cleric or an innocent, seven half-*cumals* are due from him, fifteen *séts* upon the nearest and remoter kindred as being accomplices. Three *séts* for every white blow, five *séts* for every drawing of blood, seven *séts* for every wound requiring a tent, a *cumal* for every confinement to bed, and payment of the physician besides. If it be more than that, it goes upon half-dues for killing a person. If it is a blow with the palm of the hand or with the fist, an ounce of silver (is the fine) for it. If there be a green or red mark, or a swelling, an ounce and six scruples for it. For seizing women

---

3. A *sét* was a basic unit of value.

by the hair, five wethers. If there is a fight among women with outrage (?), three wethers.

45. Men and women are equally liable for large and small dues from this on to (any) fights of women, except outright death. For a woman deserves death for killing a man or a woman, or for giving poison whereof death ensues, or for burning, or for digging under a church, that is to say, she is to be put into a boat of one paddle as a sea-waif(?) upon the ocean to go with the wind from land. A vessel of meal and water to be given with her. Judgment upon her as God deems fit.

46. If it be charms from which death ensues that any one give to another, the fines of murder followed by concealment of the corpse (are to be paid) for it. Secret plunderings and. . . . which are traced (?) to (one of) the four nearest lands, unless these four nearest lands can lay them on any one particularly, they swear by the . . . of their soul that they do not know to lay it upon any one and pay it themselves. If they suspect any one and prove it, it is he who shall be liable. If the probability lie between two or a greater number, let their names be written upon leaves; each leaf is arranged around a lot, and the lots are put into a chalice upon the altar. He on whom the lot falls is liable.

47. If offenders who violate the Law do not pay, their kindred pay full fines according to the greatness of his crime, and after that (the offender) becomes forfeited, and is banished until the end of the law. One-half of seven *cumals* for accompliceship upon every direct and indirect kindred afterwards. If there be assistance and shelter and connivance, it is death for it; but such as the fine (of the principals) was such shall be that of the accomplices.

48. A further enactment of the Law: they shall feed the stewards of Adamnan's Law, whatever their number, with the good food of their people, viz. five men as guarantors, and the feeding of every one who shall levy the dues of the Law shall be according to the wealth of every one, both chieftain and church and people. A *cumal* for leaving any one of them fasting, while fines are being levied, and offenders with regard to feeding, and they sustain a joint contract of debts unless they feed them. Two *cumals* to them from offenders.

49. This is the exemption of every guarantor who comes to levy this tribute, viz. the guilt of their family does not come upon them so long as they support guarantors and while they are in possession and do not escape; but their own guilt (comes upon them) or the guilt of their offspring and of their children and of their retainers.

50. If it be rape of a maiden, seven half-*cumals* (is the fine) for it. If a hand (is put) upon her or in her girdle, ten ounces for it. If a hand (is put)

under her dress to defile her, three ounces and seven *cumals* for it. If there be
a blemish of her head or her eyes or in the face or in the ear or nose or tooth
or tongue or foot or hand, seven *cumals* are (to be paid) for it. If it be a
blemish of any other part of her body, seven half-*cumals* for it. If it be tearing
of her dress, seven ounces and one *cumal* for it.

51. If it be making a gentlewoman blush by imputing unchastity to her or
by denying her offspring, there are seven *cumals* (to be paid) for it until it
comes to (the wife of) an *aire désa* [rent-paying free man]. Seven half-
cumals if it be the wife of an *aire désa*. From her onwards to a *muiri* [local
headman], seven ounces.

52. If women be employed in an assault or in a host or fight, seven *cumals*
for every hand as far as seven, and beyond that it is to be accounted as the
crime of one man. If a woman has been got with child by stealth, without
contract, without full rights, without dowry, without betrothal, a full fine
for it. Whatever . . . which is of hand-produce, great or small, whatever of
dye-stuff, or woad or beans. If it be red dye of a cloak, . . . of a cloak for it.

53. Three guarantors for every chief church for the Law of Adamnan,
viz. the prior and the cook and the steward; and a guarantor of the Law from
(every) parent-family throughout all Ireland; and two guarantors of the Law
from high chieftains, and hostages to be held for its payment, if there be the
proof of women.

THE PENITENTIAL OF ST. COLUMBANUS

Ed. and trans. L. Bieler (Dublin, Institute for Advanced Studies, 1963),
pp. 97–107.

1. True penance is not to commit things deserving penance but to lament such things as have been committed. But since this is broken by the
weakness of many, not to say of all, the measures of penance must be known.
A scheme of these has been handed down by the holy fathers, so that in
accordance with the greatness of the offences the length also of the penances should be ordained.

2. Therefore, if anyone has sinned in thought, that is, has desired to kill
a man, or to commit fornication, or to steal, or to feast in secret and be
drunken, or indeed to strike someone, or to desert, or to do anything else
like this, and has been ready in his heart to carry out these sins: let him do
penance for the greater ones half a year, for the lesser ones forty days on
bread and water.

3. But if anyone has sinned in act with the common sins, if he has committed the sin of murder or sodomy, let him do penance for ten years; if he has committed fornication once only, let him do penance three years, if oftener, seven years. If a monk has deserted and broken his vows, if he repents and returns at once, let him do penance three forty-day periods, but if after a period of years, three years.

4. If anyone has stolen, let him do penance for a year.

4a. If anyone has perjured himself, let him do penance for seven years.

5. If anyone has struck his brother in a quarrel and spilt blood, let him do penance for three years.

6. But if anyone has got drunk and has vomited, or, being overfed, for this reason has vomited the sacrifice, let him do penance forty days. However, if he is forced by ill health to vomit the sacrifice, let him do penance seven days. If anyone has lost the sacrifice itself, let him do penance for a year.

7. If anyone has defiled himself, let him do penance for a year, if he is a junior.

8. If anyone has borne false witness knowingly, let him do penance for two years, together with the loss or restitution of the object in dispute.

So much about matters of importance; now about small matters of disorderly behavior.

9. He who does something by himself without asking, or who contradicts and says: "I am not doing it," or who murmurs, if the matter is serious, let him do penance with three special fasts, if slight, with one. Simple contradiction of another's word is to be punished with fifty strokes; if out of contention, with an imposition of silence. If it is made in a quarrel, the penance should be for a week.

10. He who slanders or willingly hears a slanderer, let him do penance with three special fasts; if it concerns the superior, let him do penance for a week.

11. He who has despised his superior in pride, or has spoken evil of the rule, is to be cast out, unless he has said immediately: "I am sorry for what I said"; but if he has not truly humbled himself, let him do penance for forty days, because he is infected with the disease of pride.

12. The talkative is to be punished with silence, the restless with the practice of gentleness, the gluttonous with fasting, the sleepy with watching, the proud with imprisonment, the deserter with expulsion; let each suffer exactly in accordance with his deserts, that the just may live justly. AMEN.

Diversity of offences causes diversity of penances. For doctors of the body also compound their medicines in diverse kinds; thus they heal wounds in one manner, sicknesses in another, boils in another, bruises in another, festering sores in another, eye diseases in another, fractures in another, burns in another. So also should spiritual doctors treat with diverse kinds of cures the wounds of souls, their sicknesses, [offences], pains, ailments, and infirmities. But since this gift belongs to few, namely to know to a nicety all these things, to treat them, to restore what is weak to a complete state of health, let us set out even a few prescriptions according to the traditions of our elders, and according to our own partial understanding, for we prophesy in part and we know in part.

First we must enact concerning capital sins, which are punished even by the sanction of the law.

1. If any cleric has committed murder and killed his neighbor, let him do penance for ten years in exile; after these, let him be restored to his native land, if he has performed his penance well on bread and water, being approved by the testimonial of the bishop or priest with whom he did penance and to whose care he was entrusted, on condition that he make satisfaction to the relatives of the slain, taking the place of a son, and saying: "Whatever you wish I will do for you." But if he does not make satisfaction to his relatives, let him never be restored to his native land, but like Cain let him be a wanderer and fugitive upon the earth.

2. If anyone has fallen to the depth of ruin and begotten a child, let him do penance as an exile for seven years on bread and water; then only, at the discretion of the priest, let him be restored to the altar.

3. But if anyone has committed fornication as the Sodomites did, let him do penance for ten years, for the three first on bread and water, but for the seven others let him refrain from wine and meat, and let him never again live with the other man.

4. However, if anyone has committed fornication with women, but has not begotten a child, and it has not become known among people: if he is a cleric, three years, if a monk or deacon, five years, if a priest, seven, if a bishop, twelve years.

5. If anyone has perjured himself, let him do penance seven years, and never take an oath again.

6. If anyone has destroyed someone by his magic art, let him do penance three years on an allowance of bread and water, and for three other years let him refrain from wine and meat, and then finally in the seventh year let him be restored to communion. But if anyone has used magic to excite love, and

has destroyed no one, let him do penance on bread and water for a whole year, if a cleric, for half a year, if a layman, if a deacon for two, if a priest for three; especially if anyone has thus produced abortion, on that account let each add on six extra forty-day periods, lest he be guilty of murder.

7. If any cleric has committed theft, that is, has stolen an ox or a horse, a sheep or any beast of his neighbor's, if he has done it once or twice, let him first make restitution to his neighbor, and do penance for a whole year on bread and water; if he has made a practice of this, and cannot make restitution, let him do penance three years on bread and water.

8. But if any cleric or deacon, or a man in any orders, who in the world was a layman with sons and daughters, after his profession has again known his mate, and again begotten a child of her, let him know that he has committed adultery, and has sinned no less than if he had been a cleric from his youth, and had sinned with a strange girl, since he sinned after his vow, after he consecrated himself to the Lord, and made his vow void; therefore let him likewise do penance seven years on bread and water.

9. If any cleric has struck his neighbor in a quarrel and spilt blood, let him do penance for a whole year; if a layman, for forty days.

10. If anyone has defiled himself or sinned with a beast, let him do penance two years, if he is not in orders; but if he is in orders or under a vow, let him do penance three years, if his age does not forbid.

11. If anyone desires a woman and cannot commit the act, that is, if the woman does not admit him, let him do penance half a year on bread and water, and for a whole year let him refrain from wine and meat and the communion of the altar.

12. If anyone has lost the sacrifice, let him do penance for a year. If through drunkenness or greed he has vomited it up and cast it carelessly aside, let him do penance three forty-day periods on bread and water; but if through ill health, let him do penance seven days. But these provisions are made for clerics and monks collectively; now for laymen.

13. Whoever has committed murder, that is, has killed his neighbor, let him do penance three years on bread and water as an unarmed exile, and after three years let him return to his own, rendering the compensation of filial piety and duty to the relatives of the slain, and thus after making satisfaction let him be restored to the altar at the discretion of the priest.

14. If any layman has begotten a child by another's wife, that is, has committed adultery in violating his neighbor's bed, let him do penance for three years, refraining from the more appetizing foods and from his own wife, giving in addition the price of chastity to the husband of the violated wife, and thus let his guilt be wiped off by the priest.

15. But if any layman has committed fornication in sodomite fashion, that is, has sinned by effeminate intercourse with a male, let him do penance for seven years, for the three first on bread and water and salt and dry produce of the garden, for the remaining four let him refrain from wine and meat, and thus let his guilt be remitted to him, and let the priest pray for him, and so let him be restored to the altar.

16. But if any of the laity has committed fornication with women who are free from wedlock, that is, with widows or virgins, if with a widow, let him do penance for one year, if with a virgin, for two years, provided that he pays her relatives the price of her disgrace; yet if he has no wife, but has lain as a virgin with the virgin, if her relatives agree, let her be his wife, but on condition that both first do penance for a year, and so let them be wedded.

17. But if any layman has committed fornication with a beast, let him do penance for a year, if he has a wife; yet if he has not, for half a year; likewise also let him do penance who, having a wife, has defiled himself with his own hands.

18. If any layman or lay woman has misused their child, let them do penance for a whole year on bread and water, and for two others let them refrain from wine and meats, and so first let them be restored to the altar at the discretion of the priest, and then let such a husband use his bed lawfully. For the laity must know, that in the period of penance assigned to them by the priests it is not lawful for them to know their wives, except after the conclusion of the penance; for penance ought not to be halved.

19. If any layman has committed theft, that is, has stolen an ox or a horse or a sheep or any beast of his neighbor's, if he has done it once or twice, let him first restore to his neighbor the loss which he has caused, and let him do penance for three forty-day periods on bread and water; but if he has made a practice of stealing often, and cannot make restitution, let him do penance for a year and three forty-day periods, and further undertake not to repeat it, and thus let him communicate at Easter of the second year, that is, after two years, on condition that, out of his own labor, he first gives alms to the poor and a meal to the priest who adjudged his penance, and so let the guilt of his evil habit be forgiven.

20. If any layman has perjured himself, if he did it out of greed, let him sell all his property and give it to the poor, and devote himself wholly to the Lord, and receive the tonsure, bidding farewell to the entire world, and until death let him serve God in a monastery; yet if he did it, not out of greed, but in fear of death, let him do penance for three years on bread and water as an unarmed exile, and for two more let him refrain from wine and meat, and thus by offering a life for himself, that is, by freeing a slave or maid-

servant from the yoke of bondage, and by doing many alms throughout two years, in which he may quite lawfully use all foods except meat, let him communicate after the seventh year.

21. If any of the laity has shed blood in a brawl, or wounded or maimed his neighbor, let him be compelled to restore all the damage he has done; but if he has nothing to pay with, let him first attend to his neighbor's work, while he is sick, and call in a doctor, and after his recovery, let him do penance for forty days on bread and water.

22. If any layman has become intoxicated, or eaten or drunk to the extent of vomiting, let him do penance for a week on bread and water.

23. If any layman has desired to commit adultery or fornication with a married woman, and has lusted after his neighbor's wife, and not committed the act, that is, has not been able to, because the woman did not admit him, yet he was ready to fornicate, let him confess his guilt to the priest, and so let him do penance for forty days on bread and water.

24. But if any layman has eaten or drunk beside temples, if he did it through ignorance, let him undertake forthwith never to do it again, and let him do penance forty days on bread and water; but if he did it in derision, that is, after the priest has declared to him that this was sacrilege, and if then he communicated at the table of demons, if it was only through the vice of greed that he did or repeated it, let him do penance for three forty-day periods on bread and water; but if he did it in worship of the demons or in honor of idols, let him do penance for three years.

25. If any layman in ignorance has communicated with the followers of Bonosus or other heretics, let him rank among the catechumens, that is, separated from other Christians, for forty days, and for two other forty-day periods in the lowest rank of Christians, that is, among the penitents, let him wash away the guilt of his unsound communion; but if he did this in derision, that is, after he was warned and forbidden by the priest not to pollute himself with the communion of an evil faction, let him do penance for a whole year and three forty-day periods, and for two other years let him refrain from wine and meat, and thus after imposition of hands by a Catholic bishop let him be restored to the altar.

Finally we must deal with the minor sanctions for monks.

26. If anyone has left the enclosure open during the night, let him do penance with a special fast; but if during the day, with twenty-four blows, if others were not following behind when he left it open. If someone has gone immediately in front of himself, let him do penance with a special fast.

27. If anyone, desiring a bath, has washed alone naked, let him do penance with a special fast. But if anyone, while washing lawfully in presence of

his brethren, has done this standing, unless through the need for cleansing dirt more fully, let him be corrected with twenty-four strokes.

28. But if anyone, even while sitting in the bath, has uncovered his knees or arms, without the need for washing dirt, let him not wash for six days, that is, let that immodest bather not wash his feet until the following Lord's Day. Yet a monk, when standing privately alone, is permitted to wash his feet; while a senior even publicly, but with another washing his feet, is permitted to be washed standing.

29. But before sermon on the Lord's Day let all, except for fixed requirements, be gathered together, so that none is lacking to the number of those who hear the exhortation, except for the cook and porter, who themselves also, if they can, are to try hard to be present, when the gospel bell is heard.

30. It is ordained that confessions be made carefully, especially of mental disturbances, before going to Mass, lest perhaps any should approach the altar unworthily, that is, if he does not have a clean heart. For it is better to wait until the heart is healed, and becomes a stranger to offence and envy, than rashly to approach the judgment of the throne. For Christ's throne is the altar, and His Body there with His Blood judges those who approach unworthily. Therefore, just as we must beware of mortal and fleshly sins before we may communicate so we must refrain and cleanse ourselves from interior vices and the sicknesses of the ailing soul before the covenant of true peace and the bond of eternal salvation. THE END.

B. *France and Its Borders*

The official conversion of the Germanic invaders of Gaul, Spain, and (later) Italy to Catholicism allowed the Church to carry much further the Christianization of the countryside. In France Clovis' descendants not only refounded or founded bishoprics and monasteries but summoned missionaries from Aquitaine to Belgium and the Rhineland. A new impetus had been given by Irish monks and especially by St. Columban (see above, p. 122). His vivid preaching and ascetic prowess stirred up many disciples, both in France, where his monastic foundation of Luxueil soon created other monasteries, and in Italy, where his monastery of Bobbio played an important part in the Lombards' conversion from Arianism. Frankish monks carried on Columban's work, among them St. Amand (d. 675), the first effective missionary to Flanders.

Apart from Gregory of Tours we have some forty lives of saints written in

France between about 550 and 750—a far larger number than survive for the rest of Western Europe, Britain, and Ireland put together. The *Life of St. Amand* may be compared to the *Life of Caesarius of Arles* (translated in part, above, pp. 32–43). The later *Life* is anonymous. It was based on oral traditions (several witnesses are cited by name) and was written, either in Amand's monastery of Elnone or by a cleric of the diocese of Noyon-Tournai where he had worked, within about thirty years of his death. Some elements in the *Life*, the elaborate humility of the prologue, the visions and miracles, the use of biblical quotations to reinforce the comparison of Amand to Christ, are mainly interesting as being representative of the genre. Among nonbiblical sources Sulpicius Severus' *Life of Martin of Tours* and Gregory the Great's *Dialogues* (see pp. 18, 86, above) have been used and help to provide a model. In general the *Life* gives us, as Professor Wallace-Hadrill remarks, "an authentic picture of the career of a remarkable man, as difficult in his way as Columban or Boniface."[1] It is a portrait of a "man of God," a "holy man" (as the *Life* continually describes him), whose blessing or curse possesses power (*virtus*), equally active in intervening between criminals and judges, in denouncing a king's abuses to his face, in destroying sacred trees (or rather in making their worshipers destroy them), and in saving his fellow travelers from shipwreck. The insistence in Amand's authentic "Will" (below, p. 149) on the fact that his body should be buried within the monastery of Elnone and not moved to any other church clearly attests his fame.

Amand's birth, evidently of a rich family, in the relatively Romanized Aquitaine, his training as a recluse at Bourges, his connection with the shrine of St. Martin at Tours (see above, p. 31), and with several leading bishops, all this is no doubt historical. Other sources document Amand's connection with Columban's disciples. Amand's decision, early in life, to spend his life "in exile" (chap. 4) is directly in the Irish tradition of "pilgrimage for Christ," a tradition understood by him, as the "Will" puts it, as a mission "through all provinces and nations for the love of Christ." Amand's journey across the Danube to evangelize the Slavs (chap. 16) and his preaching to the Basques (chap. 20) illustrate his conviction of a universal mission. To this is added the connection with Rome, which appears in Amand's two journeys there, his visions of St. Peter, and his commission, probably by Pope Boniface V (619–25), to preach in France (chap. 7). A surviving letter from the later Pope Martin I (649–55) shows that the papacy did feel a direct tie to Amand.

Amand's two far-flung missions, to Slavs and Basques, were aimed at peoples under Frankish influence (though not control). His more enduring mission to Flanders was also directed at a border area of the Frankish kingdom. In Flanders the direct support he received from Merovingian rulers is especially apparent. His main monastic foundation, Elnone on the Scarpe (a tributary of the Scheldt), now St-Amand-les-Eaux in the French Département du Nord, received 10,000 hectares. As his "Will" states, Amand owed this land to

1. J. M. Wallace-Hadrill, *The Frankish Church* (Oxford, 1983), p. 90.

"royal largess," probably that of King Dagobert (623–39). In the account of the evangelization of the region of Ghent—the only relatively detailed episode in the *Life*—Amand is seen acting with the support of Bishop Acharius of Noyon-Tournai, who had been trained at Columban's foundation of Luxueil, and with that of Dagobert, from whom Acharius obtained, at Amand's request, a royal edict enforcing baptism on pagans (though, judging by the treatment the missionary received from the Flemings he preached to, this document does not seem to have been much use to him). Amand's tactic of buying slaves and training them as missionaries (chap. 9) was probably widely practiced. It bridged the linguistic gap which must have separated a missionary from Aquitaine, whose native speech was a type of Old Romance, from Flemings. Amand's resuscitation of an apparently dead man (chap. 14) may also have appealed particularly to a recently subjugated population, under the foreign and often arbitrary rule of Frankish counts.

Connections and differences between Amand and later Anglo-Saxon missionaries will be touched on later (D, below). His *Life*, with all its lacunae and some probably legendary elements (though the opposition of a local bishop in chap. 23 and the violent form it took is not in itself improbable at this time), is interesting because it shows that the seventh-century Frankish Church had not lost the impetus received from Ireland. A wandering abbot-bishop from Aquitaine could carry Christianity to the countryside of Northern France in a way hardly envisaged by the urban-oriented Gallic Church of the sixth century. Amand was not alone. His younger contemporaries, notably Dado (later Audoenus) and Eligius, both mentioned as members of the royal court in chap. 17, were also at work as bishops in Normandy and Noyon, respectively. Their connections with Columban and Eligius' use of Martin of Braga's sermon to the rustics (see above, pp. 57–64) are worth noting. The most enduring results achieved by the seventh-century Frankish Church were, however, due to monks not bishops. Some 230 new monasteries were established between 625 and 700 in Northern France, most of them outside towns. It was through these monasteries and especially through the network of small churches built in the vast domains given them by kings and nobles, and through the chapels founded on all major lay estates that Christianity began slowly to affect the life of the countryside.

A Traveling Bishop: St. Amand (d. c. 675)

Vita S. Amandi, episcopi et confessoris, ed. B. Krusch, MGH, SRM, V (Hannover, 1910), pp. 428–49.

Prologue. Being about to write the Life of Blessed Amand, I invoke the Holy Spirit, who dwelt in him, so that He who gave him his wondrous powers, should also grant me the speech to narrate them, both that I may fulfill the duty I owe to Your Charity and lest he be unknown to those who should imitate him. Although I am utterly unworthy in talent and am oppressed by the weight of my trifling and idleness, I trust in Him who said: "Open your mouth and I will fill it" (Psalm 80:11) and am most of all dependent on your prayers, that what I cannot obtain by my merits [I may achieve] with Your Holiness' prayers, so that, by Divine Grace, I may begin such an arduous task. First of all I wish you to know that I am not in the least able to attain knowledge of all the wonders which the Lord chose to work through him, but, as He shall give me strength, I shall attempt to set down briefly a few out of many. For it is wrong that one should be silent about such a man, when the Pious Disposer of things made him a signal worker in the field of the Church and by his diligent wielding of the hoe of faith the crop of Christ increased a hundredfold (see Matthew 13:23). Great are the remedies devised by God for the human race when such a man is chosen for the illumination of the fatherland. . . . As Truth Himself said, "a city set on a hill cannot be hid" (Matthew 5:14). If I may say this without offence to all the saints, he whose powers we have known is second to none. And so, lest prolix speech may excite disgust and generate boredom in the reader, I shall seek to hand down the life of St. Amand, how he lived from boyhood to maturity, how he acted before his episcopate and in it, how he achieved a blessed end, what discipline of mind and design were his. Although I write in rustic and plebeian speech, I do so because of his example and [to encourage] imitation of his acts.

1. The most holy Amand was born in the region of Aquitaine, not far from the shore of the [Atlantic] Ocean. He was the son of Christian and noble parents. His father was named Serenus, his mother Amantia. When, passing through adolescence to a manly strength, burning with immoderate desire in love of Christ, he left his country and his parents for the Ile d'Yeu, which is forty miles off the [Atlantic] shore. Arriving at the door of a monastery he was received with great joy by the brethren. And since he had studied sacred letters from infancy he grew daily in the things of God.

2. And so, one day, when he had been ordered to walk across the island, there suddenly appeared to him (as the man of God was used to relate) a serpent of extraordinary size, more great and terrifying than had ever been seen before (or has been seen since) in the island. When the boy, terrified by the sight, did not know what to do, Divine Grace suggested recourse to prayer. When he had prayed for some time, prostrated on the ground, he opposed the Sign of the Cross to the monster and ordered it to return at once to its lair. Obeying the sign of the man of God and fleeing rapidly back to its cave, it never again appeared in the island. By the prayer of the

Blessed Amand God freed the island from imminent danger. This beginning of his signs (see John 2:11) reached us, born by fame.

3. Then, since he was still a boy, his father began to lure him with kind speeches to leave the monastery and again assume secular dress. When he sought to persuade the boy—adding that, unless he at once agreed, he would lose the paternal inheritance—he is said to have replied: "Nothing, father, seems to me more my own than the service of Christ. He is my lot and my inheritance (see Numbers 18:20). I want none of the family riches. Only allow me to enter Christ's army."

4. Persisting in this resolve and leaving his native land and his parents he journeyed to Tours. Prostrated in prayer and tears at the tomb of the Most Holy Martin, he asked the holy man with his whole heart that he should obtain from the Lord that he [Amand] might never be permitted to return to his own land but might spend his whole life in exile. Rising up from prayer he at once cut off his hair and received the honor and grace of the clerical state.

5. With the blessing of the abbot and brethren [of St. Martin's] he traveled to Bourges, to the holy bishop Austregisilus, who was then outstanding and famous in divine things. He was received by the bishop and by his archdeacon (later bishop), the most holy Sulpicius, with great kindness. They made a cell for him beside the church in the higher wall of the city.

6. He remained for many days in this cell for the love of eternal life. Clothed in a goat's skin and covered in ashes, worn down by fasts and hunger, he was content with barley-bread and a little water. Abstaining entirely from beer and wine, he supported rather than nourished his body. He remained thus in God's service for about fifteen years. Then, again inflamed by heavenly desire, the thought came to him that he should journey to the thresholds of the most blessed apostles Peter and Paul. Taking with him only one companion and traveling through remote and rough ways, he at last reached Rome. There, accomplishing his holy desire, covering with kisses the thresholds of the apostles, he visited the churches of the city by day and by night returned to the Church of St. Peter.

7. One day, as evening approached, although the guardians had as usual searched the church and made all the faithful leave, the man of God Amand succeeded in remaining there alone, intending to keep vigil all night. But one of the guardians found him and expelled him from the church, treating him with contempt and insulting him. Amand sat down on the steps before the door of the basilica. While he was lost in ecstasy St. Peter suddenly appeared to him. Addressing him kindly and gently he told him to return to Gaul and take up the office of preaching. Filled with joy at this vision,

Amand returned happily to Gaul after he had received the apostolic bene-
diction [from the then pope] and had been provided with relics.

8. After a short time Amand was forced by the king [Lothar II] and bishops to be consecrated bishop himself. He began to proclaim the Gospel to
the pagans and in all things to show himself as an example of good works.
Serene in countenance, a great almsgiver, chaste in body and sober in
sense, careful in speech, given to vigils and prayer, he held himself in the
middle between rich and poor, so that the poor saw him as poor, the rich as
superior to themselves.

9. If he found captives or boys from across the sea [from Britain], he redeemed them at a price, baptizing them and having them taught letters.
Once they had been freed he sent them to different churches. We have
heard that some of them later became bishops, priests, or distinguished
abbots.

10. One should not omit the account of the man of God Amand's return
from Rome after his second journey there. He had boarded a ship and
reached Centumcellae [Cività Vecchia]. At night, when he was, as usual,
engaged in solitary prayer, an unclean spirit laid hands on one of the saint's
followers and sought to drag him overboard. As the boy was drawn along he
began to shout: "Christ, help me! Christ, help me!" But the evil spirit replied insultingly: "What sort of Christ [do you mean]?" When the boy was
unable to reply, St. Amand called out: "Tell him, son, 'Christ the Son of the
Living God, the Crucified.'" At the sound of his voice the Enemy vanished
as smoke.

11. Soon afterwards, while the ship was well out at sea, and Amand was
preaching the word of God to the sailors, a fish of extraordinary size appeared and was caught in a net. While the sailors were feasting and rejoicing
a sudden tempest arose which changed all their joy into grief. In the hope of
reaching land the sailors began to throw everything overboard, including
their provisions and even the ship's tackle. Nothing was of any use. The ship
was shaken to and fro by the waves. Despairing of their lives the sailors ran
to the servant of God Amand, begging him to intercede with the Lord to
save them from imminent danger. Amand, consoling them, told them to
trust in the Lord's mercy. The sailors, exhausted by their toil, lay collapsed
here and there. The saint remained alone in the poop.

12. St. Peter, unexpectedly appearing, spoke to him there, saying gently:
"Do not fear, Amand! You will not perish nor will those with you." When he
had spoken the tempest ceased and a great calm returned (see Matthew
8:26). In the morning all those traveling with the man of God landed safe
and sound.

13. While the man of God, impelled by his zeal for souls, was engaged on his travels, he heard of a region situated across the River Scheldt, to which antiquity had given the name of Ghent. This region was so caught up in the devil's nets that its inhabitants offered worship to trees and pieces of wood instead of to God; they built shrines and adored idols. Because of the savagery of its people and the infertility of the soil no bishop had preached there nor had anyone dared to proclaim the word of God. When he heard this the holy man, rather pitying [the pagans'] error than fearing for his life, went to Acharius, then bishop of Noyon, and humbly asked him to go as soon as possible to King Dagobert and obtain letters from him, stating that if anyone did not freely choose to be reborn by the waters of baptism, he should be forced by the king to receive this sacrament. This was done. Provided with power from the king and blessing from the Church the man of God Amand went intrepidly forth. Who could do justice to the tale of the injuries he suffered for the name of Christ, how often he was beaten by the inhabitants of the land, how he was repulsed, with insults, by the very women and rustics, often, even, thrown into the Scheldt? Accounting all this as nothing the holy man did not cease to preach the word of God, for he remembered the Gospel saying, "Greater love hath no man than when he lays down his life for his friends" (John 15:13). His companions, who had followed him in brotherly love, returned to their own country because of their hunger and the barrenness of the land. He was left there alone. Continuing his preaching mission, he prepared his food with his own hands. Redeeming many captives he washed them in sacred baptism and exhorted them to persist in good works.

14. We thought it worth adding to this account what we learnt from the venerable presbyter Bonus, who testified he was present on the occasion. A Frankish Count, by name Dotto, was holding court before a large assembly of Franks. Suddenly an accused was brought before him whom the whole crowd cried out was worthy of death. Savagely tortured, cruelly beaten, he was only half-alive. When Dotto decreed he should be hung the man of God Amand began resolutely to beg that his life might be spared. But since the Count was more cruel than any beast, Amand could obtain nothing. At last the man was hung up by the executioners and died. Dotto, surrounded by popular acclaim, returned to his palace while the holy man hastened to the scaffold and found the man already dead. Taking him down, he had him carried to the cell where he used to pray. Making the brethren go out he began to pray over the body of the dead man. He poured out prayers and tears until, by God's command, the soul returned to the body. As the time for Matins had come and the brethren were assembled, he ordered water to

be brought. They supposed that it was to wash the body before burial. But, entering the cell, they saw the same man they had left dead, well, sitting up and speaking to the man of God. They marveled greatly to find him alive whom they had left dead. The man of God began to impress on them that they should never reveal to anyone what God had done by him, for he asserted that it was not due to his power but to God's mercy, which is always present to those who trust in Him. The man's body was washed, the scars healed, no trace appearing of the wounds he had suffered, and so Amand, sending him back to his own house restored him safe and sound to his kindred.

15. When this miracle was diffused far and wide, the inhabitants of the region rushed to Amand and humbly begged that he should make them Christians. They destroyed with their own hands the temples, where, until then, they had worshiped, and all turned to the true worship of God. Where the temples had stood the man of God Amand, thanks to royal munificence and to the alms of devout men and women, built monasteries or churches, and, feeding the people with the sacred food of the word, illumined the hearts of all men with heavenly mandates.

16. When the holy man saw a number converted by his preaching, burning with still greater desire to convert others, he heard that the Slavs, sunk in great error, were caught in the devil's snares. Greatly hoping he might gain the palm of martyrdom, he crossed the Danube and, journeying round, freely preached the Gospel of Christ to the people. But, when a very few had been reborn in Christ, seeing that he was achieving little and that he would not obtain the martyrdom he always sought, he returned to his own flock, and, caring for them, led them by preaching to the heavenly kingdom.

17. Meanwhile King Dagobert, excessively given to the love of women, inflamed by filthy passion, had no offspring. He turned to God for aid and begged that a son should be given him, who might rule his kingdom after him. By God's grace this was granted him. When he was told that the Lord had given him a son he was filled with great joy. He began to consider to whom he should entrust the boy so that he might be reborn in sacred baptism. Immediately, calling his ministers, he wisely ordered them to search out St. Amand. (For, a little while before, the bishop having reproved the king for his capital crimes—something which none of the [other] bishops had dared to do—Dagobert, inflamed with rage, had ordered him to be expelled from the kingdom and Amand, traveling through remote places, had preached the word of God to the pagans.) When at last Amand was discovered by the king's ministers and ordered to present himself before the king, he remembered the precept of the apostle that one should obey the higher

powers (Romans 13:1) and came to the king, who was living at the villa of Clichy. When the king saw Blessed Amand he was filled with great joy. Prostrated at the feet of the saint he asked him to forgive the great crime he had committed against him. But Amand, very gentle and patient, hastened to raise the king from the ground and granted him the pardon he asked. Then the king said: "I greatly repent of having acted foolishly towards you. I beg you, do not remember the injury I did you and do not disdain the petition I address to you. The Lord—not because of my own merits—has given me a son and I ask you to baptize him and take him into your arms as your spiritual son." The man of God vehemently refused for he knew the Scripture says: "The soldier of God should not be involved in secular affairs" (2 Timothy 2:4). He should live in solitude, remote from the world, and should not frequent royal palaces. So he went out from the king's presence. But the king soon sent to him the Illustrious man Dado and the Venerable Eligius, who were then living in the royal palace in secular dress but who later, as the world knows, became bishops famous for their merits, miracles, and virtues. They humbly asked the man of God to assent to the king's petition and to agree to wash his son in the sacred font and bring him up in the divine law. They said that if the man of God did not refuse to do this, thanks to his familiarity with the king he might more easily obtain permission to preach in his kingdom or wherever he chose, and that, through royal favor, he might conquer many nations for Christ. Worn out in the end by the prayers of the two messengers, Amand gave his consent. Hearing that the saint no longer refused his wishes, the king immediately had the boy brought. It is said that he was only forty days old. The holy man took him into his arms, blessed him and made him a catechumen. Since none of the crowd standing round answered "Amen" to his prayer, the Lord opened the boy's mouth and everyone heard him clearly answer "Amen." St. Amand immediately baptized him, giving him the name of Sigebert, to the great joy of the king and of all the court.

18. When these things had been done, the bishop of Maastricht passed happily to Christ. Then the king summoned St. Amand and, calling together a great number of bishops and people, put him forward as ruler of the church in question. The saint refused, declaring he was unworthy, but all those present cried out with one voice that he should accept the bishopric, not for money but because of his zeal for souls. Forced by the king and bishops, he accepted the episcopal throne. And for almost three years he journeyed round the small towns and fortified centers, continually preaching the Lord's word to all men. It is almost wicked to record that many priests and deacons refused his preaching, disdaining to hear him, but he, following the

Gospel precept (Mark 6:11), shaking off the dust from his feet as witness against them, hastened on to other parts.

19. Finding a small island called Calloo by the River Scheldt, he worked there for some time with his spiritual brethren. But for some two years a great disaster fell on those who had despised the word of God. Houses collapsed, fields were made into solitudes, even small towns and forts were destroyed, and hardly anyone remained in these regions of those who had despised the preaching of the man of God.

20. Not long after, the holy man was asked by the brethren whom he had left in different places to carry out the cure of souls, to visit them and feed them with the food of the word. He heard from them of a people formerly known as Vaceians, now vulgarly called Basques. They were so plunged in error that, given up to auguries and other superstitions, they adored idols instead of God. This race is spread throughout the Pyrenees in rough and inaccessible country and, by its daring and mobility in battle, often raided the Frankish borders. The man of God Amand, taking pity on their error, labored earnestly to rescue them from the devil's hold. While he was preaching the divine word and the Gospel of Salvation one of those present, a light, lubricious fellow, proud also and cackling words apt to move men to laughter (what the vulgar call a jester) rose up and began to scoff at the servant of Christ and to rate the Gospel he was preaching as nothing. But that very hour, seized on by the demon, the wretch began to tear himself with his hands and was forced to confess publicly that he had deserved to suffer this for the injury he had done the servant of God. In the middle of these torments he gave up his life.

21. The Basques remaining in their blindness, the holy man came in his travels to a certain city. Honorably received by the bishop, while the latter, as is customary with hosts, was pouring water over Amand's hands, he secretly told his assistant to take the water in which the man of God had washed his hands into the sacristy of the church and keep it carefully. He did this because he trusted that the man of God's blessing could heal. At that time a blind man (who had lost his sight long ago) sat begging before the doors of the church. The bishop of the city said to him: "Man, if you have faith wash your eyes with the water in which the man of God Amand washed his hands. I trust that by his sanctity you will recover your former health." When the blind man had washed his eyes with that water, by God's grace he immediately recovered his sight so that he saw all things clearly.

22. The man of God returned to the [northern] borders of the Franks and chose for himself a fit place for preaching [Elnone], where he built a monastery with the brethren who had suffered many things with him in different

regions for the Name of Christ. Many of these brethren we have seen later become abbots or leading men.

23. The holy man of God Amand went to king Childeric [II] and humbly asked him to give him a place in which to build a monastery, not out of ambition but for the love of souls. The king gave him the place named Nant and there the man of God began to build a monastery. But a certain Mummolus, bishop of the city of Uzès, took it very ill that the man of God should have received this gift from the king. Inflamed with envy he sought to dislodge the man of God. He sent some active men to him to eject him from the place (after having covered him with insults) or else to inflict punishment on him there. The messengers, attempting to trick him, told him that they would show him a place suitable for a monastery. He had only to come with them. Thanks to God their malice could not be hidden. Amand was aware of the place where they had decided to kill him. They arrived at the summit of a hill where they meant to cut off his head. The man of God had not wished to tell his brethren beforehand since he was most willingly going to martyrdom. But suddenly a tempest arose. Rain and hail and a thick cloud covered the whole mountain. The bishop's agents who had been sent to kill Amand could see nothing. In despair they prostrated themselves at the saint's feet, asked for pardon and humbly begged him to allow them to leave alive. The man of God had recourse to his usual arms, to prayer. Shedding many tears he prayed until the weather became clear again and light returned. Stupefied with fear the bishop's satellites returned home leaving Amand unharmed.

24. The faithful testimony of the venerable priest Erchangesilus should not be passed over. When the man of God Amand was preaching in the county of Beauvais he came to a place called Ressons on the River Aronde. There was a blind woman there, who had lost her sight a long time ago. Entering her house the man of God began to ask her how this blindness had come upon her. She replied that the only reason was that she had always venerated auguries and idols. She then indicated the place where she used to pray to her idol, a tree dedicated to the demon. The man of God said: "I am not amazed that you became blind for this folly but I wonder that the mercy of God has sustained you so long. For when you should adore your Creator and Redeemer, you adore demons and dumb idols, who cannot do you or themselves any service. Now take an axe and cut down this abominable tree by which you have lost your bodily sight and your soul's salvation. I trust that, if you firmly believe, you may receive the sight you once had from the Lord." With her daughter leading her by the hand the woman hastened to the tree and endeavored to cut it down. Then the man of God called her to

him, made the Sign of the Cross on her eyes and, invoking Christ's Name, restored her to her former health, instructed her how she should act, and left her. Changing her life for the better, she spent the rest of her days chastely and soberly.

25. An event by which the Lord deigned to show forth the perfection of Amand's virtues should not be clothed in silence. When he had sent an order to a certain monk named Chrodobald, then provost of the monastery, to prepare carts to bring wine to the monastery for the use of the brethren, the provost is said to have proved disobedient. But the same night divine punishment overtook him. For while he was journeying to excuse himself to the man of God because he could find no carts, his whole body is said to have been so paralyzed that he could move neither hand nor foot. His vital force only continued in his breast. In a feeble voice he confessed he deserved this for his disobedience and contumacy. The brethren placed him in a boat to take him to the monastery of Elnone, to the man of God. In the evening, after Vespers, when the saint had, as usual, gone to eat, it was told him how this monk had fallen sick. He is reported to have remarked, smiling slightly, "He will undergo still worse dangers for he is too much given to boasting and disobedience." But he ordered a certain faithful priest to take a cup of wine and a little bread to the monk, saying, "Go and tell him to eat part of the bread and wine and tomorrow, when I come to visit him, by God's grace he will come to meet me." All this took place. Once the monk had received his father's blessing his whole body returned to health, so that it showed no injury. When the holy man arrived he met him and began to speak with him, the brethren greatly wondering that they saw him alive and well whom they had thought dead. The man of God, having pardoned him, warned him to amend his ways and sent him healed to the monastery.

26. There are many other things which the Lord deigned to work by him but they are unknown to us though known to God. "But if I wished to recount all that has come to my ears the day, I think, would end before my tale" (Gregory the Great, *Dialogues*, I, prologue). For what signs did the Lord not show forth by him, when he gave the dead life, the blind sight, the paralyzed the ability to walk, lepers cleansing, the deaf hearing, and restored those oppressed by demons to health?

The great saint of God Amand, his course faithfully completed, filled with the fruit of all good works and coming to the day of his most holy passing, went happily to Christ. He is buried with great honor in the place called Elnone. There many benefits are obtained through his prayers and there all praise the Name of the Lord Jesus Christ, to whom, with the Eternal Father and the Holy Spirit be power and honor, glory and dominion and praise for endless ages of ages. Amen.

St. Amand's Will

Copy of the Petition or Conjuration of St. Amand, with regard to his body, ed. B. Krusch, MGH, SRM, V, pp. 483f.

In the Name of Our Lord Jesus Christ, I Amandus, most wretched sinner.
We believe that the Divine Piety designs to rule and, of its clemency, to save us. Before all ages God foreknew our entry into the world and our time of leaving it. No one is ignorant of how I have traveled far and wide through all provinces and nations for the love of Christ, to announce the word of God and administer baptism, and of how Divine Clemency has saved me from many dangers and has deigned to preserve me down to the present day. But now, worn out by my labors, in extreme old age, my body half dead, I hope soon to leave this world. Since God has willed to lead me to this humble place of Elnone, where I have built a monastery with my own labor on land given by royal largess, I ask, and, in the presence of Jesus Christ, the Son of God, I dare to conjure that, if God has decided that I should leave this world here, no bishop or abbot or secular person or any power may oppose my body resting in this monastery, among my brethren, to whom I have already commended my body and soul. And if the end of my life shall come on a journey or elsewhere, may the brethren and abbot of Elnone have permission to bring my body back there.

If anyone wishes, out of temerity, to go against this or to take my body by force out of the monastery, may he first incur the displeasure of the Holy Trinity and be excommunicated by all Catholic churches and made a stranger to the society of saints. May he undergo the damnation of Dathan and Abiram (Numbers 16:33), when Hell swallowed them up alive, and be Anathema, Maranatha, that is condemned at the Coming of Our Lord Jesus Christ (1 Corinthians 16:22). And may he be unable to change our will but may our resolution remain for ever firm and inviolate. That you may more certainly believe [my will], I have subscribed this act with my own hand and have asked all God-fearing men to subscribe it and have asked our brother Baudemond to draw up this letter.

This letter was drawn up in the monastery of Elnone in the second year of our Lord the Glorious King Thierry, on the 15th Kalends of May [April 17, 674 or 675].

I Amand, sinner, have consented to this my letter and have subscribed it. [Other signatures follow: they include those of the Metropolitan of Reims, the bishops of Noyon and Cambrai, and the famous Abbot Bertin of Sithiu—later St. Bertin.]

C. *The Roman Mission to England*

The correspondence of Pope Gregory the Great (590–604) reveals the considerable part the papacy was beginning to take in the affairs of the West. Its success varied from country to country. In Spain all Gregory could do was welcome the conversion of the Visigoths (p. 89). Gregory corresponded with the Merovingian rulers, urged church reform upon them, and sent his representatives to France, but the results were not striking. The Spanish and French churches were too directly subject to their rulers for papal intervention to be effective. Italy had been invaded by the Lombards in 568; they were continually gaining ground from the Byzantines. Gregory could not bring about their conversion from Arianism. But, by the mission he sent in 597 to England, Gregory opened a new world to the papacy. This was the first papal mission to a pagan people. (St. Patrick was originally sent to Ireland about 432 to minister to existing Christians there; he received no help or encouragement from the clergy or secular rulers of the fifth-century Roman West.)

It was very important for the future that Gregory sent monks to England. The character of the conversion of Northwest Europe and its later culture were greatly influenced by the fact that it was converted by monks. By 600, since there were no schools in the outside world, a school in each monastery had to teach new recruits—by this time usually children—to take part in church services and read the Bible. Monks necessarily imbibed some Latin culture and communicated it to the peoples among whom they were sent. Ireland had long been Christian. Its vigorous Church was centered on monasteries which possessed a strong Latin as well as vernacular culture. In England monastic missionaries from Ireland and Gregory's Italian monks met; after some conflict their traditions blended. In the seventh and eighth centuries Irish- and, later, Roman-trained Anglo-Saxon monks were mainly responsible for the revival of the French Church and the conversion of Germany (p. 169).

Gregory kept in constant touch with the monks he had dispatched, sending their leader, Augustine, who became Archbishop of Canterbury, advice and reinforcements. Gregory's advice that pagan temples should be turned into churches—though not always followed in England, where many temples were destroyed—canonized general practice. But the way Gregory in Rome could envisage conditions in England is remarkable.

After Gregory's death in 604 the Roman mission soon came to a halt. By 660 it had hardly advanced outside Kent. Meanwhile, Irish monks from Iona in the Western Isles of Scotland and from Ireland evangelized Northumbria and much of Southern England. The Irish Church was separated from Rome— on disciplinary, not doctrinal questions. At Whitby in 664 the leading Anglo-Saxon king, Oswiu of Northumbria, was won over to the Roman view on these matters. This decided the definite adherence of England to the papacy. By the 680's all the Anglo-Saxon kingdoms were converted to Christianity.

Christianity in the North

The Anglo-Saxon Church was ruled by Roman discipline in firmly organized dioceses by men who were basically lawgivers and administrators. But Irish influence did not disappear. The Anglo-Saxon Church was monastic as well as diocesan, inspired with much of Irish scholarship and zeal for conversion.

Bede's *History of the English Church and People* and his other historical works record England's conversion.[1] Bede, the most learned man of Western Europe in his day, was sent to the monastery of Wearmouth in 680 at the age of seven. About 685 he went to nearby Jarrow, where he spent the rest of his life. His many works were written from 703 until his death in 735.

Bede's *Lives of the Abbots* of the two united monasteries of Wearmouth and Jarrow describe the moment when Gregory the Great's mission began to make a serious impact on Northumbria. The decision taken at Whitby was implemented mainly by three men, Theodore of Tarsus, Archbishop of Canterbury (669–90), Wilfrid of Ripon (d. 709), and Benedict Biscop, the founder of Bede's monasteries. Theodore reorganized the Church in England and bound it closely to Rome. Wilfrid, by his liberal founding of monasteries, encouraged learning in Northern England. But it was Biscop who really introduced Roman monasticism into Northumbria, where Irish monasticism had existed since 635.

Biscop's creation of stone buildings, with glass and pictures, in a land where royal palaces were built of wood, certainly impressed Northumbrians. His great contribution for the future was his importation of large libraries. This at once placed the Anglo-Saxon Church in a privileged position with respect not only to Ireland but to most of Western Europe.[2] Biscop greatly helped to inspire a civilization blending Celtic, Anglo-Saxon, and Roman influences. Stone churches, carved crosses, and illuminated manuscripts of great beauty show the level this civilization reached. Very rapidly, too, there developed in England a new ecclesiastical Latin, which in Bede attains almost classical purity. Bede's *Lives* stand out among contemporary lives of saints for their factual and yet, at times, poetic account of life in Biscop's monasteries: miracle stories are—astonishingly for the time—entirely absent. Only two or three generations separate Biscop's death (690) from Bede's *Letter* to his former pupil, Bishop Egbert of York (734), but the idyllic age has gone.

Bede's writings reveal some of the ways England was converted. The people were swayed by their rulers, by miracles wrought by saints, living or dead, by legends, by feats of asceticism, by simple catechesis, by church chant, by images such as Augustine brought with him in 597 (Bede, *History*, I, 25). The general result may be called more collective than individual conversion and education in Christianity. Bede was less interested, however, in describing the actual situation than in recommendations for its improvement. His aim was

---

1. Bede, *A History of the English Church and People*, trans. Leo Shirley-Price (Baltimore, Md., 1965).
2. See M. L. W. Laistner, in *Bede*, ed. A. Hamilton Thompson (Oxford, 1935).

the sanctification of the individual Christian. Egbert took up some of his heritage. Under him York replaced Wearmouth-Jarrow as a center of studies: from there came Alcuin, the leading scholar of the Carolingian Renaissance. But Bede's proposals for church reform do not seem to have been carried into effect.

THE NECESSARY METHODS

Pope Gregory the Great, *Epistle* XI, 56, trans. J. Barmby, "A Select Library of Nicene and Post-Nicene Fathers, Second Series," XIII (Oxford and New York, 1898), pp. 84–85.

To Mellitus, Abbot in France [on the way to England, 601].

Since the departure of our congregation, which is with you, we have been in a state of great suspense from having heard nothing of the success of your journey. But when Almighty God shall have brought you to our most reverend brother the Bishop Augustine, tell him that I have long been considering with myself about the case of the Angli; to wit, that the temples of idols in that nation should not be destroyed, but that the idols themselves that are in them should be. Let blessed water be prepared, and sprinkled in these temples, and altars constructed, and relics deposited, since, if these same temples are well built, it is needful that they should be transferred from the worship of idols to the service of the true God; that, when the people themselves see that these temples are not destroyed, they may put away error from their heart, and, knowing and adoring the true God, may have recourse with the more familiarity to the places they have been accustomed to. And, since they are wont to kill many oxen in sacrifice to demons, they should have also some solemnity of this kind in a changed form, so that on the day of dedication, or on the anniversaries of the holy martyrs whose relics are deposited there, they may make for themselves tents of the branches of trees around these temples that have been changed into churches, and celebrate the solemnity with religious feasts. Nor let them any longer sacrifice animals to the devil, but slay animals to the praise of God for their own eating, and return thanks to the Giver of all for their fullness, so that, while some joys are reserved to them outwardly, they may be able the more easily to incline their minds to inward joys. For it is undoubtedly impossible to cut away everything at once from hard hearts, since one who strives to ascend to the highest place must needs rise by steps or paces, and not by leaps. Thus to the people of Israel in Egypt the Lord did indeed make Himself known; but still He reserved to them in His own worship the use of the sacrifices which they were accustomed to offer to the devil, enjoining them to immolate animals in sacrifice to Himself; to the end that, their hearts being changed, they should omit some things in the sacrifice and retain others, so that, though the animals were the same as what they had been accustomed to offer, nevertheless, as they immolated them to God and not to idols, they should be no longer the same sacrifices. This then it is necessary for Your Love to say to our aforesaid brother, that he, being now in that country, may consider well how he should arrange all things.

THE IMPLANTING OF ROMAN MONASTICISM IN NORTHUMBRIA

Bede, *Vita Beatorum Abbatum* (c. 730), I, 1–11, ed. C. Plummer, *Venerabilis Baedae Opera historica*, I (Oxford, 1896), pp. 364–76.

1. The devoted servant of Christ Biscop, surnamed Benedict, by God's aid, built a monastery in honor of the Most Blessed Prince of the Apostles, Peter, by the mouth of the River Wear, on the north side, with the aid of the Venerable and Most Pious King of that people, Ecgfrith, who gave the land. Benedict carefully governed this monastery for sixteen years [674–90] with the same devotion with which he had founded it, among innumerable labors in journeys and many illnesses. To use the words of the Blessed Pope Gregory [I], in which he praises the life of an abbot with the same surname: "There was a man of venerable life, Benedict by name and grace, with the heart of an old man from his boyhood up, surpassing his age by his customs, keeping his soul from any pleasure" (*Dialogues*, II, 1). Biscop was born of a noble family among the Angles but, with no less nobility of soul, he was raised up to merit forever the company of the angels. When he was a thegn of King Oswiu and received, by his gift, a grant of land corresponding to his rank, being about 25 years old, he despised that transitory possession so as to acquire eternal good. He disdained earthly service, with its corruptible reward, that, serving the True King, he might deserve to enjoy an eternal kingdom in the heavenly city. He left his house, his parents, and country for Christ and the Gospel, that he might receive a hundredfold and possess eternal life (see Matthew 19:29). He refused to enter on a carnal wedding that, shining with the glory of virginity, he might follow the Lamb in celestial kingdoms (see Apocalypse 14:4). He would not procreate mortal children of the flesh for he was predestined by Christ to bring up for Him in spiritual doctrine immortal sons for heavenly life.

2. So, leaving his country, he traveled to Rome [in 653] and took care to visit and adore the places where the bodies of the Blessed Apostles [Peter

and Paul] lie, with love of whom he had always burned. Soon returned home, he did not cease to love, venerate, and diligently proclaim to whom he could the ordinances of ecclesiastical life he had seen. At that time Alchfrith, the son of the foresaid King Oswiu, also intending to go to Rome to worship at the Apostles' shrines, took Biscop as his companion on the journey. When the prince's father recalled him and made him live in his country and kingdom, Biscop, as a young man of good native qualities, at once finished the journey he had begun, returning to Rome with great speed, at the time of Pope Vitalian [657–72]. Having, as on his first visit, drunk not a little of the sweetness of saving doctrine, departing after a few months from Rome he arrived at the Island of Lérins [off Southern France], and there joined the company of monks, received the tonsure, and, marked with the vow of a monk, observed regular discipline with due care. After two years' training there in the monastic life, he was again overcome by love for Blessed Peter, Prince of the Apostles, and decided to revisit the City made sacred by the presence of his body.

3. Not long after, with the arrival of a merchant ship, he satisfied his wish. But at that time Ecgberht, King of the Kentish, had sent from Britain a man by name of Wighard, elected to the episcopal office, who had been well trained in all ecclesiastical discipline in Kent by Roman disciples of the Blessed Pope Gregory. The King wished him to be ordained bishop at Rome so that, having a bishop of his race and tongue, he and the peoples under him might be more perfectly instructed in the language and mysteries of the Faith, since they would receive these things not through an interpreter but through the tongue and hand of one of their own race and tribe. But this Wighard, coming to Rome, fell ill with all his companions and died before he could receive the rank of bishop. The Apostolic Pope [Vitalian], lest this religious embassy should fail to attain its object by the death of the ambassadors, took counsel and chose from among his clerics, to send as Archbishop to Britain, one Theodore [of Tarsus], a man learned both in secular and ecclesiastical philosophy, and this in both languages, Greek and Latin, giving him Abbot Hadrian, a man as active and prudent as himself, as colleague and counselor. And since the Pope perceived the Venerable Benedict would be wise, industrious, religious, and noble, he commended the ordained bishop and all his companions to him, and ordered him to give up the pilgrimage he had taken up for Christ, and, in consideration of a higher good, to return to his country, taking with him the teacher of truth whom England was earnestly seeking. He could serve him on the journey or during his teaching there as at once interpreter and guide. Benedict did as the Pope commanded. They came to Kent [669] and were received most kindly. Theodore ascended the episcopal see [of Canterbury]. Benedict took over the rule

of the monastery of the Blessed Apostle Peter, of which the foresaid Hadrian was later made Abbot.

4. When Benedict had ruled the monastery for two years, starting on his third journey from Britain to Rome [671], he completed it with his usual success and brought back with him not a few books on all branches of divine learning, either bought or given him by his friends. At Vienne, on his way back, he recovered the books he had bought there and lent to friends. Arriving in Britain, he thought he should confer with Cenwalh, King of the West Saxons, whose friend he had been and who had helped him. But when Cenwalh was removed at that time by a premature death [672], Benedict, turning his steps at last to his native race and the land where he was born, went to Ecgfrith, the King of the region across the Humber [Northumbria]. He recounted all he had done since he left his country as a young man. He did not conceal the desire for religion which consumed him; he set out what he had learnt of ecclesiastical and monastic observance at Rome or anywhere about, and revealed the quantity of holy books and relics of the Blessed Apostles or Martyrs of Christ he had brought with him. He found such gracious friendship in the King that he at once gave Benedict 70 hides of royal land and commanded him to build a monastery there to the first pastor of the Church. This was done, as I recalled in the prologue, at the mouth of the River Wear, on the north side, 674 years from the Incarnation of the Lord, in the Second Indiction, in the Fourth Year of the rule of King Ecgfrith.

5. Not more than one year after the monastery was founded, Benedict crossed the ocean to Gaul [675]. He sought, found, and brought back with him masons who could build a stone church for him, according to the Roman manner which he always loved. He displayed such zeal in the work, for the love of Blessed Peter, in whose honor it was done, that within a year from the laying of the foundations the roofs were on and you could see the solemnity of the Mass celebrated there. As the work grew to completion he sent messengers to Gaul to bring back makers of glass, craftsmen unknown to Britain until then, to make the windows of the church, of its portico and clerestory. This was done; they came; they not only completed the work Benedict wanted but taught Angles the knowledge of this craft, one very fit for the lamps of the church and its cloisters, and for many kinds of vessels. But since Benedict could not find at home the holy vessels and vestments which were needed for the ministry of the altar and the church, this religious purchaser took care to bring them from across the sea.

6. When he had set up the monastery according to rule, Benedict, tireless in providing for his church, so as to obtain for it from Rome and its region the ornaments and books which could not be found even in Gaul,

undertook a fourth journey [from Britain, 678?] and returned laden [from Rome] with a much more copious burden of spiritual goods than before. First of all, because he brought back an innumerable supply of books of every kind; secondly, abundant grace in relics of the Blessed Apostles and Martyrs of Christ for the profit of many churches of the Angles. Thirdly, because he introduced into his monastery the order of chanting, of singing the psalms, and of ministering in church according to the Roman manner, having asked and received, from Pope Agatho, John, Archchanter of the Church of the Blessed Apostle Peter and Abbot of the Monastery of Blessed Martin, whom he brought, a Roman to the Angles, as the future master of his monastery in Britain. When John arrived he not only handed on by oral teaching to his students of ecclesiastical things what he had learnt at Rome but also left not a few directions in writing, which are preserved in the library of the monastery to the present day for the sake of his memory. Fourthly, Benedict brought no mean gift, a letter-privilege from the Venerable Pope Agatho, received by the license and consent and at the desire and wish of King Ecgfrith, by which the monastery Benedict had made was rendered safe and free forever from all external attack. Fifthly, Benedict brought back pictures of the images of the saints for the adornment of the Church of the Blessed Apostle Peter which he had constructed, that is an image of the Blessed Mother of God and Ever Virgin Mary, and also [images] of the Twelve Apostles, with which to adorn the church's arch, stretching a board from wall to wall; images of the Gospel story with which to decorate the south wall of the church; images of the visions of the Apocalypse of Blessed John, with which to adorn the north wall—so that those entering the church (even all those who were illiterate), wherever they turned, should either see the gracious aspect of Christ and His Saints, although only in images, or should recall more attentively the grace of the Lord's Incarnation [through the representations of the Gospel story], or, having the separation [of men] at the Last Judgment as if before their eyes, should remember to examine themselves more strictly.

7. Therefore, King Ecgfrith, very pleased by the virtue, industry, and devotion of Venerable Benedict, seeing that the land which he had given him to build the monastery had been well given and had borne fruit, added a gift of 40 hides more. There, a year later, Benedict sent about seventeen monks under Ceolfrid as abbot and presbyter, and, with the advice or rather the command of the foresaid King Ecgfrith, he built [at Jarrow] a monastery of Blessed Paul the Apostle, on the condition that both places should always preserve peace and concord, friendship and kindness, so that, as a body cannot be separated from its head, by which it breathes, and the head cannot forget the body, without which it could not exist, in the same way no one

should attempt to divide one from the other these monasteries joined in the brotherly association of the two chief apostles. Now this Ceolfrid, whom Benedict made abbot, had been in every way his most energetic assistant from the very first beginnings of the earlier monastery, and had gone with him to Rome at a suitable time, both to learn what was necessary and to worship. At the same time Benedict, choosing the presbyter Eosterwine abbot from the monastery of Blessed Peter, gave him that monastery [Wearmouth] to rule, so that, as Benedict could not bear the labor alone, he might support it better in the company of his beloved fellow soldier. Nor let it seem strange to anyone that one monastery should have two abbots at the same time. This was done because of Benedict's frequent journeys for the monastery's good, his frequent journeys across the sea, and the uncertainty of his return. For history relates that the Most Blessed Apostle Peter instituted two bishops at Rome under him to rule the Church, because of necessity. And the great Abbot Benedict himself, as the Blessed Pope Gregory writes, set twelve abbots over his disciples, as he considered useful, without any detriment to brotherly love but to its increase.

8. Therefore, Eosterwine took on the charge of ruling the monastery [of Wearmouth], the ninth year after its foundation [682], and held it for four years, until his death. He was a man noble in the world but he used his rank not as an occasion for boasting, as some do, and of despising others, but turned it to a greater nobility of soul, as it is right for God's servant to do. He was indeed a cousin of his Abbot Benedict, through his father, but such was the noble character of both of them that this worldly nobility was esteemed as nothing, so that neither did Eosterwine enter the monastery to seek some honor above others, because of his blood relationship to Benedict or his noble rank, nor did Benedict think of offering it to him [for such reasons], but the young man, eating out of the same plate as his brethren, took delight in observing regular discipline in all things. And indeed, when he was a thegn of King Ecgfrith, he had abandoned secular affairs once for all, laid down his arms, and assumed spiritual service. He continued so humble, so like to the other brethren, that, joyful and obedient in all the work of the monastery, he rejoiced to winnow and thresh with them, to milk ewes and cows, to work in the bakery, the garden, the kitchen. And when he had assumed the name and rank of abbot, he commanded all men in the same spirit as before, according to what a certain wise man said: "They have made you ruler, be not puffed up but act towards them as if one of them" (Ecclesiasticus 32:1), gentle, kind, and affable to all. But when he found it opportune he corrected sinners with regular discipline, but more by careful admonition, sprung of his great natural affection, so that no one wanted to sin and cloud the most clear light of his abbot's countenance by the shadow

of his instability. In looking after the monastery's affairs he would often slightly diverge from his course to where he found the brothers working; he used to join their work at once, either taking the plough's handle to guide its course, or shaping iron with a hammer, or shaking a winnowing fork, or something of the kind. For he was a young man, both strong of body and soft of speech, but joyful of soul, generous in his gifts, and handsome in appearance. He always ate the same food as the other brothers, in the same building with them, and slept in the same common dormitory as before he was abbot, so that even when seized by disease and already aware by certain signs of his coming death, he still remained two days in the brothers' dormitory. For the last five days until the hour of his departure he remained in a more private building. Coming out from there one day and sitting in the open, he called all the brothers to him, and, as they were weeping for the departure of such a Father and shepherd, out of his merciful nature he gave them all the kiss of peace. He died on [March 6] at night, the brothers occupied in the psalmody of Matins. He was 24 years old when he came to the monastery; he lived there twelve years, seven as presbyter, for four of which he ruled the monastery, and so, "leaving earthly limbs and dying members" (see Virgil, *Aeneid*, VI, 732) he sought the heavenly kingdom.

9. Now we have briefly spoken of the life of the Venerable Eosterwine, let us return to the order of our narrative. When Benedict had made him abbot of the monastery of the Blessed Apostle Peter [Wearmouth] and Ceolfrid of the monastery of Blessed Paul [Jarrow], not long after, hastening to Rome from Britain for the fifth time [c. 684–86] he returned, as always, enriched with innumerable gifts for the churches, with a great supply of sacred volumes indeed, but, as before, with no less a quantity of holy images. For it was then that he brought back the pictures of the Lord's history, to place around the whole church of the Blessed Mother of God which he made in the larger monastery [Wearmouth]. He also displayed images to adorn the monastery and church of Blessed Paul the Apostle [Jarrow], representing extremely well the harmony of the Old and New Testaments, for instance pictures of Isaac carrying the wood with which he was to be sacrificed (see Genesis 22:6) and the Lord also carrying the Cross on which He was to suffer were placed close together, one above the other. Again he compared the Son of Man raised upon the Cross to the Serpent raised by Moses in the desert (Numbers 21:9; see John 3:14). He brought, among other things, two silk palls of incomparable artistry, with which he later bought from King Aldfrith and his counselors (for he found Ecgfrith already slain when he returned) three hides of land south of the River Wear, beside its mouth.

10. It is true that with the joy he brought with him he found sadness in the house. The Venerable Presbyter Eosterwine, whom Benedict had made

abbot before he set out, had already left the world together with a large part of the company committed to him, because of a plague raging everywhere. But there was the consolation that in the place of Eosterwine he found the deacon Sigfrid, a man equally venerable and gentle, had already been substituted by the joint election of his brothers and his co-abbot Ceolfrid. He was a man well trained in the knowledge of the Scriptures, adorned with excellent customs, possessing a marvelous power of abstinence, but greatly hindered in sustaining the strength of his spirit by his bodily weakness, laboring under a noxious and incurable lung illness in his attempts to preserve the innocence of his heart.

11. And not long after Benedict also began to be wearied by the assault of illness. That the virtue of patience might be added, to give conclusive proof of such great zeal for religion, Divine Mercy laid them both up in bed by temporal illness that, after sickness had been conquered by death, God might restore them with the endless rest of heavenly peace and light. For both Sigfrid, punished, as we said, by long internal suffering, drew toward his last day, and Benedict, during three years, gradually became so paralyzed that all his lower limbs were quite dead, only his upper parts, without which man cannot live, were preserved, to exercise him in the virtue of patience. Both men sought in their suffering always to give thanks to their Creator, and always to be occupied with the praises of God and with teaching the brethren. Benedict was often active in encouraging the brothers who came to him to keep the Rule he had instituted. "For do not think," he said, "that I set forth the decrees I gave you untaught, out of my own heart. For all the best things I found in seventeen different monasteries in my long and frequent journeys to and fro I learnt to know and I have given them to you to observe for your advantage." He commanded that the splendid and plentiful library which he had brought from Rome, and which was necessary for the teaching of the church, should be carefully preserved entire, not ruined through neglect or dispersed abroad. He also used to repeat carefully this command to his monks, that, in choosing an abbot, they should not think of looking for nobility of descent but rather for probity of life and doctrine. "And indeed," he said, "I tell you that in comparison of the two evils, it is much more tolerable to me that all this place, where I have built a monastery, should be reduced, if God so chooses, into eternal solitude, than that my brother in the flesh, whom we know has not entered the way of truth, should succeed me in ruling here as abbot. And so always take care, brethren, not to seek a Father for yourselves according to descent or from outside [the monastery]. But, following the Rule of the great Abbot Benedict [of Monte Cassino, *Regula*, 64] and what our Privilege decrees, inquire by common counsel in your congregation who, by the merit of his life and wisdom of his

doctrine is found more fit and worthy to fulfill such a ministry, and whoever you all unanimously, after a loving inquiry, know and choose as the best; seeking out the bishop ask him to confirm him for you as abbot with the usual blessing. For those who, in the carnal order, procreate fleshly sons, must look for fleshly and earthly heirs for their carnal and earthly inheritance. But those who procreate spiritual sons to God by the spiritual seed of the Word, all they do must be spiritual. Let them think him the greater among their spiritual children who is more fully endowed with spiritual grace, as earthly parents, when they divide their property, usually consider the child born first the head of the rest and prefer him to the others."

NORTHUMBRIA IN 734: THE NECESSITY TO GO DEEPER

Bede, *Epistula ad Ecgbertum Episcopum* [of York], ed. Plummer, I, pp. 405, 408–23.

1. To the Most Beloved and Most Reverend Bishop Egbert, Bede, servant of Christ, sends greeting.

I remember that last year, when I spent some days in your monastery with you for the purpose of study, you said that you wished, when you came there again this year, to converse with me on our common interests in learning. If, by God's Will, that could have been, there would have been no need to write to you now, since I could more freely, in private conversation, have put forward my thoughts on whatever I wanted or thought necessary to say. But since this cannot be, as you know, my attack of bodily infirmity preventing it, I have however tried to do what I could in brotherly response to your affection, sending in writing what I was unable to convey in speech at my coming. And I beg you, by the Lord, not to see in this letter a sign of arrogance but rather a true offering of humility and devotion. . . .

5. Since the regions which are under your diocese are too large for you to be able to visit them all yourself, even in a year, and to preach the Word of God in each village and hamlet, it is very necessary for you to take on many helpers in the sacred work, that is by ordaining presbyters and choosing teachers, who shall be active in preaching God's Word in each village and consecrating the Heavenly Mysteries, and especially in baptizing, when occasion shall arise. In this preaching to the people I consider that what you should most of all insist on is that you should engrave in the memory of all men under your charge the Catholic Faith, which is contained in the Symbol [Creed] of the Apostles, and the Lord's Prayer, which the Holy Gospel teaches us. And indeed all who have learnt to read Latin have certainly also

learnt these things perfectly, but make the uneducated, that is those who only know their own language, learn these things in their own tongue and repeat them often. This should be done not only with laymen, that is those still living a secular life, but also with clerics or monks who are ignorant of the Latin language. And so the whole company of the faithful may learn how they should believe, and, how, by firm belief, to protect and arm themselves against the attacks of unclean spirits, and the whole choir of God's worshipers may know what should most of all be sought from the Divine Mercy. Because of this I have often given to many uneducated clergy these two things, that is the Creed and Lord's Prayer, translated into the English language. For the Holy Bishop Ambrose, speaking of Faith, admonishes that the faithful should always repeat the words of the Creed at the office of Matins, and thus fortify themselves as with a spiritual antidote against the Devil's poison, which he may have cast at them with malignant craft by day or night. Our own custom of constant prayer and genuflexion has taught us to repeat the Lord's Prayer often.

6. If your pastoral authority in ruling and feeding Christ's sheep achieves the things we have suggested, it cannot be said how great a heavenly reward you will have prepared for yourself in the future from the Shepherd of shepherds. By as much as you find fewer examples of this most holy work among the bishops of our race, by so much you will receive higher rewards for your singular merit, since, moved by fatherly piety and concern, you will have kindled the people of God, by frequent repetition of the Creed and the Lord's Prayer, to knowledge, love, hope, faith, and searching after the heavenly gifts which both set forth. And so, on the contrary, if you fulfill the business given you by the Lord less diligently, you will have your part in the future with the wicked and idle servant because you have withheld the talent [given you] (see Matthew 25:26, 30), most especially if you dare to require and take temporal goods from those to whom you are shown not to have given heavenly gifts in return. For when the Lord, sending His disciples out to preach, said: "As you go, preach, saying the Kingdom of Heaven is at hand" (Matthew 10:7), He added a little later: "Freely you have received, freely give: do not own gold or silver" (ibid. 8–9). If, therefore, He ordered them to preach the Gospel freely and did not allow them to take gold or silver or any temporal reward from those to whom they preached, what peril, I ask you, threatens those who behave in a contrary manner?

7. Notice what a grave crime they commit who both most diligently require earthly gain from their hearers, and do not attempt to spend any pains on their eternal salvation, by preaching, exhorting, or reproving. Most Beloved Bishop, weigh this carefully and with close attention. For we have heard and rumor is that there are many small towns and villages of our race

in inaccessible mountains and wooded valleys, where for many years no bishop has been seen, who might perform some episcopal act or confer some heavenly grace. However, not one of these places can be immune from paying tribute to the bishop. Nor is the bishop alone lacking in such places, to confirm the baptized by laying on of hands, but any teacher, who might teach them either the truths of the Faith or the difference between good and evil actions. And so it is that some bishops not only do not preach or confirm without charge but even, what is worse, having taken money from their hearers—which the Lord forbade them to do—disdain to exercise the work of preaching, which the Lord commanded. [1 Samuel 12:2–4 and Psalm 99:6–7 cited.]

8. For if we believe and confess that some advantage is conferred on the faithful by the laying on of hands, by which the Holy Spirit is received, it follows, on the contrary, that this advantage is lacking to those who have not received confirmation. Who does this deprivation of good more clearly point at than the very bishops, who promise to be the rulers of men, when they either neglect them or are unable to fulfill the duty of their spiritual office toward them? The whole cause of this crime is nothing more than avarice. The Apostle disputing against this, in whom Christ spoke, said: "The root of all evils is greed" (1 Timothy 6:10). And again: "Neither shall the avaricious possess the Kingdom of God" (1 Corinthians 6:10). For when a bishop, drawn by love of money, has taken under his nominal rule a greater number of people than he can in any way, in a whole year, travel through or round and preach to, he is shown to be the cause of fatal danger both to himself and to those over whom he is falsely called prelate.

9. In suggesting these things briefly, Beloved Bishop, to Your Holiness on the calamity under which our race so wretchedly suffers, I beg you earnestly that what you perceive to be most wrongly done, you attempt to bring back, as far as you can, to the right norm. For you have, I believe, a most ready helper in such a just work, namely King Ceolwulf, who for his inborn love of religion, will at once both attempt to give steady assistance to what belongs to the rule of piety, and, most of all, aid the completion of those good things which you, his most beloved kinsman, have begun. On this account I wish you to admonish him carefully, so that in your days you see that the state of the Church of our race is improved from what it has been. This cannot be done in any better way, as it seems to me, than if more bishops are consecrated for our race, and we follow the example of the lawgiver [Moses], who, when he could not alone sustain the disputes and burden of the people of Israel, chose, with the help of Divine counsel, and consecrated 70 elders, by whose efforts and aid he could more freely bear the burden imposed on him

(see Numbers 11:16–17). For who cannot see how much better it would be to divide such an enormous weight of ecclesiastical rule among a number of men, who could bear it more easily, when it was divided, than for one man to be oppressed under a load which he cannot carry? For the Holy Pope Gregory [the Great], too, when he sent letters to the Most Holy Archbishop Augustine [of Canterbury], on the faith of our race (which was still laid up for the future in Christ), decreed that twelve bishops should be ordained here [in Northern England], after [our ancestors] had been converted. Among them the Bishop of York should be Metropolitan, receiving his pallium from the Apostolic See. I wish Your Holy Paternity to seek now earnestly to carry into effect this number of bishoprics, with the aid of the foresaid most pious King, beloved of God, so that, there being enough masters, the Church of Christ may be more perfectly grounded in those things that pertain to the care of holy religion. We know indeed that by the carelessness of preceding kings many most foolish donations have been made, so that it is not easy to find a vacant place where a new episcopal see can be set up.

10. On this account I would consider it useful, after holding a greater counsel and obtaining its agreement, that, by simultaneous episcopal and royal edicts, some site of a monastery should be sought out, where an episcopal see could be created. And lest perhaps the abbot or monks attempt to go against this decree and resist it, they should be given license to elect one of their number to be ordained bishop and have the episcopal charge of the adjacent places, which belong to the same diocese, as well as of the monastery itself. Or, if perhaps a man fit to be ordained bishop cannot be found in that monastery, still, according to the canonical statutes, the choice of the bishop of the diocese shall rest with the monks. If, with the Lord's aid, you carry out what we suggest I think that you will very easily obtain that, in accordance with the decrees of the Apostolic See, the Church of York shall have a Metropolitan Bishop. And if it is found necessary that a monastery, in order to sustain a bishopric, should have some increase in its lands and possessions, there are innumerable places, as we all know, most absurdly bearing the name of monasteries, but having nothing at all of monastic life. Of these I wish some to be transferred, by synodical authority, from luxury to chastity, from vanity to truth, from the intemperance of the stomach and gullet to continence and piety of heart, and to be used to assist the episcopal see which shall be newly created.

11. And since there are very many large places of this sort, which, as is popularly said, are of no use to God or men, because, that is, neither is regular [monastic] life observed there, according to God, nor are these places

held by soldiers or thegns of the secular powers, to defend our race from the barbarian [Picts], if anyone, to meet our present needs, set up an episcopal see in these same places, he will not be held guilty of betrayal of trust but rather to have done a good deed. For how can it be thought a sin if the unjust judgments of princes are corrected by the just judgment of better princes, and the lying pen of wicked scribes be effaced by the prudent sentence of wise priests, and reduced to nothing? [This would be] according to the example of Sacred History, which, when describing the times of the kings of Judah from David and Solomon to the last King Zedekiah, designates indeed some of them as religious men but many as reprobates, and, by turn about, now the impious reject the deeds of the good rulers, who preceded them, now, on the contrary, the just, as was right, by the help of God's Spirit, by the holy prophets and priests corrected most earnestly the wicked actions of the impious who preceded *them*, according to the Blessed Isaiah, commanding and saying: "Loose the contracts of exchanges made by force. Set free the oppressed and break every unjust agreement" (58:8). Following this example, your Holiness, together with the religious King of our race, should tear up the irreligious and wicked acts and writings of your predecessors, and provide for those things which may be of advantage to our province, either to God's service or according to the world, lest either, religion ceasing in our time, the love and fear of our inward judge should disappear, or, the number of our worldly forces sinking, there are none who can protect our borders from barbarian attack. It is disgraceful to have to say this but, as you yourself know very well, men who are entirely ignorant of monastic life have taken control of so many places, under the *name* of monasteries, that there is no place at all where the sons of nobles or of veteran soldiers can receive land. And so, when they have become men, they remain idle and unmarried, without any intention of living continently, and, on this account, either, crossing the sea, leave their Fatherland, for which they should fight, or, more impudently and criminally, those who have no intention of living chastely serve luxury and fornication, and do not abstain from the very virgins consecrated to God.

12. But others, by a still more serious sin, although themselves laymen and with no training in the monastic life or love of it, giving money to kings, buy lands for themselves, under the pretext of constructing monasteries, where they may more freely give rein to lust. Moreover they have these lands assigned in royal edicts as their hereditary possession, and have these letters of their privileges confirmed, as if really worthy of God, by the subscription of bishops, abbots, and secular powers. And so, having usurped hamlets or villages for themselves, free from now on from both divine and

human service, they only serve their own desires, laymen in command of monks. But in fact they do not assemble monks there but whoever they happen to find wandering about anywhere, expelled for the fault of disobedience from true monasteries, or those they succeed in luring away from their monasteries, or at least those of their hangers-on they persuade to receive the tonsure and to promise them monastic obedience. They fill the cells they build with these misshapen cohorts and, a most hideous and unheard of sight, the same men [that is, nominal abbots] now occupy themselves with their wives and with begetting children, and now, rising from their beds, busy themselves with necessary affairs within the monastic enclosure. And, with similar impudence, they acquire places for their wives, to build monasteries, as they say, and, with equal stupidity, these women allow themselves, though lay women, to be rulers of Christ's handmaids. The common saying fits them well, that wasps can indeed build nests but they do not store honey there but rather poison.

13. Thus, for about thirty years, that is from the time King Aldfrith was taken from human things [705], our province has been out of its senses with this insane error. There has scarcely been one reeve who has not, during his office, bought a "monastery" of this kind, and has not bound his wife at the same time with equal guilt in this noxious traffic. This most evil custom prevailing, the very thegns and servants of the king have had their hands deep in it. And so, by a perversion of right order, there are innumerable men to be found who call themselves at the same time abbots and reeves or thegns or servants of the king, who, as laymen, even if they could learn something of monastic life (not by practicing it but by hearing about it) still have no part of the character or profession which should *teach* it. And indeed such men, as you know, receive the tonsure suddenly, of their own pleasure, and, by their own judgment, from laymen are made, not monks, but abbots. But since they are shown not to possess either the knowledge [of monastic life] nor the zeal [necessary for it], what is fit for them but the Gospel curse: "If the blind leads the blind, both will fall into a ditch" (Matthew 15:14)? This blindness could surely be brought within some bounds and be curbed by regular discipline and driven far from the confines of Holy Church by episcopal and synodical authority, if the bishops themselves were not known rather to assist and agree with crimes of this kind. They not only do not seek to break such unjust decrees by just decisions but, as we said, are rather active in confirming them by their subscriptions, the same greed inspiring them to confirm the evil documents which impels the buyers to establish "monasteries" of this kind.

I could tell you many more things in this letter of these and similar transgressions by which our province is most wretchedly plagued, if ; did not know that you knew these things very well. For neither have I written thus as if to teach you things you did not already know but so as to advise you by a friendly exhortation to correct errors which you knew very well with the greatest possible zeal and diligence.

14. And again and again I earnestly beg and implore you in the Lord that you carefully protect the flock committed to you from the assault of ravening wolves. Remember you are not appointed to be a mercenary but a shepherd who displays his love for the Supreme Shepherd by careful pasturing of his sheep, and is ready, if need be, with the blessed Prince of the Apostles, to lay down his life for his flock. I earnestly beg you, beware, lest, when the same Prince of the Apostles and the other leaders of the faithful flocks offer the great fruit of their pastoral care to Christ in the Day of Judgment, some part of your flock deserves to be set apart among the goats, on the left of the Judge, and to go, accursed, into eternal punishment (see Matthew 25:33, 41). But may you rather deserve to be numbered among those of whom Isaiah says: "The least will be among a thousand and a little one among a very strong nation" (60:22). For it is for you to examine most diligently what is done well and what badly in each monastery of your diocese, so that neither an abbot ignorant or contemptuous of monastic rules, nor an unworthy abbess should be set in judgment over the male and female servants of Christ. And again, lest a contemptuous and undisciplined crowd of contumacious hearers rebels against the orders of their spiritual masters. You are especially responsible because, as the report goes, you bishops are accustomed to say that what should be done in each monastery should only be inquired into and judged by bishops and not by kings or any other secular princes (unless perhaps someone in a monastery is shown to have sinned against the princes themselves). It is your duty, I say, to see that the Devil does not usurp power in places consecrated to God, that discord does not oust peace, quarrels devotion, drunkenness sobriety, fornication and murder charity and chastity. Let there be none found among you of whom it may be rightly inquired and said: "I saw the wicked buried, who, when they lived, were in the holy place, and were praised in the city, as though they were men of just works" (Ecclesiastes 8:10).

15. It is also necessary for you to take due care of those who are still encompassed in the life of the world. As we advised you at the beginning of this letter [see 5 above], remember to give them enough teachers of salvation and make the people learn, among other things, by which works to please God most and from what sins those who wish to please God should

abstain; with what sincerity of heart they must believe in God; with what devotion they should address the Divine Mercy in prayer; with what frequent diligence they have to protect themselves, and all that is theirs, with the Sign of the Lord's Cross, against the continual attacks of unclean spirits; how saving to every class of Christians is the daily reception of the Lord's Body and Blood, according to the practice which, you know, the Church of Christ in Italy, Gaul, Africa, Greece, and the whole East wisely follows. This form of devotion and of devout sanctification to God is so far from almost all the laity of our province and almost foreign to them—because of the neglect of their teachers—that those laymen who seem more religious do not presume to communicate in the Holy Mysteries except at the Lord's Nativity and at Epiphany and at Easter. Yet there are countless boys and girls, young men and virgins, old men and women of innocent and chaste life who, without any shadow of debate, could receive Communion every Lord's Day and also on Feasts of the Holy Apostles and Martyrs, as you yourself have seen done in the Holy Roman and Apostolic Church. Even married people, if anyone would show them the measure of continence and teach them the virtue of chastity, could freely and would willingly do the same.

16. I have taken pains, Most Holy Bishop, to set down these things briefly, both out of regard for your affection and for the general good, greatly desiring and exhorting you to try to draw our race from its ancient errors and to guide it onto a more certain and direct way of life. And if there are some men, of whatever rank or degree, who attempt to prevent and impede your good beginnings, still seek to bring your holy and virtuous intention to an assured end, remembering your heavenly reward. For I know that some will strongly oppose our exhortation, and especially those who feel that they are themselves caught up in the crimes from which we warn you to abstain, but you should remember the Apostolic reply, that: "We ought to obey God rather than men" (Acts 5:29). For God's commandment is, "Sell what you possess and give alms" (Luke 12:33), and "Unless a man renounces all he has he cannot be my disciple" (Luke 14:33). But there is a new tradition of certain men who claim to be God's servants, not only not to sell their possessions but even to acquire new ones. . . . Or perhaps we think the Apostle was deceived and wrote a lie when, admonishing us, he said: "Brethren, be not deceived," and at once added: "Neither the avaricious, nor the drunken, nor the grasping shall possess the Kingdom of God" (1 Corinthians 6:9, 10). And again: "But know this, that no fornicator or unclean or avaricious or rapacious man, which is idolatry, shall inherit in the Kingdom

of Christ and of God" (Ephesians 5:5). Therefore, when the Apostle clearly calls avarice and covetousness idolatry, how are we to think they are deceived who have either withheld their hand from subscribing to traffic in avarice, even when the king commanded it, or have put their hand to weeding out useless documents and their subscriptions?

17. . . . And if men bring forward charters drawn up in defense of their desires, and confirmed by the subscription of noble persons, I beg that you never forget the Lord's sentence, in which it is said: "Every plant which My Heavenly Father has not planted shall be rooted up" (Matthew 15:13). And indeed I wish to learn from you, Beloved Bishop, when the Lord declares and says that "the gate is wide and the way is broad that leads to perdition, and there are many who enter in there, and the gate is narrow and the way confined that leads to life, and there are few who find it" (Matthew 7:13, 14), what hope you have of the life (or eternal salvation) of those who, all their life, are known to have entered by the wide gate and broad way, and not, even in the smallest things, have opposed or refused any pleasure to their body or soul because of heavenly reward. Unless perhaps we are to believe they are absolved from their sins through alms to the poor, with which they interspersed their daily desires and delights, although the hand itself and the conscience which offers a gift to God should be clear and absolved of sin. Or indeed are we to hope they may be redeemed by others when they are already dead by the Mystery of the Holy Sacrifice [Masses for the dead], of which they, while they lived, had shown themselves to be unworthy? Or perhaps this sin of desire seems small to them? . . . May the Grace of the chief Shepherd, Most Beloved Bishop in Christ, keep you always safe for the saving feeding of His sheep. Written on the Nones of November, in the Third Indiction [November 5, 734].

D. Boniface and the Conversion of Germany

Anglo-Saxon missions to the continent of Europe built on the achievements of the Irish and of their Frankish disciples in the seventh century. This is particularly clear in Flanders.

The first effective Anglo-Saxon missionary to Flanders, Willibrord (658–719), was a disciple of Egbert, who had spent many years in Ireland. Willibrord and his band of Anglo-Saxon supporters came from Ireland to Flanders

(Bede, *History*, V, 13). They arrived there about 690, only a few years after the death of St. Amand (see B, above), and appear to have used the church Amand had set up in Antwerp. Willibrord's private liturgical calendar attests his veneration for Amand. Like Amand, Willibrord was supported by the Frankish monarchy and nobility and the papacy. The same aims and the same support continue on to Boniface, who, in his early years as a wandering monk-bishop, resembles the earlier Amand. It was his later attempts to establish new dioceses which differentiated Boniface (*c.* 675–754) from his predecessors and which lost him the support of the Frankish bishops and nobility. The Anglo-Saxons differed from the Irish and from a wandering bishop such as Amand in their success in establishing a stable episcopal hierarchy. Their methods were very close, however, to those of their predecessors.

Missionaries began by addressing themselves to the local ruler. Amand obtained a royal order enforcing Baptism on pagans. Boniface did not do this but he was protected by the Mayors of the Palace, Charles Martel and his sons, who had taken over Merovingian power. Protection was essential for missionaries who wished to cut down sacred trees, destroy idols, and pagan temples. That idols did not punish attacks on them was bound to impress pagans. (See Bishop Daniel's letter, comparable to Gregory the Great's to Mellitus.) Boniface, like Amand, ransomed prisoners and slaves, who were useful as missionaries and interpreters—although Anglo-Saxons could learn South German dialects without much difficulty, and spoke the same language as the Saxons further north.

Churches arose in pagan areas, replacing temples as meeting places for the population. Monasteries were essential as spiritual centers and as schools for native clergy. From 625 to 650 almost fifty monasteries were founded in Belgium. Boniface founded many in Germany. This vast extension of church property clearly assisted the spread of official Christianity among the dependent peasantry.

Boniface was constantly in touch with England. He relied largely on Anglo-Saxon helpers, monks, and nuns. Those who came with him trained native pupils. English convents helped provide the manuscripts Boniface needed for teaching. (See the letter to Eadburga.) Boniface had seven Anglo-Saxon bishops under him in Germany. He had found the existing native clergy hopelessly pagan and corrupt.[3]

From 722 Boniface acted as a direct agent of the papacy in Hesse and Thuringia, regions under Frankish rule but only nominally Christian. In 739–41 Boniface organized four dioceses in the independent duchy of Bavaria and established four more sees covering Hesse, Thuringia, and Franconia. As "Archbishop of East France" he presided over these eight bishoprics.

3. *The Anglo-Saxon Missionaries in Germany*, ed. C. H. Talbot (New York, 1954), contains contemporary lives and more of Boniface's letters.

When Charles Martel died in 741 his eldest son, Carloman, succeeded him in Austrasia (including Frankish Germany), his younger son, Pepin (III), in Western France. The brothers invited Boniface to restore church discipline in France as well as Germany. A series of reforming Councils and laws insisted on the re-establishment of the diocesan bishop's authority and on clerical discipline. In 751, Carloman having become a monk, Pepin III was anointed King, his dynasty formally replacing the Merovingians. Boniface performed the ceremony, which was repeated by Pope Stephen II in 754. Boniface's reforms were not fully realized in France but, by his determined loyalty to the papacy and to Roman discipline, he had established principles accepted in England; in Europe the Frankish "Landeskirche," hitherto dependent almost entirely on the local ruler, was brought into vital touch with Rome. A stable church hierarchy now existed in Germany and monastic foundations from which many other monasteries were soon founded. All this survived Boniface's martyrdom (754) in Friesland. Boniface's work ends the age that began with Clovis' conversion. With Pepin III and Charlemagne a new age begins for the Catholic Church and for Western Europe: in it the alliance between the Carolingians and the papacy, which Boniface had largely helped to forge, was to play a central role.

"The word 'Christianization' covers many and different things." To paraphrase Professor Tessier, if, by Christianization, one understands the reception of Baptism and certain ritual practices—such as attendance at Mass on certain days—then England, France, Belgium, and much of Germany were "Christianized" by 750. Bede's *Letter to Egbert* shows how limited this "Christianization" was in England. The Church's war on pagan superstitions had to continue for centuries throughout Western Europe. Boniface's monasteries were important cultural centers, but the very nature of monasticism cut monks off from the people, especially after the Carolingian reformers sharply separated monks from pastoral responsibility. An effective parish system only developed slowly in Northern Europe. But by 750 the *first* Christianization of most of Western Europe and the British Isles had been achieved and the preconditions for deeper penetration of Christianity established. The enormous losses the Latin Church had suffered to Islam since 650—North Africa and Spain—had been redeemed to an extent by the new world of Northern Europe which Clovis, Gregory the Great, and Boniface had given to Rome.

The letters given here are from *The Anglo-Saxon Missionaries in Germany*, translated and edited by C. H. Talbot. Copyright 1954 by Sheed and Ward Inc., New York, now Andrews, McMeel and Parker, Fairway, Kansas, pp. 71–72, 75–78, 84–86, 91–92, 93–95.

POPE GREGORY II COMMENDS BISHOP BONIFACE TO THE CHRISTIANS OF GERMANY (DECEMBER 1, 722)

Bishop Gregory, servant of the servants of God, to all the very reverend and holy brethren, fellow-bishops, religious priests and deacons, dukes, provosts, counts and all Christian men who fear God.

Knowing that some of the peoples in the parts of Germany that lie on the eastern bank of the Rhine have been led astray by the wiles of the devil and now serve idols under the guise of the Christian religion, and that others have not yet been cleansed by the waters of holy Baptism, but like brute beasts are blind to their Creator, we have taken great care to send the bearer of these letters, our reverend brother and fellow-bishop Boniface, into these parts to enlighten them and to preach the word of faith, so that by his preaching he may teach them the way of eternal life, and when he finds those who have been led astray from the path of true faith or been misled by the cunning of the devil he may reprove them, bring them back to the haven of salvation, instruct them in the teachings of this Apostolic See and confirm them in the Catholic Faith.

We exhort you, then, for the love of our Lord Jesus Christ and the reverence you bear to His Apostles, to support him by all the means at your disposal and to receive him in the name of Jesus Christ, according to what is written of His disciples: "He who receiveth you, receiveth me." See to it that he has all he requires; give him companions to escort him on his journey, provide him with food and drink and anything else he may need, so that with the blessing of God the work of piety and salvation committed to him may proceed without hindrance, and that you yourselves may receive the reward of your labors and through the conversion of sinners may find treasure laid up for you in heaven.

If, therefore, any man assists and gives succor to this servant of God sent by the Apostolic See for the enlightenment of the heathen, may he enjoy through the prayers of the princes of the Apostles the fellowship of the saints and martyrs of Jesus Christ.

But if (which God forbid) any man should attempt to hinder his efforts and oppose the work of the ministry entrusted to him and his successors, may he be cursed by the judgment of God and condemned to eternal damnation. . . .

CHARLES MARTEL TAKES BONIFACE UNDER HIS PROTECTION (723)

To the holy lords and apostolic fathers, bishops, dukes, counts, regents, servants, lesser officials and friends, Charles Mayor of the Palace, hearty greetings.

Let it be known that the apostolic father Bishop Boniface has come into our presence and begged us to take him under our protection. Know then that it has been our pleasure to do this.

Furthermore, we have seen fit to issue and seal with our own hand an order that wheresoever he goes, no matter where it shall be, he shall with our love and protection remain unmolested and undisturbed, on the understanding that he shall maintain justice and receive justice in like manner.

And if any question or eventuality arise which is not covered by our law, he shall remain unmolested and undisturbed until he reach our presence, both he and those who put their trust in him, so that as long as he remains under our protection no man shall oppose or do him harm. . . .

Bishop Daniel of Winchester Advises Boniface on the Method of Converting the Heathen (723–24)

To Boniface, honored and beloved leader, Daniel, servant of the people of God.

Great is my joy, brother and colleague in the episcopate, that your good work has received its reward. Supported by your deep faith and great courage, you have embarked upon the conversion of heathens whose hearts have hitherto been stony and barren; and with the Gospel as your ploughshare you have labored tirelessly day after day to transform them into harvest-bearing fields. Well may the words of the prophet be applied to you: "A voice of one crying in the wilderness, etc."

Yet not less deserving of reward are they who give what help they can to such a good and deserving work by relieving the poverty of the laborers, so that they may pursue unhampered the task of preaching and begetting children to Christ. And so, moved by affection and good will, I am taking the liberty of making a few suggestions, in order to show you how, in my opinion, you may overcome with the least possible trouble the resistance of this barbarous people.

Do not begin by arguing with them about the genealogies of their false gods. Accept their statement that they were begotten by other gods through the intercourse of male and female and then you will be able to prove that, as these gods and goddesses did not exist before, and were born like men, they must be men and not gods. When they have been forced to admit that their gods had a beginning, since they were begotten by others, they should be asked whether the world had a beginning or was always in existence. There is no doubt that before the universe was created there was no place in which these created gods could have subsisted or dwelt. And by "universe" I mean not merely heaven and earth which we see with our eyes but the whole extent of space which even the heathens can grasp in their imagination. If they maintain that the universe had no beginning, try to refute their arguments and bring forward convincing proofs; and if they persist in arguing, ask them, Who ruled it? How did the gods bring under their sway a universe that existed before them? Whence or by whom or when was the first god or goddess begotten? Do they believe that gods and goddesses still beget other gods and goddesses? If they do not, when did they cease and why? If they do, the number of gods must be infinite. In such a case, who is the most powerful among these different gods? Surely no mortal man can know. Yet man must take care not to offend this god who is more powerful than the rest. Do they think the gods should be worshiped for the sake of temporal and transitory benefits or for eternal and future reward? If for temporal benefit let them say in what respect the heathens are better off than the Christians. What do the heathen gods gain from the sacrifices if they already possess everything? Or why do the gods leave it to the whim of their subjects to decide what kind of tribute shall be paid? If they need such sacrifices, why do they not choose more suitable ones? If they do not need them, then the people are wrong in thinking that they can placate the gods with such offerings and victims.

These and similar questions, and many others that it would be tedious to mention, should be put to them, not in an offensive and irritating way but calmly and with great moderation. From time to time their superstitions should be compared with our Christian dogmas and touched upon indirectly, so that the heathens, more out of confusion than exasperation, may be ashamed of their absurd opinions and may recognize that their disgusting rites and legends have not escaped our notice.

This conclusion also must be drawn: If the gods are omnipotent, beneficent and just, they must reward their devotees and punish those who despise them. Why then, if they act thus in temporal affairs, do they spare the Christians who cast down their idols and turn away from their worship the inhabitants of practically the entire globe? And whilst the Christians are allowed to possess the countries that are rich in oil and wine and other commodities, why have they left to the heathens the frozen lands of the north, where the gods, banished from the rest of the world, are falsely supposed to dwell?

The heathens are frequently to be reminded of the supremacy of the Christian world and of the fact that they who still cling to outworn beliefs are in a very small minority.

If they boast that the gods have held undisputed sway over these people from the beginning, point out to them that formerly the whole world was given over to the worship of idols until, by the grace of Christ and through the knowledge of one God, its Almighty Creator and Ruler, it was enlightened, vivified and reconciled to God. For what does the baptizing of the children of Christian parents signify if not the purification of each one from the uncleanness of the guilt of heathenism in which the entire human race was involved? . . .

POPE GREGORY III TO BONIFACE (732)

. . . Since, as you say, you are unable to deal with all the matters involved in imparting the means of salvation to the multitudes of those who, by the grace of God, have been converted in those parts, we command you in virtue of our apostolic authority to consecrate bishops wherever the faithful have increased. This you must do in accordance with the sacred canons, choosing men of tried worth so that the dignity of the episcopate may not fall into disrepute. . . .

Those whom you say were baptized by pagans and the case is proved should be baptized again in the name of the Trinity.

You say, among other things, that some eat wild horses and many eat tame horses. By no means allow this to happen in future, but suppress it in every possible way with the help of Christ and impose a suitable penance upon offenders. It is a filthy and abominable custom.

You ask for advice on the lawfulness of making offerings for the dead. The teaching of the Church is this—that every man should make offerings for those who died as true Christians and that the priest should make a commemoration of them [at Mass]. And although all are liable to fall into sin, it is fitting that the priest should make a commemoration and intercede for them. But he is not allowed to do so for those who die in a state of sin even if they were Christians.

It is our command that those who doubt whether they were baptized or not should be baptized again, as also those who were baptized by a priest who sacrifices to Jupiter and partakes of sacrificial offerings. We decree that each one must keep a record of his consanguinity to the seventh degree.

If you are able, forbid those whose wives have died to enter into second marriages.

We declare that no one who has slain his father, mother, brother or sister can receive the Holy Eucharist except at the point of death. He must abstain from eating meat and drinking wine as long as he lives. He must fast on every Monday, Wednesday and Friday and thus with tears wash away the crime he has committed.

Among other difficulties which you face in those parts, you say that some of the faithful sell their slaves to be sacrificed by the heathen. This, above all, we urge you to forbid, for it is a crime against nature. Therefore, on those who have perpetrated such a crime you must impose a penance similar to that for culpable homicide. . . .

BONIFACE ASKS ABBESS EADBURGA TO MAKE HIM A COPY OF THE EPISTLE OF ST. PETER IN LETTERS OF GOLD (735)

To the most reverend and beloved sister, Abbess Eadburga, Boniface, least of the servants of God, loving greetings.

I pray Almighty God, the Rewarder of all good works, that when you reach the heavenly mansions and the everlasting tents He will repay you for all the generosity you have shown to me. For, many times, by your useful gifts of books and vestments, you have consoled and relieved me in my distress. And so I beg you to continue the good work you have begun by copying out for me in letters of gold the epistles of my lord, St. Peter, that a reverence and love of the Holy Scriptures may be impressed on the minds of the heathens to whom I preach, and that I may ever have before my gaze the words of him who guided me along this path. The materials [gold] needed for the copy I am sending by the priest Eoban.

Deal, then, my dear sister, with this my request as you have so generously dealt with them in the past, so that here on earth your deeds may shine in letters of gold to the glory of our Father who is in heaven. . . .

POPE GREGORY III WRITES TO BONIFACE ABOUT THE ORGANIZATION OF THE CHURCH IN BAVARIA (OCTOBER 29, 739)

To our most reverend and holy brother Boniface, Gregory servant of the servants of God.

A sentence of the teacher of all nations, the celebrated Apostle St. Paul, tells us that everything helps to secure the good of those who love God. Therefore when we learned from your report that God in His mercy had loosed a great number of the German people from the toils of paganism and had brought as many as a hundred thousand souls into the Church through your efforts and those of Prince Charles, we raised our hands in prayer and thanked God, the Giver of all good, for having opened the gates of mercy and love to make known to the West the path of salvation. Glory be to Him forever.

You tell us that you have made a journey into Bavaria and found the people there living in a manner contrary to the ordinances of the Church, and that, because they have no bishops except Vivilo, whom we consecrated some time ago, you have, with the approval of Odilo, Duke of Bavaria, and the nobles of the province, consecrated three other bishops. You say also that you have divided the province into four districts, so that each bishop may have his own diocese. In carrying out our commands and in performing the task that was enjoined upon you you have acted wisely and well.

Continue, reverend brother, to teach them the holy, Catholic and apostolic traditions of the See of Rome, so that the ignorant may be enlightened and may follow the path that leads to eternal bliss.

As to the priests whom you have found there, if the bishops who ordained them are not known to you and a doubt remains whether they were true bishops or not, let them be ordained by a bishop and fulfill their sacred charge, provided they are Catholics of blameless life, trained to the service of God, well versed in the teachings of the Church and fitted to hold office.

Those who were baptized with a formula expressed in a heathen tongue, provided their Baptism was performed in the name of the Trinity, should be confirmed with sacred chrism and the laying-on-of-hands.

Bishop Vivilo was consecrated by us. If, however, he has deviated from othodox teaching in any point, correct and instruct him according to the traditions of the Church of Rome, as you have learned them from us.

We command you to attend the council which is to be held on the banks of the Danube and, vested with Apostolic authority, to act as our representative. As far as God shall grant you strength, continue to preach the word of salvation, so that the Christian faith may increase and multiply in the name of the Lord.

You have no permission, brother, to remain in one district once your work there has been completed. Strengthen the minds of your brethren and the faithful who are scattered throughout the West and continue to preach wherever God grants you opportunity to save souls. When the need arises consecrate bishops according to canon law in your capacity as our representative, and instruct them to observe apostolic and Catholic doctrine. In this way you will assure yourself of a great reward and win over to Almighty God a perfect people. Do not shrink, beloved brother, from difficult and protracted journeys in the service of the Christian faith, for it is written that small is the gate and narrow the road that leads on to life.

Continue, then, brother, the exemplary work you have begun, so that in the day of Christ you may be entitled to say in the presence of the saints at the day of judgment: "Here stand I and these children the Lord has given me. I have not lost any of them whom thou hast entrusted to me." And again: "It was five talents thou gavest me, see how I have made profit of five talents besides." Then you will deservedly hear the voice of God saying: "Well done, my good and faithful servant: since thou hast been faithful over little things, I have great things to commit to thy charge: come and share the joy of thy Lord."

4

LITURGY: THE ORDERING OF THE CHRISTIAN COMMUNITY

THE FIFTH AND LATER CENTURIES SAW RAPID CHANGES IN THE PUBLIC WOR-
ship of Christians in the West. By about 750 different, though interrelated,
liturgies had evolved in Spain, France (the Gallican Liturgy), and Rome; all
these rites were subject to considerable influence from the Byzantine East.

The changes in the liturgy reflected the theological thinking of the time (see
p. 86, above). It is difficult to assess the impact of these changes on the laity.
By 600—at least in the more settled parts of Latin Christianity—infant Baptism had become the norm. The dismissal of adult catechumens (see the
description of the Mass, below) was now an anachronism that needed explanation. Men and women did not, as in earlier centuries, become Christians by a
conscious decision. They grew up as members of an officially Christian society
that laid much less stress on their active participation in their religion than on
adhesion to accepted norms. The Church also made little effort to simplify its
liturgy for an increasingly uneducated public. It is unlikely that the elaborate
prayers of the time were fully intelligible to ordinary Christians, who were now
often separated by screens from the clergy. Despite these difficulties, Christians
of the seventh and eighth centuries remained part of a community open to the

sacraments and teaching the clergy conveyed in the services of the Church. The use of art (see p. 151, above) and of music supplemented prayers. The evolution of ceremonial stressed the mystery and transcendence of God. Sermons emphasized the importance of performing basic duties, which included frequently visiting church or the saints' shrines (p. 63, above), and of the Church's "rites de passage," such as those for adolescence or marriage.

In an age when Latin education was increasingly confined to their ranks, the importance of the clergy in the community inevitably grew. It became necessary to regulate clerical duties. One of the attempts to do so is contained in the *Letter to Leudefred*, translated here. Formerly ascribed to Isidore of Seville (d. 636), it is now thought to have been "probably written in Visigothic territories in the late seventh or eighth century" (R. E. Reynolds). The *Letter* regulates not only the major orders (subdeacon, deacon, priest, and bishop) but the minor, which are here five in number, including the psalmist, as well as the four which became standard, the doorkeeper, acolyte, exorcist, and lector (reader). The popularity of this *Letter* in later centuries was due to its inclusion in collections of canon law. What is notable here—apart from the details on the different offices—is the elaborate chain of command established and the attempt to assign clear responsibility not only for the conduct of the liturgy, but for the general running of the urban and rural churches of the diocese. The aim was to ensure a competent and well-disciplined clergy. The *Letter* reflects an established church, rich in possessions and prepared for lawsuits. Little is said, except at the end, of the spirituality which should animate the clerical body. These ideals are more clearly expressed in a short document, kown as the Hibernian Chronological Ordinal, written about 700, either in Ireland or by an Irish pilgrim on the continent.

The Ordinal is one of a series of texts in which Christ is seen as fulfilling all the ecclesiastical grades (orders). A biblical example is provided for each grade, except for that of exorcist, where the source is probably a life of Mary Magdalen. The idea of drawing up these Ordinals was first developed in the Eastern Church and may have reached the West largely through Spain. As with grammatical treatises and biblical exegesis, so also in this field, Spain soon passed on the models it received to Ireland. While the detailed application of the idea may seem forced, it is interesting as one of the many attempts to instill the imitation of Christ. All grades of the clergy, from doorkeeper to bishop, were intended to feel their work was justified by Christ's example. Here, as with the new Penitentials (see 3, A, above) and the missionary aims expressed by Columban and Amand (3, B) the Irish infused a new spirit into the somewhat legalistic continental church.

Apart from two longer works by Isidore of Seville, the only fairly complete attempt to explain the central rite of Christianity, the Mass, which survives from this age, is to be found in the first of two *Letters* ascribed to Bishop Germanus of Paris (d. 576). In fact, the *Letters* were written in the late seventh or early eighth century and represent general Gallican usage at this time. The unknown author's aim was to bring out the inner or spiritual meaning of the liturgy. The use of allegory is constant. Modern scholars would prefer more detail on the actual conduct and contents of the liturgy of the time. The writer sketches the course of an episcopal Mass, from the antiphon sung during the bishop's entrance, through the later chants (notably the thrice repeated Greek "Aius") and biblical canticles, and the readings from the Old Testament, the Epistles and Gospels, the sermon (or the homily drawn from one of the Fathers of the Church which often replaced it), the lengthy prayers, the processions of the Gospel and Offertory, the exchange of the kiss of peace, down to the fraction of the Host, the communal recitation of the Lord's Prayer, the blessing imparted by bishop or priest, and the concluding Trinitarian chant. The exposition gives us some glimpses of how the different clerical offices, described in the *Letter to Leudefred*, actually took part in a solemn liturgy. The role of the deacon in leading prayers and dismissing catechumens becomes particularly clear. The liturgy described in the *Letter* of Pseudo-Germanus is related in some ways to the Roman rite but it is (as Quasten showed) much closer to contemporary Eastern liturgies. One may instance the use of Greek chants, the system of readings from the Old Testament as well as the New, the "Prayer" (14), which is an equivalent of the diaconal litany of the East, and especially the emphasis on processions, particularly that bearing the offerings, which are referred to as if they were already consecrated (17–18). This corresponds to the Byzantine "Great Entrance."

Much of the celebrant's role, especially the prayers of consecration (which were perhaps not said aloud) is only indicated and not described. Everything is seen from the point of view of the congregation. What was important for the writer was to explain the visible gestures and ritual of the Mass. He tries to show the connection between the Bible (the Old as much as the New Testament) and the Church of his day, and stresses the miraculous "transformation" (while the later term transubstantiation is not used, the meaning is the same) of bread and wine into the Body and Blood of Christ. Hence the insistence on the texts from John 6 and also the use of the crude legend (of Eastern origin) cited in 24a. Although the people were not frequent communicants at this time—Mass really ended with the blessing stressed in 26—the Church sought to make the Mass a central fact in their lives. It aimed at their emotions (by chants, processions, and mystical comparisons), but also at their minds. Great emphasis is laid on reading and teaching, and especially on expounding—if only, because of the lack of education of the average clergy, by using older sermons—the Bible to the people, "in clearer speech" (13).

With the directions for a papal procession translated here we move to the center of Western Christendom. The description of the procession is taken from the oldest of the *Ordines Romani*, a series of handbooks drawn up for the conduct of ritual in papal Rome. *Ordo I* was apparently composed about 700. At this time the pope still lived, in normal times, in the Lateran palace, not in the Vatican, and it was there that his treasury and vestiary were kept. It was possible for him to celebrate Mass in a different church (a "station") on all Sundays and major feasts, a practice recorded in the rubrics of the Roman Missal as it survived until recently. On Easter Sunday, as our document states, the pope celebrated Mass at one of the four great Roman basilicas, Santa Maria Maggiore. The elaborate, ritual character of the procession escorting the pope was influenced by the fact that Rome in 700 was under strong Byzantine influence. The city had a Byzantine garrison and was full of Eastern ascetics, one of whom even lived (like the Eastern stylite or pillar saints) on top of Trajan's column. The pope in 700 was the Syrian Sergius I. But despite the mounted escort and the splendor of gold and silver which made the procession a papal successor to the military triumphs of pagan Rome (cf. p. 19, above), one is struck by the relative ease with which ordinary Romans or pilgrims to Rome could approach the pope in person and present petitions to him. Thus the procession not only recalls imperial triumphs but also the simpler practice of Republican times, when the "clients" of a great man would attend his levee at dawn and then escort him through the streets of the capital.

At the moment of death, when Judgment approached and the choice between Heaven and Hell was imminent, the Church, in prayers of great beauty, invoked God's mercy and protection for the departing soul. The prayers translated here are from the Sacramentary of Gellone, which was probably written in France at the Benedictine monastery of Meaux, about 760. Parallels to these prayers exist in other older and contemporary liturgies. They have been used, with little change, by the Catholic Church down to the present day. The first two prayers were used—slightly rephrased—by Cardinal Newman in his poem, *The Dream of Gerontius*. In them, as in the exposition of the Mass which is also translated here, one sees a feeling of continuity between the Old Testament and the New. The Psalms—the most popular of all the books of the Bible—are used continually. The imagery of the Apocalypse is invoked. Perhaps it is here, in these prayers for the dying, that the Church of the eighth century stands out most clearly as a praying community, entrance into which could link the least educated peasant with the great heroes of the past, Noah and Moses, Job and Daniel, angels and martyrs. Nor were these prayers the final expression of the Church's concern for its members. After the body's death the soul could be assisted by burial beside or in one of an expanding network of rural churches. It could be helped by the prayers the dead man's relatives were exhorted to offer, and, most especially, by Masses celebrated in increasing number and on whose efficacy the greatest teacher of the age, Gregory the Great, insists most emphatically (*Dialogues*, IV, 57).

The last text translated here, the *Vision of Barontus*, is a strictly contemporary account (written probably in 679) of what a monk, who had been unconscious for twenty-four hours, recalled, when he awoke, of a visionary tour of Heaven and Hell. Barontus was a recent recruit to a monastery founded about thirty years earlier under Irish influence, St. Peter's, Longoretus (later known as St. Cyran-en-Brenne) in the diocese of Bourges, and the nearby sister foundation of Méobeque were examples of over 200 rural monasteries founded in Northern France in the seventh century (see above, 3, B, p. 139). The text as we have it was probably written by a monk of Méobeque (hence the apparent digression of chapters 5–6) but it incorporates Barontus' own story, as told by him to his brethren at Longoretus. It is written in rustic Latin, probably close to the actual speech of the time, and was intended for monks. These monks were not entirely otherworldly in their interests. Together with the stress on the Psalms and the references to the Apocalypse which recall the prayers for the dying, texts taken from Gregory the Great's *Dialogues* and from his equally popular *Homilies on the Gospels* are clearly central to the writer, but it is the actual experiences of Barontus which, it is hoped, will be even more successful in convincing monastic "unbelievers" (chaps. 6, 20).

The *Vision* is one of the earliest examples of the many descriptions of the other world which culminate in Dante's *Divine Comedy*. Barontus' vision may have been influenced by the slightly earlier *Vision* of the Irish St. Fursey (who had settled in France and died there about 650) but it is more down-to-earth. We have less spiritual teaching on the vices which take men to Hell and much more on the way a monk could "ransom" himself by almsgiving. The people Barontus meets in Paradise behave very much as a monk might imagine their doing in daily life. The question of whether to keep the church lights burning all night (using up expensive olive oil, which had to be brought from Southern France), and the need to keep tombs in church clean occupy a greater place than does doctrine. The condemnation of the last bishop of Bourges to Hell (17)—perhaps because of his opposition to the acquisition of property by Longoretus and its claims, on the Irish model, to immunity from his jurisdiction—is contrasted with the praise heaped on the present abbots of the two sister monasteries (5, 10). The earliest surviving manuscript contains some illustrations which display the battle of Saints Peter and Raphael with the demons for the soul of Barontus (St. Peter's keys—given the crucial role they play in that battle—are rightly represented in great detail). While the *Vision* indicates the hopes seventh-century men entertained of the future life, it also sheds light on the struggling but growing Christianity coming into existence by that time in the monasteries of Northern France.

THE DUTIES OF THE CLERGY

Epistula beati Isidori iunioris episcopi Spalensis eclesie ad Leudefredum episcopum Cordubensis eclesie directa [late seventh or eighth century], ed. R. E. Reynolds, *Mediaeval Studies*, 41 (1979), pp. 260–62.

When I had read Your Holiness' letters I rejoiced to hear of your good state of health. With regard to those matters which you raise, I thank God that you are concerned with the duty of pastoral care and how ecclesiastical offices are ordained. Despite the fact that you are perfectly aware of all these questions, since with paternal affection you consult me I will reply as best I can and discuss all the grades of the Church.

To the doorkeeper there belongs the [care of the] keys of the church, that he may close and open the temple of God, take care of everything inside and outside, receive the faithful and exclude the excommunicated and infidels. To the acolyte there pertains the preparation of lamps in the sanctuary, of the side tables [for Mass] and of the eucharistic chalice for the subdeacon. He is to carry the candles [during the liturgy]. The exorcist has to memorize the formulas of exorcism and lay his hand on the catechumens to be exorcised [before Baptism]. The psalmist's duty is to chant, to recite the blessings, the psalms, lauds, the responses during the Mass and whatever else belongs to the skill of the chanter. The lector [reader] has to read the lessons and [especially] those from the Prophets [of the Old Testament].

The subdeacon has to bear the chalice and paten to Christ's altar and hand them over to the deacons and assist them. He is to hold the pitcher, the aquamanile and towel, and provide water for the bishop, the priests, and deacons to wash their hands at the altar.

The deacon has to assist the priests and minister in all matters concerning Christ's Sacraments, in Baptism, in anointing, and with the paten and chalice. He has to bring the offerings to the altar and arrange them there, arrange and dress the Lord's table, carry the cross [in procession] and read aloud the Gospel and the Apostle [the Epistle]. For just as the reading of the Old Testament pertains to the readers so that of the New belongs to deacons. It is also the deacon's task to lead the prayers and recite the names [of those to be prayed for]. He is to turn men's minds to the Lord, to exhort them to pray, to call out [to catechumens to leave the church], and to announce the [kiss of] peace.

The priest has to consecrate the sacrament of the Body and Blood of the Lord at God's altar. He is to recite the prayers and bless the people.

The bishop's task is to consecrate churches, to anoint altars, to bless chrism, and to confer the offices we have mentioned. He blesses sacred virgins. While each rank has its own duty, his are general. These are the orders and duties of the clergy. The bishop's authority is distributed, however, among the offices of archdeacon, secretary, and treasurer.

The archdeacon commands subdeacons and deacons. It is for him to see that the altars are clothed by deacons, and that incense and the offerings to be taken to the altar are prepared. He is to see that the subdeacons carry out their duty of providing what is necessary for the Eucharist. The archdeacon has to select the deacon who will read the Epistle and Gospel, who will lead the prayers or responses on Sundays and feast days. He has to see to quarrels between parishioners and suggest to the bishop what churches need repair. He is to visit the parishes and enquire into the ornaments and possessions of the parish churches; all this as the bishop's deputy. He is to take to the bishop matters concerning the defense of ecclesiastical liberties. He receives the money collected in parishes and hands it over to the bishop, distributing among the clergy what is due to them. He is to inform the bishop of the misdeeds of deacons, to notify priests of fast days, and to announce fast and feast days publicly in church. When the archdeacon is absent the next senior deacon is to perform these duties.

The secretary has to direct the acolyte, exorcist, psalmist, and lector. He has to give the sign to begin the office; he is to supervise clerical morality, meditation, and action. He is to say which cleric shall recite the lessons, the blessings, psalms, lauds, offertory prayers, and responses. He is to control the order and mode of singing the psalms in choir according to the feast and the season of the year. He is to direct the way the lamps are set out. He is to inform the bishop of what repairs are needed to churches in the city and send out (by doorkeepers) the bishop's letters, informing the parishes of fast days. He is to discipline the clergy whom he discovers going astray; those he cannot emend he is to denounce to the bishop. He appoints the custodians of churches and controls their registers. When the secretary is absent his duties are to be discharged either by the next in seniority or by the most skillful in these matters.

The treasurer is to control the custodian and the doorkeeper, the preparation of incense and making of chrism. He is responsible for arranging the baptistery, for the preparation of lamps in the sanctuary, and for that of the materials for the Eucharist. The parishes are to send to him for chrism and candles. He is to accept oblations from the people for the altar and to collect candles on feast days in churches. He has charge over the ornaments and vestments of the altar and over whatever is in use in church. He is to take care of the veils and ornaments of the urban churches which are without priests. The custodian is to bring him every month whatever candles and tapers are left over in each church. He gives a quarter of these to the custodian and divides the other three-quarters equally with the secretary and the priest who celebrates Mass in the church in question.

The steward has charge of repairing and building churches, over the Church's lawsuits, over receipt of tribute and the accounts of those who bring it in. He is responsible for the lands of the Church, for its vineyards, for its possessions, for the salaries of dependent clergy, widows, and devout poor, for payments for the clothing and food of domestic clerics, servants, and craftsmen. All these things are to be done by him under the authority and at the discretion of the bishop.

These matters were either assigned by our elders to the different offices or determined in each case by local customs. Nothing here is my own idea but is either dictated by reason or sanctioned by ancient authority.

You should choose as abbot of the monastery you came from a man commended by holy life and probity of morals, in whom, when he was subject to another, no deceit was found. In such a man is grace fulfilled, as the Lord says, "Because you were faithful in a few things, I shall set you over many things" (Matthew 25:21). For the man who lived dishonestly when he was under another's rule and did not fear to defraud his brothers will commit greater sins when he is a prelate, free and in power. Of such men the Apostle says: "But you do wrong to and defraud even your brothers. Do you not know that the wicked shall not inherit the Kingdom of God?" (1 Corinthians 6:8f.). Let it be enough to say to you that you should fulfill what you think worthy of God. I do not cease to beg your Holiness to intercede for me with God that, since I have fallen by my own fault, through you I may obtain remission of my sins. Amen.

CHRIST IN THE CLERGY

The Hibernian Chronological Ordinal [about 700], ed. Roger E. Reynolds, *The Ordinals of Christ from their origins to the twelfth century* (Beiträge zur Geschichte und Quellenkunde des Mittelalters, 7) (Berlin, 1978), p. 58.

Tell me, Why did the Lord choose to be baptized by John? The answer: For four reasons. First because, being born a man, He wished to fulfill all justice and humility. Second, that John might strengthen his baptism by baptizing Christ. Third, that John might sanctify water [for Baptism]. Fourth, that no one should disdain to be baptized by his servant, since the Lord Himself was baptized by His own servant.

Tell me, How or when did Christ fulfill the seven grades [orders]? The answer. First, He fulfilled that of lector [reader], when He opened the book of the Prophet Isaiah and said, "The Spirit of the Lord is upon Me" (Luke 4:17f.). Second, he fulfilled that of exorcist, when He expelled seven demons from Mary Magdalen. Third, that of subdeacon, when He made wine out of water in Cana of Galilee (John 2:3–11). Fourth, that of deacon, when He washed the feet of His disciples (John 13:5). Fifth, that of presbyter, when He blessed bread, broke it and gave it to His disciples (Matthew 26:26). Sixth, that of doorkeeper, when He said, "Lift up your heads, O gates, and be lifted up, you everlasting doors" (Psalm 23:9). Seventh, that of bishop, when He placed His hand on the heads of His disciples and blessed them (see Luke 24:50f.).

AN EXPOSITION OF THE MASS

Pseudo-Germanus of Paris, *epistula* 1 [France, about 700], ed. E. C. Ratcliff, *Expositio antiquae liturgiae gallicanae* (London, 1971), pp. 3–16.

We have received from the traditions of the Fathers how the solemn order of the Church is performed and with what teachings the ecclesiastical Canon is adorned.

The first and greatest of all gifts, the Mass, is sung in commemoration of the death of the Lord (for the death of Christ has become the life of the world), that by being offered it [the Mass] may work the salvation of the living and the rest of the dead.

1. *On the Prelude.* An antiphon is sung as a prelude. This represents the mystical prophecy made by the patriarchs, who lived before the Flood, of the Coming of Christ. So Enoch, "seventh from Adam," who was taken up by God, prophesied, saying "Behold the Lord is coming to execute judgment with thousands of His saints." This testimony is recorded by Jude the Apostle, the brother of James (Jude 14). Just as the patriarchs had prophesied, the Lord's hand covered the ark that He might not condemn the whole earth, so [today], while the clerics are singing the antiphon, the bishop, representing Christ, proceeds from the sacristy (as if from heaven) to the ark of the Lord, which is the Church, so that both admonishing and praying he may nourish good and destroy evil works among the people.

2. *On Silence.* The deacon calls for silence for two reasons, so that the people may better hear the word of God and that our hearts, free from any mundane thought, may receive God's truth.

3. The bishop, addressing the people, blesses them, saying: "The Lord be with you always." The blessing is returned, "And with your spirit." He receives a blessing from the mouths of all the people so that he may be more worthy to bless them in return.

4. *On the Aius [hymn].* "Aius" [Agios, Holy] is sung before the Prophecy. It is sung in Greek because—with the exception of the Apostle Matthew, who first of all the evangelists set down the Gospel of Christ in Judaea in

Hebrew—the New Testament was originally proclaimed in Greek. We therefore pay due honor to the language which first received the Gospel of Christ and first put it into writing. The bishop intones the first canticle, the *Aius* ["Holy God, Mighty God, Immortal God, have mercy upon us"], alternating Greek with Latin [i.e. he also intones the same hymn in Latin, "Sanctus Deus," etc.]. The "Amen" which follows comes from the Hebrew to signify the union of the Old with the New Testament. We thus represent the inscription in three languages which Pilate by divine inspiration placed on the Cross and by which (though in ignorance) he confessed "Jesus the Nazarene, King of the Jews" (John 19:19), that is, holy [Nazarene] and king.

5. Three children sing the *Kyrie eleison* ["Lord, have mercy"] in unison. They repeat it three times in representation of the three languages of the sacred law, Hebrew, Greek, and Latin, or of the three ages of the world, before the Law [was given to Moses], under the Law, and under Grace.

6. *On the Prophecy.* The canticle of the priest Zachariah (Luke 1:68–79) is sung next, in honor of St. John the Baptist, to show that the beginning of salvation consists in the sacrament of Baptism, the administration of which John received as a divine ministry. As the shadow of the Old Law was falling away and the light of the new Gospel was dawning, John appeared as the last Prophet and the first Evangelist. Before the face of Light itself he stood out as a shining light (John 5:35). The Church, therefore, in alternate chorus, sings the Prophecy which John's father sang at his birth.

7a. *On the Prophet and the Apostle.* A reading from the Prophets of the Old Testament follows. It castigates evil and announces things to come, so that we may understand that it is the same God who resounds in Prophecy, who teaches through the Apostle and shines forth in the splendor of the Gospel.

7b. *On the Apostle* [an Epistle written by an Apostle]. What the Prophet announces the Apostle shows has come to pass. [Instead of the Epistles] the Acts of the Apostles and the Apocalypse of John are read after Easter to celebrate the newness of paschal joy. We follow the sequence of seasons, reading the historical books of the Old Testament in Lent and the lives of holy confessors and martyrs on their feast days, so that the people may understand how greatly Christ loved his servant, whom the devout claim as patron, by showing forth in him signs of power.

8. *On the Hymn.* The Hymn of the Three Children [in the fiery furnace] (Daniel 3:52–90) is sung after these readings. It represents the ancient saints who, sitting in darkness (Luke 1:79), awaited the Lord's coming. Just as a fourth angel came to the children as they were singing and, bringing a cloud of dew, overcame the flames of fire (Isaiah 18:4), so the Son of God

came to the ancient saints as the Angel of Great Counsel (Isaiah 9:6). As the evangelist [i.e. the author of the apocryphal Gospel of Nicodemus] tells us, dashing in pieces the empire of Hell, He freed them, bringing them the joy of the Resurrection.

9. The Church does not postulate a collect between the "Benedictus" [the canticle of 8, above] and the Gospel but rather a Response, which is chanted by boys, who represent the Innocents whom the Gospel records perished at the time of Christ's Nativity (Matthew 2:16), or the other children who called out "Hosanna to the Son of David" to the Lord in the temple as He went to His passion (Matthew 21:9, 15). For the Psalmist declares (8:3): "Out of the mouths of babes and sucklings you have perfected praise."

10. *On the "Aius" sung before the Gospel.* At the entrance of the Holy Gospel the clergy sings "Aius" [see 4, above] in a measured chant, as a representation of the angels calling out before Christ's face at the gates of Hell, "Lift up your heads, O gates, and be lifted up, you everlasting doors, and the King of Glory shall come in" (Psalm 23:9).

11. *On the Gospel.* The procession of the Holy Gospel goes forth, therefore, as the power of Christ triumphing over death. During the chant of "Aius" the Gospel Book is accompanied by seven burning torches which represent the seven Gifts of the Holy Spirit or the seven lights of the Law (Exodus 25:36f.), like unto the mystery of the Cross. The procession ascends the tribunal of analogy [i.e. the ambo], as Christ ascends the throne of His Father's kingdom, so that [the bishop] may announce from there the gifts of life. When the clergy cry out, "Glory to you, O Lord," they represent the angels who, at the Lord's birth, appeared to the shepherds, singing: "Glory to God in the highest" (Luke 2:14).

12. *On the "Sanctus" after the Gospel.* As the Gospel procession returns the "Sanctus" ["Holy, Holy, Holy"] is chanted by the clergy in representation of the saints who, as the Lord Jesus Christ returned from Hell, followed Him singing [Gospel of Nicodemus], or of the twenty-four elders whom the Apocalypse of John commemorates, who sang a sweet song as they cast their crowns before the lamb (Apocalypse 4:10f.).

13. *On Homilies.* The Homilies of the Holy Fathers, which are read [aloud] are simply to serve in place of a sermon, so that whatever [the readings from] the Prophets, Apostles, or the Gospel have announced, a doctor or pastor of the Church shall set forth to the people in clearer speech, striving neither to offend the learned with rusticity nor to prove obscure to rustic ears.

14. *On the Prayer.* The prayer the deacons chant for the people has its origin in the Mosaic books. After the people has heard the sermon the Le-

vites [deacons] pray for the people and the priests, prostrate before the altar, intercede for their sins. As the Lord said to Aaron, "You and your sons and all the tribe of Levi will bear the sins of My people" (Exodus 28:38; Leviticus 10; 17; Numbers 18:1, 23), not bearing the sins as a penalty but supporting the people by their prayers.

15. *On Catechumens.* Following the ancient ritual of the Church, the deacon calls out that any catechumen is to leave the Church. This was so that Jews, heretics, and pagans, who had come as adults to be baptized and were being instructed before receiving the Sacrament, might come to church and hear the readings from the Old and New Testament. After the deacons had prayed for them and the bishop had said the Collect after the Prayer, they had to go out since they were not worthy to remain during the oblation. They were to listen to the great deeds of God prostrate on the ground outside the door. It was the duty of the deacon to admonish them to leave, that of the doorkeeper to see they did not linger, lest someone unworthy should be present in the temple, for, as the Lord says, "Do not give that which is holy to the dogs nor cast pearls before swine" (Matthew 7:6). For what on earth is holier than the making of the Body and Blood of Christ? And what is more unclean and fit to be compared to dogs or pigs than someone who is not cleansed by Baptism or fortified by the Sign of the Cross?

16. We are commanded to keep silence in the spirit, "keeping the door" [of the church closed], that is keeping ourselves from the tumult of words or vices, making the Sign of the Cross lest desire enter by the eyes or wrath by the ears, lest filthy speech proceed from our mouth. Let the heart be intent only on receiving Christ.

17. *On the "sonum."* The "sonum" [a hymn], which is sung during the procession of the offerings [for the Eucharist], has the following origin. The Lord commanded Moses to make silver trumpets which the Levites should sound when an offering was made, and this should be a sign to the people of the hour when the offering was made, and all were to bow down and adore the Lord until there came the column of fire or the cloud which would bless the sacrifice (Numbers 10:2–10; 14:14). Now, however, as the Body of Christ is borne to the altar, the Church celebrates the great deeds of Christ in sweet melody, not with trumpets but in spiritual chants.

18. The Body of the Lord is carried in [vases in the form of] towers because the Lord's Sepulcher was carved out of stone in the likeness of a tower and in it was the bed on which the Lord's Body was laid. From there the King of Glory arose in triumph. The Blood of Christ is offered in a chalice because the mystery of the Eucharist was consecrated in such a vessel "the day before He was to suffer," the Lord Himself saying, "Here is the Chalice of

My Blood, the Mystery of Faith, which shall be shed for many for the remission of sins."

The bread is transformed into flesh and the wine into blood, the Lord saying of His Body, "My flesh is food indeed" and of the blood, "My Blood is drink indeed" (John 6:55). For of the bread He said, "This is My Body" (Matthew 26:26) and of the wine, "This is My Blood" (26:28). Water is mixed with wine, either because the people should be united with the Lord or because from the side of Christ Crucified there flowed blood and water (see John 19:34), that with the one we may be cleansed from our sins and with the other prepared for the Kingdom of Heaven.

19a. The paten, where the oblation is consecrated, is so called because, by commemorating it, the mystery of the Eucharist offers up the Passion of the Lord.

19b. An [outer] pall, made of linen and wool, represents Christ's tunic without seam which was not divided by the soldiers (John 19:23f.).

19c. The oblation is placed on a corporal of pure linen because the Lord's Body was placed in the tomb, wrapped in pure linen cloths and with spices (John 19:40).

19d. The actual cover of the Sacraments is more [elaborately] adorned because the Resurrection of Christ excels any adornment, or as a symbol of the roof of heaven which now hides the Lord from our eyes. It is made of silk, adorned with gold or gems, because the Lord commanded Moses to have veils made for the tabernacle of gold and hyacinth and purple and scarlet (see Exodus 26:31), for all these mysteries anticipated the wounds of Christ.

20. *Lauds, that is "Alleluia."* After Christ's Resurrection John, in the Apocalypse, heard singing in heaven (Apocalypse 19:1, 3, 4, 6). Therefore, in the hour in which the Lord's Body is covered with a pall (as Christ was hidden by the heavens) the church is accustomed to sing the angelic song, "Alleluia," thrice over, the repetition standing for the three ages, before the Law, under the Law, and under Grace [see 5, above].

21. The names of the dead are recited at the time the pall is removed [from the offerings], because the resurrection of the dead will take place when, at Christ's coming, the heavens will be folded up as a book (see Isaiah 34:4).

22. Those present offer each other the peace of Christ, so that, [united] by a mutual kiss, they may be bound together by the spirit of love, and because, if discord arise recourse may be speedily had to grace or pardon be asked of one's neighbor. May we not incur the traitor's punishment by giving

a false peace (see Luke 22:47f.). And may the Eucharist or the Blessing we receive profit us the more when Christ sees our hearts are at peace. For so He commanded His disciples at His Ascension, "I leave you My peace, My peace I give you. I give you a new commandment that you love one another. And in this shall all men know that you are My disciples if you love each other" (John 14:27; 13:34f.).

23. The bishop admonishes us, "Lift up your hearts," so that no earthly thought may remain within us. In the hour of the sacred oblation Christ is better received in our minds when they are concerned only to attain Him.

24a. The fraction and admixture of the Lord's Body was prefigured in so many mystical ways to the holy fathers in ancient days that when the bishop breaks the host he appears like the angel of God who cut open the members of a shining boy with a knife and poured his blood into a chalice, so that men might more fully believe the Word of God, who said His flesh was food and His blood drink. [See John 6:55. The legend is taken from the *Vitae patrum*, V, 18, 3.]

24b. By this fraction the bishop wishes to increase [the Host]. He should also add [consecrated wine to unconsecrated, for the communion of the people], for thus heavenly things are joined to earthly. At the bishop's prayer the heavens are opened. During the fraction the clergy intones a plaintive antiphon, for all the elements—as the trembling of the earth testified— bore witness to their sorrow at the Lord's death (see Matthew 27:51).

25. The Lord's Prayer is placed at this point so that all our prayer may be summed up in this divine prayer.

26a. The Lord commanded priests to bless the people when He told Moses, "Say to Aaron and his sons: 'Thus shall you bless My people: May the Lord bless you and keep you,'" and the rest which follows (Numbers 6:22f.).

26b. Aaron occupied the place of a bishop, his sons that of presbyters (Exodus 29:4–9). The Lord commanded both of them to bless the people, but in order to preserve the honor of the pontiff the sacred canons ordered that the bishop give the longer, the presbyter the shorter blessing [see the Council of Orléans of 511, c. 26, p. 102 above], the latter saying, "Peace, faith and charity and the communion of the Body and Blood of Our Lord Jesus Christ be with you always." For although it is permissible for the pres- byter to give the blessing which God dictated to Moses [as 26a, above], and no one may contradict him—for, as the Lord said, "Heaven and earth will pass away; My words will not pass away" (Luke 21:33) . . . [a lacuna in the manuscript]. Therefore, a Blessing is given before Communion that the mystery of blessing may enter a vessel already blessed.

27. When Christ says in the Gospel, "If you remain in Me and My words in you whatever you ask of the Father in My Name shall be given you" (John 15:7), He shows how sweet Holy Communion is to soul and body.

28a. The [chant of the] "Trecanum" is sung [at this point], symbolizing the Catholic belief in the Trinity. . . . [This chant probably began with Psalm 33:8, "Taste and see how sweet is the Lord."]

THE PAPAL PROCESSION: ROME ABOUT 700

Ordo Romanus I, 7–23, ed. M. Andrieu, *Les "Ordines Romani" du haut moyen age*, II (Louvain, 1948), pp. 69–74.

7. On solemn days, that is on Sundays, all the acolytes of the third region and the defenders of all the regions shall meet at dawn in the patriarchal palace of the Lateran and precede the pope on foot to the stational church [of the day].

8. Lay grooms shall ride on right and left lest anyone go astray.

9. The deacons, the papal secretary, two regional notaries, the regional defenders and subdeacons precede the pope on horseback. They are to ride ahead, leaving a space between themselves and the apostolic father.

10. After the pope there come, on horseback, the majordomo of the palace, the head of the papal vestiary, the head notary, and the sub-treasurer.

11. One of the acolytes of the stational churches precedes the pope on foot, bearing the holy chrism in an ampoule wrapped in a napkin . . .

12. If anyone on horseback wishes to approach the pope, let him dismount as soon as he sees him and wait for him beside the road until he can speak to him.

13. Having asked his blessing, he should explain the matter to the head notary or the sub-treasurer and they should convey it to the pope; this should be done even if anyone comes to meet the pope without a [written ?] petition.

14. If [the petitioner] is on foot, he is to remain in his place until he is heard and blessed.

15. On the day of the Lord's Resurrection, when the pope goes to S. Maria [Maiora], the regional notary shall await the pope on the Via Merulana and, having greeted him, say: "In the Name of Our Lord Jesus Christ, last night in the church of the Holy Mother of God Mary so many male and so many female children were baptized." The pope replies: "Thanks be to

God." The notary is to receive one *solidus* from the sub-treasurer. The pope continues on to the church . . .

18. On the holy day of Easter all the acolytes [as 7, above].

19. The acolytes bear before the pope chrism, the Gospels, the corporals and purses [for the distribution of alms]; the aquamanile is to be carried after him.

20. The subdeacon who is to read the Apostle [the Epistle] is to have charge of this volume, the archdeacon of the Gospel Book.

21. The aquamanile, the usual patens, the chalice, the cups and tubes [to administer eucharistic wine to the faithful], the other gold and silver vessels for ritual use, the cullender [for eucharistic wine], the silver arms, the Gradual Book, the candelabra in gold and silver from the church of the Saviour [the Lateran], are to be taken out by the principal sacristan and carried [in the procession] by porters.

22. On feast days the greater chalice and paten and Gospel Books are to be taken out of the papal vestiary under the supervision of its head because of the number of jewels [which decorate them], so that they are not lost.

23. A lay chamberlain is to carry the pope's chair before him so that it is ready when the pope arrives in the sanctuary [of the church where he is to celebrate Mass].

THE COMMENDATION OF THE DYING

Sacramentary of Gellone (c. 760), ed. A. Dumas, *CCSL*, 159 (Turnhout, 1981), pp. 460–62.

Go forth, O soul, from this world, in the Name of God the Father Almighty who created you, in the Name of Jesus Christ, the Son of the Living God, who suffered for you, in the Name of the Holy Spirit, who was poured out on you, in the name of angels and archangels, of thrones and dominions, of principalities and powers and of all the heavenly virtues, of Cherubim and Seraphim, of the whole human race which has been taken up by God, of the Patriarchs and Prophets, Apostles and Martyrs, Confessors and Bishops, priests and deacons and of every rank in the Catholic Church, of monks and hermits, virgins and faithful widows. Today your servant's place is established in peace and his dwelling in Jerusalem on high. Receive your servant, Lord.

Free, O Lord, the soul of your servant from all the perils of hell and from the snares of sin and from all tribulations. Free, O Lord, this soul as you freed Noah from the flood, as you freed Enoch and Elijah from the common death of the world. Free him as you freed Job from his sufferings and Moses from the hand of Pharaoh, the king of the Egyptians. Free his soul as you freed Daniel from the lion's den and the three boys from the fiery furnace and the hands of the wicked ruler. Free him as you freed Jonah from the whale's belly and Susanna from false witnesses. Free him as you freed David from the hand of King Saul and from Goliath and from all his dangers. Free your servant as you freed Peter and Paul from prisons and torment. So deign to free the soul of this man and allow him to dwell with you in heaven. Through Jesus Christ.

O God, before whose sight all who are born are brought, as you are the giver of life be merciful in punishment. We ask that you grant your servant a place with your saints and an inheritance with your elect. Through.

God, with whom all those dying are alive (for in dying our bodies do not perish but are changed for the better), we humbly ask that you dispose that the soul of your servant be taken by the hands of the holy angels to the bosom of your friend, the Patriarch Abraham, to be raised again on the last great Judgment Day. Mercifully cleanse and forgive whatever evil by the devil's wiles he may have contracted in this mortal region. Through.

O Lord, grant us your aid. Of your mercy receive the spirit of your servant, beloved by us, freed from the bonds of the body, in the peace of your saints, that, escaping the place of punishment and the flames of Gehenna, he may attain the region of the living. Who reigns.

[Then there are recited the following prayers: "The just shall be in everlasting remembrance" (Psalm 111); "Do not give the soul trusting in you, O Lord, to beasts" (Psalm 73:19); "Let the just rejoice in the sight of God" (Psalm 67:4); "Precious in the sight of the Lord is the death of his saints" (Psalm 115:15); "The saints will rejoice in glory" (Psalm 149:5).]

Receive, O Lord, the soul of your servant, returning to you; clothe him with a heavenly garment and wash him in the holy spring of eternal life, that he may rejoice among those who rejoice, and be wise with those who are wise, that he may take his place among the Martyrs, and go forth among the Patriarchs and Prophets, and that he may seek to follow Christ with the Apostles, and behold God's Glory with angels and archangels, and joy among the golden jewels of Paradise, and come to knowledge of mysteries, and find God among the Cherubim and Seraphim, and hear the song of songs among the twenty-four elders (Apocalypse 4), and wash his garments among those washing their stoles in the source of light (Apocalypse 7:14), and, among those knocking, may he find the doors of the Heavenly Jerusalem lie open (Apocalypse 3:20), and may he be with those who see God face to face, and sing the new song (Apocalypse 5:9) with the singers and hear heavenly sounds with those who hear them. Through Our Lord Jesus Christ your son.

THE FUTURE LIFE

Visio Baronti monachi Longoretensis, ed. W. Levison, *MGH. SRM*, V (Hannover, 1910), pp. 377–94.

In the Name of the Lord there begins the Revelation of the blessed monk Barontus.

1. I wish to recall to you, dearly beloved brethren, what occurred recently in the monastery of St. Peter the Apostle, which is called Longoretus. A certain brother, by name Barontus, noble in origin, had recently joined the monastic order. After he had devoutly rendered praise to God at Matins in church with his brothers, on returning to his bed he was struck down by fever and reduced to the last extremity. He began to call out in anguish to his son Aglioaldus, telling him to go at once to the deacon Eudo and bring him to his aid. The boy ran off, crying loudly, and brought back the brother. But when Eudo entered the cell where Barontus lay sick and began to call him by name, Barontus could not speak but pointed with a finger to his throat and waved his hands in front of his face [to repel demons]. Eudo, trembling, had recourse to the normal weapons. He began to make the Sign of the Cross and, groaning deeply, to command holy water to be sprinkled throughout the cell, to expel the crowd of evil spirits. But Barontus, his arms fallen to his sides, his eyes closed, lay there half dead, unable to see anyone at all.

2. By then it was almost the third hour [about 9 a.m.] and the brethren assembled to pour out prayers to God for his life. When they saw him motionless, they began to weep bitterly and, dividing into groups, to take turns to recite the Psalter right through in the hope that the heavenly doctor would return the soul to the body. The uninterrupted singing of the Psalms continued throughout the day until the evening when it was time to sing the praises of God as usual in church. Brother Barontus had fallen so low that no one who saw him could believe that he would live. But God's servants, seeing this, began to redouble their chant and to beseech the heavenly Creator, who had brought his soul out of Egypt [i.e. the world] to remove it to the heavenly region. And so, going on singing all night, they came to

cockcrow. Then it was that the wonderful power of Christ was made visible in a way which should be made known throughout the Catholic Church. Those who hear the account may tremble at their sins and turn with their whole hearts to Christ's service, lest they lament at the last in perpetual pain what they failed to emend by true penance. For as the monks were singing Psalms, Barontus suddenly awoke. Rousing himself, he opened his eyes and, uttering God's praises, exclaimed repeatedly: "Glory to Thee, O God! Glory to Thee, O God! Glory to Thee, O God!" When the brethren saw this they began with great feeling to give thanks to God who had thus brought his servant back to bodily life, for by then no one expected to hear him speak.

3. Drawing round him they asked him to tell them in detail where he had been and what he had seen. As if "awaking from heavy sleep" (Genesis 45:26), he said: "When last night you saw me return to my cell after I had sung Christ's praises with you at Matins, I at once fell heavily asleep (see Luke 9:32). But immediately I was asleep there appeared two hideous demons, whose appearance I could not endure. They began to strangle me by force, trying to swallow me down and so carry me off to Hell. They went on attacking me until the third hour when there came to my aid the Archangel Raphael, shining in splendor of light, who forbade them to go on treating me so cruelly. But they resisted him proudly, saying: 'If God's glory does not take him from us, you cannot do so.' Then St. Raphael replied: 'If this is as you say, let us go together before God's Judgment Throne and there your sin will be exposed.' So they went on arguing all day until the evening, when Blessed Raphael said to them: 'I am taking this soul with me before the tribunal of the eternal judge but I leave the hope of recovery here in his body.' They objected that they would never let the soul go unless God's judgment went against them.

4. Hearing this, St. Raphael touched my throat with a finger and wretched I at once felt my soul plucked out of my body. But I will describe how small my soul seemed to me. It seemed as small as a hen's chick when it comes out of the egg. But, small as it was, it took with it my head, eyes and the rest, sight, hearing, taste, smell and touch, though it could not speak at all until I came to the test and my body received an aerial shape resembling what I had left behind here." He continued: "But there was no slight contention over my little body. St. Raphael was struggling to raise my soul to Heaven above and the demons were battling to precipitate it below. St. Raphael began to raise me from the ground and to sustain me on the right. One of the demons seized me on the left, a second kicked me severely from behind and, full of rage, exclaimed: 'I have already had you in my power once and done you great harm. Now you will be tormented for ever in Hell.'

5. While he was speaking we had risen above the wood round the monastery and the church's bell had sounded for Vespers. St. Raphael commanded the demons: 'Begone, begone, you cruel beasts, you can no longer hurt this little soul. The church bell has sounded. The brethren are assembled to pray for him.' But they would not agree but struck my side with savage blows. So we soon came over the monastery of Millebeccus. St. Raphael prayed and this verse came from him: 'Bless the Lord, O my soul, in all places of his dominion' (Psalm 102:22). And I, when I heard this, beheld and saw that monastery and recognized the brethren celebrating Vespers, and I saw one of them carrying green herbs to the kitchen. We should, beloved brethren, greatly wonder and tremble at this, that in a moment the soul may be transported from one monastery to another which is twelve miles distant. But St. Raphael, having finished his prayer, said: 'Let us visit the true servant of God [the Abbot Leodaldus], who lies sick in this monastery; he is very different, both in his humility and in the works he performs, from others in the city of Bourges.'" For indeed [the abbot] was almost dead. He could not eat anything and all the monks, despairing of his recovery, were only concerned with planning his burial.

6. But after the Archangel had visited and strengthened him, Abbot Leodaldus recounts a great miracle. It may terrify the hearts of unbelievers, who are not moved by compunction to do penance for their evil deeds and to beg St. Raphael (whose name means "divine medicine" [Gregory the Great, *Homilies on the Gospels*, 34, 9]) to come and cure them, lest the devil lead them captive to eternal punishment, from which they will not be able to escape to the bodily pleasures in which they place all their trust. For this abbot states that the hour when Brother Barontus recounts he was there with St. Raphael, he [the abbot] beheld a great glory over the cell in which he lay sick, suffering great pain in his chest. Then St. Raphael appearing, the shining light of his face illumined the whole cell. As he passed through he made the Sign of the Cross on the sick man's chest and that very hour he was healed.

7. Barontus went on: "As we were passing this monastery, four more terrible black demons came to meet us, seeking to rend me with their teeth and claws. I began to fear that they would carry me, a sinner, off from St. Raphael and plunge me into the depth of Hell. They were six and he alone could not resist them. But Blessed Raphael stood out against them and while they were in dispute, two angels clothed in white garments (see Acts 1:10) and of wonderful scent, coming swiftly, laid hold of St. Raphael's feet and began to sing the antiphon: 'Have mercy on me, O God, according to your great mercy' (Psalm 50:1). At once these demons lost their power. Two of them

fell to earth and vanished and two more soon did the same. But the two demons who were present when I was taken out of the body, never withdrew but always kept us company. And we went near Hell and saw its guards.

8. And so, after this second battle, we came to the first gate of Paradise, where we saw some of the brethren of our monastery, who were assembled there awaiting the Day of Judgment when they are to receive the fullness of eternal joys. These are their names: Corbolenus, the priest, to whom God gave good things in this world; Fraudolenus, the priest, who lived his life well; Austrulfus, the deacon, who left the world in an instant at God's command; Leodaldus, the reader, on whom God conferred a special blessing; Ebbo, the reader, God's chosen servant. When they all saw us, with the demons sticking closely to my left side, they were amazed and wished to speak to us. The evil demons in no way wished this but the great servant of God Leodaldus besought St. Raphael by the Maker of Heaven and Earth to allow me to rest a little. Then he humbly asked St. Raphael and me, unhappy as I was, from which monastery I came and in what way I had so gravely erred that demons should have such power over me. I answered: 'I am from the monastery of St. Peter at Longoreto and I do not deny that all I endure is due to my sins and crimes.' But they, when they heard I was from their monastery, were greatly saddened and began to groan and say that the devil had never dared to ensnare any soul from that house. But St. Raphael began gently to console them, saying: 'I have left the hope [of recovery] in his body. If the Heavenly Father so wills, he will return there.' The brethren humbly begged St. Raphael to kneel with them in prayer to the Lord of Mercy that He might not allow me to be devoured by the ancient enemy, and so they gave themselves up to prayer.

9. After they had prayed we soon came to the second gate of Paradise where there were countless thousands of children clothed in white (Acts 1:10), praising the Lord with one voice. When we had entered this gate, passing through the midst of these saints, we saw a small path prepared by which we began to go towards the next gate. But so great was the throng of virgins on right and left that no man but only God could see the whole. As soon as they saw us, the saints began to cry out: 'A soul is going to judgment!' And then: 'Conquer, Thou Warrior Christ, conquer, and let not the devil take him down to Hell!'

10. Then we came to the third gate of Paradise, and this gate had the appearance of glass (see Apocalypse 21:18). And within there was a multitude of saints wearing crowns, with shining faces, seated in their dwellings and on their thrones, always praising God. And there was there a multitude of priests, excellent in merit, 'whose houses were built of gold bricks,' as St.

Gregory [the Great] states in the *Dialogues* [IV, 37, 9]. And many more mansions of great splendor and honor were being built; their inhabitants were not yet there. But he builds mansions in Heaven who does not cease to give bread to the hungry [on earth] (Psalm 145:7). While I was looking fixedly at all this, one of our brethren, Corbolenus [see 8, above], who had already died, appeared and showed me a house built with great honor and said: 'This house the Lord has rightly prepared for our Abbot Francardus.' I shall briefly recount what I know of his deeds, for he [Francardus] brought me up from infancy. He was a man who feared God and was instructed in sacred reading. Because of his zeal and charm the monastery has been given good lands, which may support God's servants and pilgrims. He was the teacher and educator of noble sons. God has prepared for him, now he is purified by long illness, eternal joys to follow his good deeds.

Entering the third gate, we went swiftly on our way. When the holy martyrs saw us they also called out without ceasing: 'Conquer, O strong Warrior Christ, who has redeemed us by shedding Thy Blood. Let not the devil take this soul down to Hell.' I recount all this truthfully. I decided to do so, so that the saints' voices should resound throughout the world.

11. Then we reached the fourth gate of Paradise, and there we recognized one of our brethren, Betolenus by name, who used to lie at the gate of the monastery, contorted in great pain, but who now enjoyed great consolation. He told me that by St. Peter's ordinance he had been given the charge of the lighting of the churches in the whole world, and he began to scold me because in our church, which is dedicated to St. Peter, the light goes out at night and does not burn without ceasing and he [Peter] is certainly aware of this. We did not have permission to go any further [into Paradise] but I beheld such great splendor and glory all round me that I could scarcely see with my eyes closed.

12. Then St. Raphael summoned one of the angels and sent him to ask Peter the Apostle to come swiftly to him. He appeared without delay, saying: 'Why, Brother Raphael, have you sent for me?' St. Raphael replied: 'The demons accuse one of your little monks and are not willing to let go of him.' At which Blessed Peter, addressing the demons, asked politely: 'What crime do you have against this monk?' The demons said: 'Major sins!' Peter: 'Recount them!' They replied: 'He had three wives, which was not permitted. He has also committed other adulteries and many other sins which we persuaded him to,' and they went over in detail all the sins I had committed from infancy onwards, including those which I had totally forgotten. Peter then asked me: 'Is this true, brother?' I answered: 'Yes, Lord.' Blessed Peter said to them: 'Even if he has done some bad deeds, he has given alms—alms

free men even from death (see Tobias 4:11)—and he has confessed his sins to priests and done penance. Moreover, he has deposited his hair [been tonsured] in my monastery, and has given up all his possessions for God and given himself to Christ's service. These good deeds outweigh all the evil actions you recount. You cannot take him from me now. Know clearly that he is not your companion but ours.' But they stubbornly resisted him, saying: 'Unless God's glory takes him from us, you cannot do so.' Then St. Peter was moved to wrath against them and adjured them twice or thrice, saying: 'Begone, evil spirits, begone, enemies of God and always opposed to Him, let him go!' Since they were still not willing to release me, Blessed Peter—having three keys in his hand, of which you have a drawing here [included in the oldest manuscript]—sought to strike them on the head. But, spreading their wings, they began to fly rapidly, wishing to return whence they had come. This Blessed Peter the Apostle forbade, calling out: 'You have no permission, you foul spirits, to go out that way!' Confined by his command, they took flight above the gate and fled through the air.

13. After the demons had been driven away, St. Peter, turning to me, said: 'Ransom yourself, brother!' Trembling greatly I asked: 'O good shepherd, what can I give? I have nothing here at hand.' He answered: 'When you return to your own place of pilgrimage you are to bring out and show everyone the twelve *solidi* you kept hidden, without permission, when you entered the monastery. Hasten to give up the money. Beginning on the 1st of April, each month throughout the year place one *solidus* [twelve pennies] in the hand of a poor man. Have it weighed properly and marked by a priest, so that you have proper witnesses [to prove] that you keep nothing back. As I said, put the money in the hands of pilgrims and through them transmit your ransom to the heavenly fatherland. Beware that you never fall back into those sins which you committed through human frailty. Take great care that when the year is over you are not left with one penny (*denarius*). If, from now onwards, you are negligent you will greatly repent it when you die and your ruin will be worse than what you have already endured.' A certain old man of excellent appearance and venerable aspect, who was standing near Blessed Peter, asked him: 'Lord, if he gives all this, are his sins forgiven him?' St. Peter replied: 'If he gives what I told him to give, his evil deeds are forgiven him at once. And if he firmly believes, he will accept my judgment.' And so I accepted it. And Peter said to the old man: 'This is the price of the rich man and of the poor, twelve *solidi*.' After this warning St. Peter commanded two boys, beautiful in aspect and clothed in white stoles (see Apocalypse 7:9), to escort me to the first gate where the brothers of our monastery were peacefully residing. They [the brethren] were to lead me

through Hell so that I might behold all the torments endured by sinners and might know what I should tell our other brethren. Then they were to take me on, unharmed, to our monastery. The boys promptly obeyed and brought me with wonderful speed to the place commanded them.

14. When the brethren saw me, they gave great praise and thanks to the heavenly doctor who had freed me from the devil's jaws. They then received the command to take me back to my transitory fatherland, to my own place of pilgrimage. They began to discuss which of them should carry out this task. They chose one of their number, Framnoaldus, who, by God's permission, had died as a boy in our monastery and lies buried there at the threshold of St. Peter's church. They earnestly besought him to take me back to the monastery and also gave him a promise, saying: 'If you bring this brother back to the monastery he will take care to brush the dirt off your tomb every Sunday and he will also sing the psalm "Have mercy on me, O God" (Psalm 50:1) over it, right through to the end.' Turning to me they said: 'Pledge yourself, brother, to fulfill these promises.' I at once promised to do so and gave my pledge. They replied: 'See that you do this and are not condemned as a liar.' Then Brother Framnoaldus said: 'I will carry out your order, so that he fulfill what he has promised.' The brethren gave God thanks for his obedience.

15. They placed a candle in his hand that he might bear it to God's servant Ebbo [8, above] in church. Ebbo was to sign the candle with the sign of Christ lest it be put out by evil spirits and our journey disturbed, for demons are always seeking to drag us down in deed and word to darkness. Brother Ebbo was celebrating the mysteries of the Apostles in church. So we went there together. When they came to him the brethren began to beg, 'Man of God, bless this candle, for St. Peter has ordered us to take this pilgrim back to the monastery. Thus he may be protected against the tricks of demons along the way.' Brother Ebbo replied: 'Beloved brethren, let us bless it together.' He began to raise his hands to make the Sign of the Cross. As he did so, great splendor shone from his arms and fingers. When I saw this I began to think what this radiance resembled. As I gazed his limbs seemed to glow like gold and jewels. This was not without cause. In as much as my poor understanding permits I will say a little about it. Ebbo was of high birth. Following the Lord's saying, 'Go and sell all you have and give to the poor, and come, follow me' (Matthew 19:21), he gave up all his earthly possessions. Then he handed himself over to Christ's service. He cut off his hair, tore away his vices, and, thus reborn, became a minister of Christ. His hands were always ready to give alms. He traded temporal payments for eternal rewards. It was because of this and other good deeds that his fingers and

arms shone with light. No one, therefore, beloved brethren, should hesitate to give alms, since by this means the Lord of Mercy brings his faithful to eternal life."

16. The account continues: "When God's servant Ebbo had blessed the candle he said to this Brother Barontus, 'Listen to me, brother! If demons lay in ambush for you on your journey, say: "Glory to Thee, O God," and they can never turn you aside from your path.' Then Blessed Ebbo asked the brethren to put me on my way, so that I might visit Hell and see and know its guardians and be able to recount all this to our brothers [in the monastery]. And he said: 'We know, brethren, that the demons cannot turn him aside for St. Peter told him to return to his own place so as to lead a better life.' The brethren began to go with me. As we were traveling between Paradise and Hell, I saw an old man of most beautiful appearance, with a long beard, sitting quietly on a high throne. When I saw him I leant towards them and asked in a low voice who that powerful and magnificent man was. They turned to me and said: 'He is our father Abraham, and you, brother, should always beg the Lord that when He commands you to leave the body, He should allow you to rest in the bosom of Abraham' (see Luke 16:22).

17. So, going on our way, we came to Hell but we did not see what was within because of the dense fog and the amount of steam going up. But I will expound what God allowed me to see through the guardposts watched over by demons. I saw countless thousands of men, strictly bound and fettered by demons, moaning and lamenting continually, like bees returning to their hives. The demons dragged souls entangled in sins to the torments of Hell and made them sit in a circle on leaden seats. I shall set out the distinctions of evil men and the groups they formed. The proud were grouped with the proud, the lascivious with their peers, perjurers with their like, homicides with other murderers, evil speakers with their kind, 'deceivers with other deceivers.' They groaned in pain; as St. Gregory says in his *Dialogues* [IV, 36, 14], 'They bound them in bundles to burn them' (Matthew 13:30) and the rest which follows. There was an innumerable number of clerics there who had transgressed against their intention and had defiled themselves with women. Caught in torments, they shrieked with pain. But it profited them nothing, for, as St. Gregory says, 'It is useless for the man who has lost the opportunity of proper penance to come and pray to the Lord' [*Homilies on the Gospels*, 12, 5]. There Bishop Vulfoleodus [of Bourges], damned as a deceiver, sat exhausted, clothed in a filthy beggar's garment. There we recognized Bishop Dido [of Poitiers] and some of our own relations. There the foolish virgins (see Matthew 25:3), who plumed themselves for their virginity in the world and brought no good works with them, were kept under

the demons' guard, lamenting bitterly enough. And I saw another thing which should instill great fear in sinners. All those who were in the demons' power and had done something good in the world, were offered manna from Paradise (looking like dew) each day about the sixth hour (see Exodus 16:14). It was placed before their mouth and nose and they were refreshed. Those who brought it looked like deacons, wearing white clothes (see Apocalypse 3:18). The rest, who had not done anything good in this world, were not offered this but, groaning, closed their eyes and struck their breasts, crying out: 'Woe to us wretches, who did nothing good when we could have!'

18. After we had seen all this evil we went on with our brethren whose names are mentioned above [8], and with other travelers, who said they were going to the city of Poitiers to visit the shrine of St. Hilary, until we landed in a pleasant countryside. Thanking God, our brethren returned to the heavenly fatherland. I and Brother Framnoaldus, who had been instructed to take me back, arrived at our monastery. There was apparent here a wonderful mystery of God for at our arrival we found the church doors open. Framnoaldus, coming in, prayed for a long time. Then we came to his tomb. Kneeling down, he prayed, 'Have mercy on me and raise me again, O Lord (Psalm 40:11) when your Kingdom comes.' He said to me, 'Here, brother, is where my body lies! If you choose to fulfill your promise you will be rewarded in full.' When he had said this he took from me the aerial body I had been given and the candle and went on his way.

19. Sinner that I am, being destitute of all aid, I was left in front of the arch of St. Peter's church, in tribulation such as I had not endured since I left St. Peter's presence. I began to drag myself along the ground and hasten back to my body. But God's boundless mercy sent a wind which lifted me up and, 'in the twinkling of an eye' (1 Corinthians 15:52) carried me to the roof of the cell where my body lay dead. As soon as I looked inside I saw the brethren keeping watch and my son Aglioaldus sitting beside my bed and holding his hand to his jaw. From sadness and exhaustion he was tottering with sleep. The wind blowing again, I entered my body through the mouth. The first words I uttered were in praise of God, 'Glory to Thee, O God,' as the servant of God Ebbo had taught me, and then I went on and recounted to our brothers all the things recorded above, in detail, as I was commanded." [The end of Barontus' account]

20. I, who have dared to write down these things, have done so not by hearsay but according to what I myself have experienced up to now. If anyone takes up this little work I have made and begins to read it, he may indeed accuse me of rusticity of expression, but not of lying. Who, dearest brethren, possesses such an iron-bound mind that the punishments de-

scribed here will not terrify him? Here we are told that demons can seize on any sinner as he leaves his body and carry him swiftly off to Hell. This is confirmed by St. Gregory [*Homilies on the Gospels*, 39, 5], who states that the Lord permits the devil to take a sinner's soul from his body that it may be compelled to learn to whom it freely gave itself in the present life. Who is so alien from the faith that he will not believe in his [Gregory's] teaching? But many do not believe because they delight more in the love of this earthly world than they do in the love of God and the society of angels and saints.

21. The Lord clamours and warns us by the prophet, "Do not delay to turn to God and do not put this off from day to day. For suddenly His wrath will come upon us, and in the time of punishment He will destroy us" (Ecclesiasticus 5:8f.). And what will what we have heaped up by our greed profit us? He calls us again, saying: "Come, my son, listen to me, and I will teach you the fear of the Lord" (Psalm 33:12). He rouses us by the Gospel, saying: "Come to me all of you who labor and are heavy laden," with the burden of sins, "and I will give you rest" (Matthew 11:28). He calls us by Himself and says: "Come, blessed of My Father, receive the kingdom which is prepared for you from the beginning of the world" (Matthew 25:34). John the Apostle preaches to us: "Brethren, do not love the world nor those things which are in it. If anyone loves the world, the love of the Father is not in him. All that is in the world, the lust of the flesh and the lust of the eyes, and the pride of this life, is not of the Father but of the world. And the world passes away and the desire for it. But whoever does the will of the Lord, remains for ever" (1 John 2:15–17). But the greed of the world hardens men's hearts as a hard stone and they cannot rise again to uprightness.

22. "May our faith, beloved brethren, warm us again to heavenly desires." Let us again bring before our eyes the sins we have committed. "Let us consider how severe a Judge is coming," who will judge not only our evil deeds "but even our thoughts. Let us turn our minds to lamentation, our life to penance" [Gregory the Great, *Homilies on the Gospels*, 14, 6; 2, 8; 32, 8], lest, because of our love of the world, we experience eternal punishment. Rather let our good deeds raise us to the eternal region so that, when we leave the body, we may deserve to have holy angels as guides to the heavenly kingdom. May He deign to grant this, who, with the eternal God the Father, lives and reigns for ages of ages. Amen.

All this was written down on the 8th Kalends of April in the sixth year of the reign of Thierry, king of the Franks [25 March, 678 or 679].

SELECTED BIBLIOGRAPHY

Age of Spirituality, Late Antique and Early Christian Art, Third to Seventh Century. Edited by Kurt Weitzmann. New York: 1979.

Beck, H. G. J. *The Pastoral Care of Souls in South-East France during the Sixth Century.* Rome: 1950.

Bowen, E. G. *Saints, Seaways and Settlements in the Celtic Lands.* Cardiff: 1969.

Brown, Peter. *Religion and Society in the Age of Saint Augustine.* London: 1972.

———. *The World of Late Antiquity: From Marcus Aurelius to Muhammad.* London: 1971.

Chadwick, N. K. *Poetry and Letters in Early Christian Gaul.* London: 1955.

La conversione al Cristianesimo nell'Europa dell'Alto Medioevo. Spoleto: 1967. Contains important articles in French, English, German, and Italian.

Courcelle, P. *Histoire littéraire des grandes invasions germaniques.* 3d ed. Paris: 1964.

Daniélou, J., and Marrou, H.-I. *The First Six Hundred Years* [of Church History]. New York: 1964.

Dawson, C. *The Making of Europe, 400–1000.* London: 1932.

de Clercq, C. *La Législation religieuse franque de Clovis à Charlemagne.* Louvain-Paris: 1936.

de Paor, M., and de Paor, L. *Early Christian Ireland.* London: 1958.

Dill, S. *Roman Society in Gaul in the Merovingian Age.* London: 1926.

————. *Roman Society in the Last Century of the Western Empire.* London: 1924.

Famulus Christi: Essays in Commemoration of the Thirteenth Centenary of the Birth of the Venerable Bede. Edited by G. Bonner. London: 1976.

Goffart, W. *Barbarians and Romans A.D. 418–584: The Techniques of Accommodation.* Princeton: 1980.

Gough, Michael. *The Early Christians.* London, 1961.

Hillgarth, J. N. *Visigothic Spain, Byzantium, and the Irish.* London: 1985.

Hughes, K. *The Church in Early Irish Society.* London: 1966.

————. *Early Christian Ireland: Introduction to the Sources.* Ithaca, N.Y.: 1972.

Hunter Blair, P. *The World of Bede.* London: 1970.

Ideal and Reality in Frankish and Anglo-Saxon Society: Studies Presented to J. M. Wallace-Hadrill. Oxford: 1983.

Irland und Europa, Ireland and Europe, The Early Church. Stuttgart: 1984. Contains very valuable articles in English and German.

Levison, W. *England and the Continent in the Eighth Century.* Oxford: 1946.

Lot, F. *The End of the Ancient World and the Beginnings of the Middle Ages.* Translated by P. and M. Leon. New York: 1931.

McKenna, S. *Paganism and Pagan Survivals in Spain up to the Fall of the Visigothic Kingdom.* Washington, D.C.: 1938.

Momigliano, A., ed. *The Conflict between Paganism and Christianity in the Fourth Century.* Oxford: 1963.

de Moreau, E. *Histoire de l'Eglise en Belgique.* 2d ed. Vol. 1. Brussels: 1945.

Nock, A. D. *Conversion: The Old and the New in Religion from Alexander the Great to Augustine of Hippo.* Oxford: 1933.

Quasten, J. "Oriental Influences in the Gallican Liturgy." *Traditio* 1 (1943).

Reynolds, R. E. *The Ordinals of Christ from Their Origins to the Twelfth Century.* Berlin: 1978.

Riché, P. *Education and Culture in the Barbarian West from the Sixth through the Eighth Century.* Translated by J. J. Contreni. Columbia, S.C.: 1978.

Smyth, A. P. *Warlords and Holy Men, Scotland A.D. 80–1000.* London: 1984.

Stancliffe, Clare. *St. Martin and His Hagiographer: History and Miracle in Sulpicius Severus.* Oxford: 1983.

Thomas, Charles. *Britain and Ireland in Early Christian Times, A.D. 400–800.* London: 1971.

van der Meer, F., and Mohrmann, C. *Atlas of the Early Christian World.* New York: 1958.

Wallace-Hadrill, J. M. *The Barbarian West, 400–1000.* Rev. ed. London: 1967.

————. *The Frankish Church.* Oxford: 1983.

————. *The Long-Haired Kings and Other Studies in Frankish History.* London: 1962.

Ziegler, A. K. *Church and State in Visigothic Spain.* Washington, D.C.: 1930.

INDEX

THE MIDDLE AGES

Edward Peters, General Editor